Praise for Jessica Shepherd and
A Love Alchemist's Notebook

"Jessica Shepherd . . . is one of the bright rising stars among the astrologers of the early twenty-first century."

—Steven Forrest,
author of *The Inner Sky* and *Skymates*

"*A Love Alchemist's Notebook* is a worldly and wise guide to finding a spiritual partner. Jessica Shepherd reveals in detail the practical magic that, if followed, will work for anyone ready to connect with great love."

—Holiday Mathis,
author of *Rock Your Stars*

"Where was this book when I was single?! Jessica's guide to attracting your soul mate delivers well-crafted prose, spells, and anecdotes in a voice that's uniquely warm and inspiring. It's filled with valuable advice about finding love—and more importantly, about learning to love yourself."

—April Elliott Kent,
author of *Star Guide to Weddings*

"Jessica's a poetic, heartfelt writer. I love the Moonkissd blog. Honestly, it's the only one I regularly read."

—Jeffrey Kishner,
creator and astrology blogger of Sasstrology.com

"Jessica's . . . writings are a tender reminder that we can create the life that we want to experience."

—Lauren Lesko, astrologer and blogger at
Astrology: The Art of Awareness, laurenlesko.com

"I am quite impressed with Jessica's 'Conjure Your Soul Mate' spell and other tips she's given me, like auspicious dates and times. Within ten minutes of doing the ritual love spell, I heard someone calling my name from the street down below. It was a dear friend in my life who matches 90 percent of the qualities I named on my soul mate list (described in the 'Dear Cupid' spell). That's a pretty amazing score!"

—Minouche G., Fairfax, California

"After the many sessions I've had with Jessica, I find myself moved, touched, and inspired to meet my true self, and challenged to live my dream and get out of the box. I trust her like no other astrologer because she is so accurate."

—Kelli M., San Rafael, California

"Having used numerous professional services, I would rate Jessica's services as the best yet and give her my highest recommendation. She had so many incisive, illuminating insights; it was almost surreal. I was asking myself, 'Is this woman a psychic, too?'"

—Gordon H., Portland, Oregon

A

Love Alchemist's

NOTEBOOK

About the Author

Jessica Shepherd is a counselor, astrologer, and teacher living in the San Francisco Bay Area. She writes for print and online publications and publishes her own astrology website, Moonkissd.com, where she animates the stars and planets through personal experiences and stories. She has studied and practiced modern astrology for eighteen years and has a private astrology practice specializing in individual and couples counseling. Clients praise her "astro-magical style of delineating the ancient art" and "nudges to live more fully and passionately." Jessica holds a BA in art and business and certificates in Evolutionary Astrology and Mechanics of Vision (clairvoyance and vision). Jessica shares a funky pink cottage with her husband, three stepdaughters, and five chickens. Her other writing credits include "Venus & Beyond," an Astrology.com column; "Sex & Soul Mates," a *Constellation* magazine column; and contributions to *Pregnancy & Newborn* magazine, Sasstrology.com, Saptarishi's Astrology, and astrocenter.com/MSN.

To Write to the Author

If you wish to contact the author or would like more information about this book, please write to the author in care of Llewellyn Worldwide and we will forward your request. Both the author and the publisher appreciate hearing from you and learning of your enjoyment of this book and how it has helped you. Llewellyn Worldwide cannot guarantee that every letter written to the author can be answered, but all will be forwarded. Please write to:

Jessica Shepherd
c/o Llewellyn Worldwide
2143 Wooddale Drive, Dept. 978-0-7387-1964-1
Woodbury, MN 55125-2989, U.S.A.

Please enclose a self-addressed stamped envelope for reply,
or $1.00 to cover costs. If outside U.S.A., enclose
international postal reply coupon.

Many of Llewellyn's authors have websites with additional information and resources. For more information, please visit our website at:

www.llewellyn.com

A Love Alchemist's NOTEBOOK

Magical Secrets for Drawing
Your True Love into Your Life

Jessica Shepherd

Llewellyn Publications
Woodbury, Minnesota

Dedicated to my Sun, my Soul Mate, proof that magic does exist.

—MOON

First Edition
First Printing, 2010

Cover design by Ellen Dahl
Cover image © IZA Stock/PunchStock
Editing by Nicole Edman
Interior lips illustrations by Llewellyn art department

Llewellyn is a registered trademark of Llewellyn Worldwide, Ltd.

Library of Congress Cataloging-in-Publication Data
Shepherd, Jessica, 1973–
  A love alchemist's notebook: magical secrets for drawing your true love into your life /
by Jessica Shepherd.—1st ed.
      p. cm.
  Includes bibliographical references.
  ISBN 978-0-7387-1964-1
  1. Man-woman relationships. 2. Mate selection. I. Title.
  HQ801.S524415 2009
  133.4'42—dc22
                                                                2009029348

Llewellyn Publications
A Division of Llewellyn Worldwide, Ltd.
2143 Wooddale Drive, Dept. 978-0-7387-1964-1
Woodbury, MN 55125-2989, U.S.A.
www.llewellyn.com

Printed in the United States of America

Contents

Acknowledgments

My gracious acknowledgments and gratitude to: Erin Reese, soul sister, for her advisement and friendship; Paul Bogle, for handholding, cheerleading, and daring; Holiday Mathis, for inspiration and mutual appreciation; Grant Jeffers, for presence of mind; wise sorcerer Steven Forrest, for magic, wisdom, and compassion; the Artist's Group—Todd Donahue, Jessica Rice, and Yasmine BarDor; Kim Patron, Emily Steele, Kelli McGowan, Irina Bilenkaya, Minouche Graglia, and Fern Feto Spring, for conversations that went from ear to page; and those who have sought my love advice and stretched my heart to answer. Thanks to Nicole Edman and Llewellyn Publications, for polishing up and beautifying this creative gem and offering it to a larger audience. Finally, thanks to the men who were in my life before I met my soul mate—their combined contribution to this book has been delightfully alchemical.

Preface

We have to stop and be humble enough to understand that there is
something called Mystery.

—Paulo Coelho

I BEGIN WRITING *A Love Alchemist's Notebook* in the majestically romantic city of Vienna, Austria, where I'll be living for the next seven weeks. I am here because I conjured up my soul mate, John, now my husband of two years.

This is our third trip to Vienna; our very first trip here was our honeymoon. Before that, I'd never been out of the continental United States. Were it not for a serious magical stretch of the imagination, I wouldn't have met John, and I wouldn't be here in Vienna. Thanks to the secrets I'm revealing to you in this book, I am having the experience of a lifetime, one of many begun by the adventures of relationships. So many things have opened up in my life since I first began using these soul mate secrets, and my world has been unequivocally blown open by love.

There are no coincidences, especially when it comes to soul mate love. Vienna captured my heart and imagination long before I came here on my honeymoon, as a city romantically immortalized in the popular movie *Before Sunrise*, starring Ethan Hawke and Julie Delpy. In this story of soul mate love, two passing strangers meet on a train and fall under a spell. Jesse (Hawke) spontaneously suggests that they hop off the train in Vienna, and Celine (Delpy) agrees. Over the next twenty-four hours, the two wander through the city, deep in conversation, exploring each other and the possibility and plausibility of their connection. Real time seems to suspend itself in collusion with their destined meeting, and magical time begins.

At one point in the film, a poet disguised as a beggar appears, offering to write the pair a poem using a word of their choice. The beggar is the archetypal Cupid, making his appearance in Jesse and Celine's love play. Eventually, Jesse and Celine must part to return to their native lands, and fans had to wait nine whole years for their reunion in *Before Sunset*. Oh, curses!

While I now know that timelessness, synchronicity, and the appearance of a Cupid-like stranger (the poet-beggar) are magical collusions, and that all do show up in real-life soul mate meetings, back when I first saw *Before Sunrise*, I only saw the tragedy of endless romantic longing and a reunion destined to never happen. The on-screen relationship was a closed book, I thought, and when the movie ended and the couple parted, I left it at that. But that book wasn't destined to remain closed.

What I didn't know then, I know now: where we feel the hole in our life—where something is missing, injured, or misunderstood—that is exactly where we need to put our focus and do our life's work. I personally needed to have my faith in love restored. When I first watched *Before Sunrise*, I understood that the soul mate would always lead us home, but I had no idea where to begin to find mine. Now I know that soul mates will find us! Even when we're impatient, when we lose phone numbers, lose touch, lose our confidence and our faith, they will eventually find us. Simply by using the techniques in this book, we become open to love and ready for our soul mate meeting.

Now, as an official Woman of the World, I've come to believe that love's purpose is to give me wings to fly. I'm claiming the same for you. I'm no different than you, and my ordinary life is testimony to the extraordinary ways love expanded my identity. How often we forget this in our search for love—single and pining for a soul mate who we think will make us happier, more content, more exciting, and far more fabulous individuals than we already are.

The wish for someone else to make your life worthwhile is a dangerous one. First, it's far too simple. We haven't moved beyond romantic longing into the particulars of the person we want, we just know we want to find love and get married. Second, when we're vague on the particulars, happiness can be pretty fickle, too. Just think how often your own requirements for happiness change over time! Romantic happiness, as a feeling, is as easily gotten from a good meal or a warm bubble bath as it is from a person, and it can be just about that fleeting. Since wishful thinking doesn't usually yield the results we want, lately some of us are taking this whole soul mate matter into our own hands.

What you hold in your hands right now is one woman's doing. This woman, myself, looked around and saw that the only love strategy currently circulating resembled more of a mission impossible than a divine missive. *A Love Alchemist's Notebook* was born from the yearning for a spiritual and soulful love and a strategy to find it. And, since I conjured up a man, I thought I might be able to help you get you one, too. A heartfelt how-to, this book is my testimony that your dream for love no longer has to remain a dream. You can draw love toward you; I have the strategy, and I'll share it with you.

I now know that destiny is not just another word for destined-to-fail meetings, but magical ones as well. The possibilities for soulful relationships are much richer and more vast than we think. A soul mate might be our best friend, a mentor who keeps our heart warm, or a companion we meet in a strange and foreign land. A true soul mate need only give us one thing (and may this be your guiding thought, bringing you infinite comfort): a soul mate gives us back a timeless piece of our self.

Through being profoundly and soulfully touched by another, we become a larger version of who we already are.

INTRODUCTION

Love's Promise

When a person really desires something, all the universe conspires to help that person to realize his dream.

—PAULO COELHO

THE JOURNEY TOWARD SOULFUL LOVE begins by thinking bigger. Love's promise is even larger than happiness. Ask your heart and it will tell you it wants nothing less than total fulfillment on all levels of your being—emotional, spiritual, material, physical, sexual, and beyond. Oh, what's that you say? You want pure bliss? Wooha! Pay attention, your heart wants what it wants, and it's very wise in that way! Total fulfillment is not only totally natural, it actually goes hand in hand with love. Why?

To become a spiritually larger, self-actualized, more magnificent individual who is capable of living her dreams, you've simply got to be loved. There's no way around it. We know this is true because we can feel the truth deep within our heart. An inner knowing tells us when we're feeling unloved; when we're with the wrong partner, we begin moving away from our self-knowledge, our wisdom, our dreams, and our authentic power.

The soul mate myths say many things, but all of them say this: the soul mate bears a gift. He or she brings back to you a timeless piece of your soul, separated from itself before birth. That's it. The soul mate's divine task is *completion*. They will help you self-actualize by bringing you closer to your heart's fulfillment on all levels. The soul mate will also deliver a few more miraculous gifts we didn't even anticipate—after all, I didn't know I wanted step-daughters until I got them! A soul mate relationship has soulfulness, and since many people deeply touch our soul in this life, we do often have more than one soul mate. That's another reason we must remain vigilantly generous, soulful, and open to the gifts that each and every relationship offers.

It all sounds great, right? That doesn't mean it's easy. For most people, the road to finding one's soul mate isn't traversed in a straight line; there are diversions, near misses, and plenty of "OMG, what was I thinking?" moments. There are problems, pitfalls, and manholes along the way, such as going out on a date but forgetting your soul at home. As an astrologer, I frequently receive letters that go something like, "I'm engaged in this holy task of finding soul mate love, and because (fill in the blank: I'm hurt, they're liars, I don't trust them), I refuse to be soulful with the people I encounter." I want to reply, "So, you're actually *surprised* that instead of stumbling into ecstasy, you're stumbling into casual sex, casual connections, and casual conversations with your girlfriends in which you can only marvel at a man or psychoanalyze him?" If you want a soul mate, you simply must be soulful with the people around you, and that might take some practice.

Honoring the Mystery

As a professional astrologer, the number one question posed to me every week by clients and readers has to do with the heart. "Is this person The One?" "When will I find my soul mate?" "I've been hurt before—will I find love again?" These heartfelt questions speak to the core of our vulnerability, because the underlying meaning is often: I'm afraid I'm not lovable.

Oh, how I can hear the pain in their voice, the desperation, the need for reassurance and hope. I've felt qualified, using the ancient technique of astrology, to take educated guesses about their concerns. I've spotted cycles of life and periods of time when personal magnetism is at an all-time high, or when we'll feel courageous and confident and therefore attractive. During such periods, a private Piscean-type hits a social upswing and can make new relationship connections, or a shy and awkward

Cancer can reach out of her shell for the first time, moving beyond her old fears and boundaries. I always encourage people to ride the upswing of these very positive periods by taking certain actions. Occasionally, I've predicted planetary periods when someone special will show up on a person's doorstep, and it's happened. I've even ventured guesses about soul mate meetings, including my own.

Great! This is all well and fine and very hopeful. Yet sometimes, despite the hype and the immaculate knowledge base at my disposal, nothing happens. Even for me.

Ah, Mystery. You gotta love it. You actually do have to love it, at least enough to stay in the game of life. Appreciate the wonder. From gazing into Mystery, I've learned there are many reasons why "nothing happens," and such reasons always have to do with our own evolving spiritual needs and our consciousness . . . or our lack thereof.

For a metaphorical hypothesis, say a handsome or beautiful person knocks on the door and you don't open it because you're indisposed (you had a date with your TiVo that night) or you're seriously unavailable (you're still finishing up old, arduous karma with a not-so-distant ex). Both are blocks to activating "I'm available and looking" energy. Maybe you're getting out of a divorce and need time to heal. Whatever the reason, there *is* a reason why nothing is happening. The frustrating piece is that we're often the last to figure out those reasons! Still, it helps to call a spade a spade and label what it is we're working with, which is psychological "soot." If we don't heed the deeper meaning of frustration, depression, or pain as an opportunity to do inner work, such soot can cloud our vision and pull our spirit down.

Consider this: the reason that nothing is happening in your love life might be that you're out of step with your soul's wish—that is, your inner knowing that your next step might not be personal love. Yet. That's because there are far more indirect steps to love than there are direct ones. Your next step might be to finish a creative art project that activates your soul purpose, and then you meet someone who will help you get the project on stage . . . where you will *then* meet someone who can truly, finally see you, your whole self, because you've shown up for yourself, and you're shining brighter, stronger, and clearer than before. The person who sees your light then proceeds to fall madly, deeply in love with you, all because you answered the call, following your inner prompting to grow!

The point is, the only choice we ever truly need to make in our search for love is to actively endeavor to spiritually grow. The rest of the love experiment—the spells, the tools, the books—is just gravy (or more like really delicious butter cream frosting). They're the finishing touches on your commitment to being an evolving, expansive, and unfolding person who's got heart and soul.

I used the Nine Soul Mate Secrets I'm about to share with you to attract my mate. You could say I magically conjured up my man! But that would be leaving out an important element: my personal growth work was the foundation for everything else. Committing to the personal process of awakening rendered every love spell magically charged. The deeper spiritual work of becoming the right person, ready and available to receive love, is probably one of life's more profound teachings. There are certainly fabulous teachers, guides, and faiths to facilitate your path of personal opening, and I hope you have them in your life. I certainly don't claim to be your love guru, or to know the answers to the mystery of your own unique heart, but I will share some tools I have found helpful on this search for soulful love.

How to Use This Book

Unless they're novels, I rarely read books from front to back. I prefer to practice casual reading divination; by flipping through the book, I'll often land on the right page and end up reading the sentence or discovering the spell I most need at that moment in time. That's one way to use this book! Yet there are many others. No matter your style, treat this as you would a manual, a love "how-to" manual. *A Love Alchemist's Notebook* is highly interactive by design. This book is experiential, experimental, and absolutely hands-on. Attention couch potatoes: you'll have to do the spells and exercises to effect change. So if you're ready to dig in, do the spells, explore the exercises, and learn about your own heart, you'll meet with success. And, you know results are possible, as it's all been tested: I've done every single one of these exercises, rituals, and spells myself!

The first tools you'll need on your journey to finding soulful love are the Nine Soul Mate Secrets. I offer these Secrets to you as a set of principles you will want to work with throughout the book, and they are introduced in the first chapter.

This manual of love also contains:

- Personal exploration exercises designed to deepen your self-awareness and mastery of the Nine Soul Mate Secrets.

- Meditations inspired to draw love toward you.

- Love spells and rituals to manifest your soul mate.

- K.I.S.S.es ("Keep It Simple, Sweetheart" sections) to bring you brief kisses of insight and encouragement along the way.

I suggest starting your own personal love alchemist's notebook immediately. Your notebook can be a designer leather-bound journal or a three-ring spiral with a dressed-up homemade collage cover; all that matters is that you fill it with care and make it yours. This notebook will also give a place for your thoughts to land and a way to chart your progress. If your perception of a person or situation changes after doing a spell, ritual, or exercise, writing in your notebook will help you keep on keeping on. Since magical work is often invisible work, it requires faith and encouragement that "it's working." During the interim between the magical work and the soul mate's appearance, it's encouraging and validating to track your heart's journey and the progress you've made along the way.

A Love Alchemist's Notebook holds the beginning of your cosmic love adventure, but it's no finished product. To make this soul mate endeavor your own, you must own everything involved in the work. Feel free to change up a spell, for instance. Take note of what you did differently and keep track of your results in your notebook. If you come across a ritual you particularly enjoy, even if it's from another source or your imagination, put it in there! You say you've got an inspirational love quote? Song lyrics that move you? A bumper sticker slogan that goes straight to the heart? Write them down! Go ahead and compose a poem, draw a picture, or paste macaroni and glitter on the cover. Your notebook will chart your spiritual progress and track the strength of your intention to attract soulful love. Writing things down is in itself magical work: the Universe knows you're committed when you sign your name and stand by your words.

Getting Started

So where should you begin? Right where you are, by loving the ones you're with. And keep in mind the following advice: start getting curious about those connections you're moved to explore beyond a coffee date. No, I'm not talking about gazing dreamily into the eyes of every casual stranger at the espresso bar, with the question, "Are you The One?" dangling in the air. Ick. This isn't about desperation! It's about regarding those encounters with people who hold some compelling chemistry for you as supremely meaningful coincidences that deserve exploration.

Here's another bit of advice, since you asked! Throughout this entire *A Love Alchemist's Notebook* experiment, you must remain vigilantly and positively expectant without losing your sense of humor or your perspective. You just never know what might come up. How should you prepare? Get ready to throw your hands up in the air. Prepare be surprised. Sometimes it's the people you would least expect who have the most to offer you. Imagine that! Actually, start imagining that everyone you meet is in service to your wish for love. About all your current connections, start asking yourself:

What gift are they bringing me?

What gift do I have for them?

They might be here to heal you! They might be here to help you! They might be here to teach you something! You might be here to give them something!

You may not have an immediate answer to those above questions, and that's okay. But that's no excuse to not treat people extraordinarily well, as messengers in service to your wish for love. Be supremely reverent toward whoever shows up (without being a doormat), and honor the whole messy package they bring you.

If you're in a messy relationship situation, consider that this person's purpose in your life is to move you out of the small, tight, closed space within which you've been boxed for way too long. This person, who is here to help you grow, may activate your fears and fill you with confusion, or even dread. If this is your experience, it is happening so that you can learn more about who and what you really want and need (bet you didn't really want to have to learn that lesson!). If you decide an exchange has completed its course for your heart, exit cleanly, clearly, and gracefully so you don't have to meet them again in another variation or—heaven forbid—in another lifetime!

Don't worry about memorizing all the nuggets of wisdom contained in *A Love Alchemist's Notebook*. You won't have to—they'll start working on their own. Once you begin folding the Soul Mate Secrets into your life, they become a part of you, capable of raising you higher and closer to love than you've ever been before. As earth begins to rise to heaven, both begin to conspire on behalf of your love wish. You may be simply awed. You'll know it's working when you begin to see your role within relationships differently. Eventually, you'll begin attracting differently, too, drawing on a whole new, subtle level. That's when you'll start launching this soul mate search to magical heights. It's a wild claim I'm making, I know, but it's not a new idea, and for good reason: this soul mate voodoo is the most heavenly drug out there, and it works.

A Love Alchemist's Notebook walks you through an individual process of growing your love consciousness. We are all at various stages in our growth. You may wish to take only what you need, adding to what you already know. I'm offering you the raw materials and a recipe for your discretionary mixing. Pretend this is a recipe for a basic golden cake, flexible enough to add in your own flavor. If you're a strawberry girl, add strawberries! Throw in a special spice that only you have, and give it a twist. The Universe digs your creativity and your individuality. So, to these love spells and exercises, please add your own personal flourish. You want your soul mate custom made for you.

Before we begin, one final word about soul mates: prepare to change your mental concept about who your soul mate is. Soul mates are really special people disguised as ordinary ones. They often appear in the unlikeliest of places. They don't always appear as romantic partners, and often we have no idea how things will turn out. Period. Question Mark. That's Mystery. And that's ultimately hopeful.

My Story

My own journey didn't begin with love. The foundation of everything I'm about to teach you began when I was eighteen years old and bedridden with an illness no one knew how to cure. That's why, when I now hear people say, "I just can't find the love I want," or they're stuck in a chronic loveless pattern, I think to myself, *it can't be any more difficult than living with a chronic disease with no real answers!*

I now know that my incapacitating "illness" at the age of eighteen was actually a spiritual emergency, and no one knew how to help. I was still a child with parents who were truly unable to help themselves. My parents divorced when I was fifteen, and I had tried for most of my young adulthood to be my own parent and make up for it. I look back at my younger self with awe: *Wow, she really had no idea of the danger she was in.* By the time I became cripplingly ill with what appeared to be a chronic flu that responded only to bed rest, I had accumulated a short lifetime of unresolved pain.

I'd get winded after a five-minute walk. I didn't graduate with my high school class, and I lost every single friend but one, who told me later that a rumor had circulated that I might have AIDS (this was in 1990).

Any serious crisis will (not so) kindly expose a person to a lack of resources. In my case, I learned that basic resources—a family foundation, proper guidance, emotional support, and financial stability—were seriously lacking in my world. My healing began when I broke away from the root dysfunction of my illness: my family. When I moved out of my mother's house, my energy instantly shot up by 50 percent. Recovering the next 50 percent of personal power took fourteen years; it was like the final stretch of a long journey back home.

When we're falling apart, whether physically or psychologically, our usual first line of response is to seek out information, to self-educate. In my case, I made like a sponge and absorbed everything I could get my hands on. I looked for learned, wise beings. I discovered astrology and the spiritual teachings offered therein. I even slept with astrology books under my pillow! I journaled constantly, putting down all my dark feelings and experiences on paper. Sure, I'd learned math in school (and was thoroughly convinced I'd never actually use geometry) but now I was learning that no one teaches you the ropes of being human. It's not even offered as an elective. I found out it's much more like a crash course.

On my path to spiritual recovery, I was ambitious to taste my own life but I was lost and hurting and in need of a tremendous amount of emotional healing. It became clear that the heavy pain I was carrying hindered my ability to choose a life direction or find a sense of home. A lack of financial resources meant I couldn't even pay the rent. All of this precluded any love relationship. Using a typical hierarchy of human needs, I needed building blocks of survival, food, shelter, money, and support first. A soul mate was last on my list, down at the very bottom. And that's where love remained for me for a long, long time.

A Return to Love

It was quite a while before the scales finally swung in favor of the empty love space of my life, but when they did, it was like being a beginner all over again. I'll be honest: from day one, I began attracting the most difficult and drama-filled relationships, and I'm pretty averse to drama. Today, a relationship with a 50/50 ratio of good-to-bad days wouldn't even rate a signature in my guest book o' love. But back in the beginning of my love quest, even a bad day spent with someone appeared better than a good day alone. Perhaps it's better to be tortured than ignored. At least, that seemed to be the theory I was operating under.

When I first started dating, I felt I needed to be open to everyone. I would consistently settle for less than I truly needed because there was scant evidence that more was available. There was suffering involved, and it was mostly mine. I learned a lot about who and what I didn't want in my life. As if I wanted to learn those lessons the hard way!

Because I hadn't really experienced love before, I also doubted my capacity to recognize love within myself, or even recognize the capacity to love in another. I had lowered the almighty bar so far that practically any man could walk over it! I believe this was divinely orchestrated so I could identify my comfort zone and define my boundaries. For example: Oh, he's dating other people, too. Ah, so we're in an open relationship. Okay, I'm a progressive, too. Hmmm, wait . . . isn't *polyamory* really just a hip word for *promiscuity*?

Yes, it was a learning curve.

Since I'm a sensitive Cancer Sun sign, a little pain goes a long way with me. Being pain-averse in the face of tortured love rendered me a quick study. I also have great intuition: I knew when I was lying to myself, when I was being lied to, and when something about shared chemistry didn't add up. I learned that if people tell you who they are, take them at their word. If they don't tell you, they will often show you fairly quickly. This may sound like soul mate boot camp, but we can waste a lot of time spinning our wheels until we're ready to take our search for intimacy to a spiritual level.

Learning the Rules of Attraction

As a result of my open-door style of dating, the love epiphanies began piling up quickly. To elucidate them, I need only take a brief trip back to a point in time when I was attracting exactly who I didn't want. I was tempted to throw in the towel on my whole love experiment. (Hmmm, I'm sure you've never experienced anything like that before . . .) But, I wondered, After all, I attracted this person . . . could he be an answer to my prayers?

"No!" my heart screamed immediately in reply.

Okay, he wasn't my soul mate, but he was in my life for a reason. So, I began asking questions (an inquiring mind is a healthy mind): Why am I so eager to throw him back in the water, when I know I'll only bait my hook and get another fish just like him? Might I explore an alternative meaning for this relationship, if not for educational or healing reasons alone? If this person had a part in my life's movie, what role would he play?

After all, this real-live beating heart of a person wasn't just a fish in the pond, nor was he just a reflection of my failed attempt to find love. This was a man, a human being looking for love, just like me, and I had forgotten this small but oh-so-important detail.

Oh, these were uncomfortable thoughts. Mainly because thinking them meant I would have to engage and examine those turn-offs, feelings, and qualities I really hated instead of just breaking off another relationship and moving on. All this self-examination was hitting close to the heart. I suddenly wanted to curl up with my blankie and call the whole soul mate search O-F-F.

An even more uncomfortable realization surfaced: even though things weren't working out the way I wanted them to, I didn't really blame him. How could I? The blame game was too thin an argument and it never stood up to the test of honest inquiry. I didn't blame him for being who he was, nor for being irreparably damaged (it was only my opinion after all, and he might be perfect for someone else). I didn't blame him for not meeting my need for him to be The One. I could truly find no fault with him, which meant that I finally, truly saw him as a human being instead of merely an extension of my own want. He was imperfectly perfect, just like me.

A profound shift in consciousness was taking place. I realized I could forgive this non–soul mate man, wholeheartedly bless him, and let him go. When I felt the rewarding sense of liberation that goes along with honesty, I was beside myself. I'd made some spiritual leaps in my lifetime, and this was the biggest win for love yet!

Still, the dilemma remained: I couldn't reconcile why I'd attracted such a man in the first place, a person who was simply not right for me. I knew I didn't want to keep repeating the pattern, attracting more of the same. So, what to do? Oh, the conflict, the agony! Luckily, when love brings us to our knees, the resolution is always nearby. Therefore, in my case, I decided to use the same tools I'd discovered during my spiritual healing journey in order to attract real love. After all, if finding soulful love wasn't a spiritual journey, what was?

Hitting Bottom

I was left with a cleansed mind, freed of limiting perceptions, and no ideas about what to fill it up with. So what did I do? As my grandma used to say, "If you don't have a recipe and you need to eat, you start from scratch." In one of my bookstore foraging sessions, I discovered metaphysics, or the science of the mind. I dabbled with the notion of doing affirmations, while secretly thinking they were silly. I procrastinated. I dubiously questioned whether the mental effort of memorizing a few sentences would produce anything other than a headache. Then, I, a person whose parents were a Unitarian and a Buddhist, who'd had no introduction to Christianity, and had never consciously or intentionally prayed a day in her life (other than "Please, if there is a lord, help me get out of this speeding ticket"), began to pray.

Metaphysics, the science devoted to meta-thinking your reality into a better one, holds this premise: physical reality follows certain laws of nature. Spiritual reality follows certain laws, too, and spiritual reality always wins. Millions of miracles exist, large and small, proving that practically anything that is needed can be imagined into existence once we understand a few basic spiritual laws. Einstein said, "Imagination is more important than knowledge." He knew imagination was more powerful than any problem; to paraphrase Einstein, he even held that creative imagination—more so than money—held the secret to curing humanity's ills. I became inspired!

Practical Magic

When it came to my search for soulful love, I wasn't desperate, but I was tired of believing that I was chronically broken in one particular spot—my heart. I remembered I'd had a similar feeling before, concerning my relationship to money, which did have a tinge of desperation mixed in, as landlords and eviction notices were usually involved. I'd also reached a similarly low place when I'd needed a job right away, as well as the time my roommate moved out and I quickly needed to find a new place to live.

So, how would I kick-start my soul mate search? I did the same thing I'd done before when reality had me between a rock and hard place: I assembled a metaphysical game plan, calling on knowledge from mystics such as Ernest Holmes, Shakti Gawain, Catherine Ponder, and other historical metaphysicians who have advocated principles of "The Law of Attraction" long before *The Secret* phenomenon of the twenty-first century. In addition to this knowledge base, I had my own direct experience with this natural law of attraction to draw from: as an astrologer, I was intimately familiar with the powers of the archetypal, attracting goddess of love—Venus herself, the planetary principle of feminine magnetism.

To add even more mystical grist to the metaphysical mill: I'd recently been examining the roots of my personal craft to discover that magic—yes, magic—lies at the very core of the ancient art of astrology. This discovery was another sign that I was on the right track, for what is love if not magical? Love and magic are both mysterious and miraculous, and both ask us to suspend our disbelief, just as the early astrologers did. These stargazing ancients had love tricks up their sleeves: they made use of specific herbs and gemstones with characteristic principles—such as love, fortune, or health—as a sort of "divine assist" for key moments of auspicious planetary energy. Ah, here's a way to court the favor of the gods! If you've harbored doubts about magic, suspecting it to be just woo-woo or New Age fluff, entertain this thought: magic was common practice during the Renaissance, which is considered the most enlightened age humanity has ever known. Notable astrologer-physician-magician Marsilio Ficino, a respected member of the prestigious School of Athens, was employed by kings, queens, and learned people of the day to perform astrological magic.

I'd used spiritual principles before in my own homegrown magic, and it worked: I'd prayed, intended, and diligently affirmed when I'd needed money, employment, and living arrangements, and I'd gratefully received. Now, in the search for soulful love, I merged magic with astrological divine timing to create my own alchemical blend. With this holistic, astro-magical love picture in mind, I figured I just might conjure me up a man. Heck, I wasn't doing anything else on Friday nights. It was worth a shot!

In the beginning of my magical work to manifest a soul mate, the results were mixed. Yes, something was afoot in my love life, one shy guy approached me at the laundromat with stars in his eyes, and no one had done that in years! Still, he was far from my "type." Soon after, another suitor asked for my number at a magic bookstore, which was less of a long shot than the lad in the laundromat, although hardly a hole in one.

Now, at this point in the game of love, I could have given up, but I didn't! Instead of becoming disheartened by these off-target encounters, I became encouraged, bolstered by the profundity of my love life going from flatline to a heartbeat of activity. I decided that the Universe really was listening to my wishes, and I likened these mixed results to a cosmic fitting, whereby the Creator was looking for a closeness of fit, maybe even getting a little testy or mischievous with me! I saw that, just like trying on a new pair of shoes, if I refused to settle for the ones that weren't quite right, each consecutive pairing offered something closer to what I was looking for. This understanding gave me not only faith, it gave me cause for sheer magical intrigue.

When the going gets really tough, the girl goes mantra. Hindus believe that mantras or devotional prayers are the solution to cracking life's toughest karma including disease, poverty, and lack of love. Who was I—whose last significant relationship had taken place in high school—to argue with the oldest living religion? So, I found a mantra for attracting my perfect spiritual partner and, as an act of faith (or out of stubbornness to convince the Universe that I knew what I wanted), I stuck with it. If repeating a mantra 108 times, twice a day for thirty days doesn't earn you faith and patience points with Cupid, what will?

And Cupid eventually rewarded my faith and patience, sending me a magical soul mate, but not until I'd accomplished some pretty serious inner alchemical transformations.

The Alchemy of Love

What is alchemy? It's a process of purification. The ancient art of converting base metals into precious ones was once a coveted and precious power. Those who knew how to change lead into gold, the alchemists, were said to possess the secrets of the Universe. Alchemy always involved an organic process (often fire) to compel transformation. That's because fire burns away impurities and purifies all things. Fire converts a base element into something else more refined, more essential, and perhaps even more valuable.

Love is the fire for which we risk who we once were for the sake of who we will become. We have no idea who that will be, so we learn to have faith and to surrender to the process. In the middle of this, we practice not knowing; in the middle of the alchemical fire of heartbreak, pain, and self-awareness, magic happens, but we may not see it until it's over.

There's a famous myth told in ancient Sumeria about this transformational process. The Sumerian goddess of love was named Inanna, a blissful light being who journeyed down into the Underworld to find her lover. Her sister, Ereshkigal, ruled the Underworld, and you could say their relationship was strained. Finding love came easy for Inanna, but Ereshkigal felt like she got the short end of the stick. Ereshkigal was everything Inanna was not. She was infertile, chronically lonely, and lacked any form of loving relationship, be it with a sibling, parent, or lover. Ereshkigal was angry about the ease and happiness her sister possessed. So she kidnapped Inanna's lover and made it extremely hard for Inanna to get him back.

Ereshkigal made Inanna pass through the seven gates of hell to get to the Underworld. At each gate, Inanna was asked to surrender something precious. At first it was her superficial possessions, her jewels, makeup, shoes, and clothes; but as she descended deeper, her very essence was stripped. She surrendered her magic girdle, which contained the magic of love and her identity as love goddess. She was told to surrender her heart's warmth, then her will to live. Finally, she was told she must surrender her connection to her higher self, her ability to hear the voice of the Divine. In total psychological and physical darkness, and without spiritual connection, there Inanna stood naked. Her sister then proceeded to hang her on a meat hook, leaving her body there to rot.

Some might say Ereshkigal was an obvious bitch who was nursing a grudge and that she betrayed Inanna, but that's not the end of the story, nor is it the point. There's no blame. Just as in real life, blame doesn't serve anyone; resourcefulness does. Inanna's dark sister struck a magical deal: she would return Inanna to her queen-dom if she sacrificed someone precious in return. Fittingly, when Inanna returns home to discover her lover cavorting carelessly with others in her absence, the die was cast: Inanna sent him in her place. Sometimes, after the descent into darkness, we learn to see right through other people. It seems, after a traumatic trip like this, nothing in life can remain the same.

The harrowing Underworld journey gives an all-new meaning to "Feel the burn," and puts a new twist on the saying, "You've come a long way, baby!"

So what's the point? The earliest versions of this myth say the goddess of love isn't motivated to visit the Underworld by the loss of a loved one, but by the desire to learn about darkness and death so she can become a whole person. How many people do you know who will volunteer to do that?! Still, we need loss and pain to put us in touch with our depth, our resourcefulness, and the part of our self that is bigger than our personality and its problems. Through being stripped of our superficial values—and sometimes stripped of everything and everyone we love—we discover our eternal self, the one that won't be broken. It seems loneliness, loss, and pain will teach you more about your self than you ever thought you wanted to know!

But darkness is fascinating. Doesn't a little darkness make you a deeper, richer, more interesting and varied person? There's no one more interesting to be around than the person who's seen pleasure and pain. People who have been to hell and back are an inspiration to the rest of us because they are so strong. And after a descent into darkness, we always discover that we are stronger than we think.

Just as Inanna's dark sister was really her friend, the journey to soulful love will ask us to regard our enemies differently. This journey to soulful love is an invitation to greet your adversary as an initiator of change.

So, you're going on a journey to love. What will you bring with you? Nothing at all. A journey like this requires only your vulnerability and a very open mind. There will be pivotal points to navigate, crossroads to traverse, and dragons to slay. Yet we survive. Often, we thrive.

In seeking soulful love, we're stripped down and changed, often into someone more self-aware and strong. Stripped of ornaments—our mascara, our drama, our "ideal love relationship," our unrealistic expectations—we bring love back to Earth in a purer form. We leave all those trappings to discover our essence. And in a world of artifice and confused romantic longing, only our own soulfulness can bring us back to reality.

Paradoxically, we still love our ornaments and we still wear them. But once we've found our essence, we can put on our jewels and our little black dress, and wear them, instead of having them wear us. This time, when we get dressed up to go out, we wear our essential self. This time, we wear inner authority and self-knowing— the most coveted accessories in the Universe.

Exploring the Nine Soul Mate Secrets

Soul Mate Secret No. 1

You don't need to be healed enough to be worthy of love, but you may need to heal before you're ready for your soul mate. You deserve love, as broken or complete as you are.

Talk about meeting your soul mate . . . I truly feel I have been given that gift. And believe me, I wasn't some lightweight package. I'm, like, the package that didn't just come with luggage—I had trunks.

DEMI MOORE

EVERYONE NEEDS A FOUNDATION FOR love, and to set that foundation, I sought out and discovered the Nine Soul Mate Secrets. Well, actually, it was more like they discovered me! No, I didn't channel them, and no, they didn't come to me in a dream. These Secrets were illumined: as I wrote, they sprang from the page, ringing so true to experience that they called for placement in honorary bold-faced type. The kernels of insight contained therein were impossible to ignore, and they elegantly communicated, in a nutshell sort of way, the very essence of my entire journey to soulful love. Yet the power of the Nine Soul Mate Secrets is far grander than nutshell thinking: each one contains a very real seed of Universal Truth. While this was my personal journey to love, I recognized these Secrets were coming from a timeless place, far beyond my own mind (perhaps from Venus herself?). The Nine Soul Mate Secrets, I discovered, are actual Truths with a capital *T*. These are Truths that anyone can understand and integrate to fully activate the magic offered in *A Love Alchemist's Notebook*.

You'll want to refer to these Secrets often: when you're stuck, when you're waiting, when you're wondering what you need to muster in the moment, return to the Nine Secrets. You can even use them as a divination tool by closing your eyes and reopening this first chapter, focusing on the first Secret you see. When that pressing question arises ("What now?" or "What next?"), allow the Nine Soul Mate Secrets to guide you to the next step toward love. Look at the Secrets and ask yourself which one you need to investigate further, and you will have your answer. Then, you can deepen your understanding by reading the corresponding chapter and doing the exercises and spells.

The Nine Soul Mate Secrets reinforce a precious tenet of *A Love Alchemist's Notebook*, which is to remember who you truly are, beyond your person and your personal story. This is a bold endeavor, but in order to find our heart's desire, endeavor we must. When we get stuck in our personal story, our own daily miseries, we tend to push away the wisdom we know to be true. Often, we do a backward spiral in the process, and that's not an elegant new swimming style, either! This can happen in a variety of ways: for example, when we experience rejection without an explanation, we're especially challenged to remember who we truly are and not fall into the trap of thinking we're eternally doomed to a loveless eternity. As you allow the Nine Soul Mate Secrets to enter your life, even if you find yourself in a painful relationship, you'll realize that every player and every inning in the game of love has a purpose, and there is no such thing as backsliding.

In the search for soulful love, as in every holy quest, the challenge is to keep returning to what is true. We will experience ups and downs, near misses, and almost-but-not-quite-rights. The Nine Soul Mate Secrets remind us that this quest is bigger than finding a mate; it's a journey to total happiness and fulfillment. The Secrets help to widen your lens and give you pause to reconsider love's journey from another angle.

Finally, the Nine Soul Mate Secrets are a gentle reminder that self-discovery is built into the love mix, and that which you discover is unique to you. After all, these Secrets are one mortal woman's revelations of Truth. You will have your own additional revelations.

To unearth your own Truths on the journey to soulful love, in addition to your love alchemist's notebook, I heartily advise keeping a dose of discovery on hand and childlike innocence within reach. After all, love arises from our willingness to see the world through youthful eyes. Especially in against-all-odds moments, children open their hearts crazy-courageously! They entertain oddities and investigate peculiarities with wonder, and they expect minor miracles. Hang out in this childlike place of innocence and bemusement. Let this attitude of personal discovery frame your explorations and, without a doubt, you'll arrive at your own soul mate Truths.

The Power of Nine

Why are there Nine Secrets? Nine is the number of months it took to manifest my soul mate. The human gestation cycle is nine months from the point of conception to the baby's first breath. Actually, once you start this soul mate work, it feels very much like a pregnancy; you'll know something is growing inside you, even if you or others don't see it yet. You may even feel some physical nausea, perhaps the release of thoughts and behaviors you can't digest any longer, or that "type" you used to settle for now giving you indigestion. And those flutters in your belly? Hey, maybe that's your intuition finally kicking in!

As nature holds many obvious secrets, cooperating with the most natural cycle of life, the nine-month birth cycle, is reasonable. Should anything as miraculous as love take less time than that?

In mystical teachings, the number nine is symbolic of completion, spiritual fruition, and attainment. Aha! The number nine represents a culmination, a birth. The ancient art of numerology teaches us to flow with the number nine by stepping outside the box, being experimental, and considering stubborn problems from another angle. We are spiritually aligned with the number nine when we are self-reflective, using our intelligence and our inventiveness to overcome stuck patterns and the things in life that vex us. On multiple levels, the number nine fits the manifesto of *A Love Alchemist's Notebook*: you'll be breaking down old patterns, learning intelligent new ways of attracting and, ultimately, manifesting the results of your commitment by giving birth to a whole new relationship to love.

Of course, this number nine business is conceptual, not actual, so it's silly to put a time line on something as mysterious and personal as love. Why? First, as an astrologer, I know people have their own natural cycles to grow through involving karma and other fun lessons. These are organic processes that take varying amounts of time and patience to master. Second, I'm not a believer in the quick love fix. *Au contraire*, I believe in becoming more natural and less uptight about attracting our soul mate. It may or may not happen overnight, so we might as well relax into the process.

Soul Mate Secret
No. 1

You don't need to be healed enough
to be worthy of love, but you may need to
heal before you're ready for your soul mate.
You deserve love, as broken or complete as you are.

*Y*ou need to commit to your own spiritual growth, healing, and self-love, but not to land a soul mate. Yes, you read that right. You need to do this for your very self and no one else, not even your soul mate. Others will see your love light shining confidently and brilliantly, but that's not the point. Healing the split between your head and your heart, between your real-life dreams and your dream for love—that's the point.

Healing is defined as the restoration of wholeness. In a fascinating twist, soul mate love does something restoratively similar by giving us a piece of our essence back. This fuzzy distinction may be the reason we get so confused in our search, why the air surrounding us grows thick with desperation, and why even the simplest relationship conundrums short-circuit us (though we see right through those problems in other people's lives). When we confuse the search for the worthiness and wholeness we crave within ourselves with "I'm looking for a soul mate!" energy, we court what I call a healing or karmic relationship—a relationship designed for our healing only. Understanding this Soul Mate Secret is an essential first step, and that's why this Secret is the foundation for all the other Soul Mate Secrets and thus the Secret for the first chapter. If we don't accept that we are already worthy, we attract a mate from a place that is unhealed and unfinished . . . and you are probably already familiar with the fun and games that brings.

Soul Mate Secret
No. 2

A soul mate relationship is joyful.
When a relationship skips the love and goes directly
to wounding, it is a clear signal this relationship is
for your healing resolution and not for ever-after.

oul mate relationships are joyful. That's because they bring qualities of soulfulness, healing, and integration. Sure, we experience periods of stress and even healing crisis with our beloved, but suffering and pain from the get-go or as an overriding quality of a relationship is just not on the soul mate's agenda. When a relationship moves from joy to suffering in zero to sixty seconds flat, you've lost ground with your soul. Likewise, if you're perpetually questioning whether your relationship du jour is from heaven or hell, that's no soul mate relationship, either. Trust your intuition here. Even if you have an abnormally high tolerance for pain, I know you can still discern the difference.

Just as it is necessary for the body to recognize a foreign pathogen, you need to learn how to recognize the people who are not your soul mate. They might be karmic mates, stuck to you with invisibly strong glue. Karmic mates are not soul mates, they are people we've joined up with to complete a contract. These relationships aren't always painful . . . until they are. Karmic relationships often bear a time-date stamp, coming into our life at an important life passage, like college graduation, divorce, or that "it's time to get married" moment, and they have all the requirements we think we want. Unfortunately, the attrition of this painful mismatch takes its toll on the soul, and these relationships expire.

Soul Mate Secret
No. 3

The energy of abundance attracts love.
Lack is the opposite of love.
Anytime you feel lack, do something that
makes you feel abundant, opulent, and rich.

*G*rowing in love, like growing anything else, does require thinking in terms of abundance. And it also requires the basic nutrients of a prosperous life, like sunshine (energy), water (emotional flow), and earth (a strong foundation). If you've got those physical reality bases covered, even on minimal levels (you feel basically healthy, safe, and cared for), you're in a good position to plant a seed of love. Finding a soulful love means taking a holistic approach toward your entire life. If you can't meet these basic levels of self-care, you are sending out a weaker signal and have to work within a real deficiency. While it's not impossible to attract from this place, it may take more time, support, and creativity.

Once we have our basics met, it's our beliefs about what we have or don't have that challenge our ability to attract and receive love. Lack is unattractive on so many levels. I've never been more "un-attractive" in my life than when I felt or believed I was emotionally, physically, or spiritually poor. Impoverishment is a huge turnoff. We may have to get more creative during periods of apparent scarcity, but that's way more fun than walking around with a big sack of lack, which is a block to receiving. Likewise, you've probably never happily dated a guy who was desperate, right? To flow with love, identify your abundance and keep your well full. This includes loving yourself, and, the most important part, doing that abundantly well.

Soul Mate Secret
No. 4

To pull love toward you, tap your Venus magnetism.
We can attract the person we desire most by
holding a mental picture of who we want and
imagining them into existence.

No need to try to move a river by pushing on it (which would be pretty much impossible) in an effort to find love when there's a far more elegant and natural way to pull love toward you. In astrology, Venus is a resonant force of femininity and spirituality; she's the principle of magnetic desire. Venus is constantly at play in the Universe, and both genders tap Venus energy to relate or connect to that which we love or to those we love. Yes, everyone has a Venus! Venus is the basis for all those laws of attraction you've practiced or heard about. Despite the newfound popularity of her laws, the earliest teachings of Venus date all the way back to ancient Sumeria. Attract-ability has always been where it's at.

Still, we women have misunderstandings to clear up about our femininity and attract-ive powers. To clear those up for yourself, you may need to distinguish the Divine dish herself from pop-tart propaganda. For me, that took astrology's take on the goddess of love, beauty, and happiness, as well as Venus myths and magical tools for attracting. Restoring Venus to her ancient lineage was like unearthing a hidden Venus de Milo at an ancient site that was covered by a modern dump. There, I discovered that Venusian femininity is magnetic desire embodied, and her goals are timeless: love, peace, and happiness. Sure, maybe her sublime sparkle is covered with superficial slime, but anyone can restore the magic to this misunderstood muse! As with any power, it's all in how you use it.

Venus has many tools to share, but the more you get to know what makes you truly and organically happy, the more magnetically receptive you'll become. A state of imagination, relaxation, and joy for life precipitates all attract-ive power. And so armed with a newfound enthusiasm for all things love-ly, ask yourself: What gets me in the mood? Yes, you can imagine your soul mate into existence and attract him. Is that too big of a leap to make? It's a leap of imagination. It's a leap of love.

Soul Mate Secret
No. 5

If you're in a difficult relationship,
you may be experiencing the
consequence of a choice you made yesterday.
You are a different person today, and you
can choose to have a new experience of love.

Chances are, if you're in a difficult relationship and reading this, you have a strong feeling that this person is not your soul mate. You have some new choices to make. If you're single and have felt stuck and unhappy in your previous relationships instead of ecstatically in love, as you crave, you have some new choices to make, too. There are many reasons to make a new choice today, but the best one I've found is karma. From the perspective of cause and effect, prolonging the present-day pain of a difficult relationship doesn't just affect today, it sends a ripple into the future. Unhappiness repeats, just like a skipped record, for lifetimes.

Taking responsibility for your love life is serious business when you view your entire life through the lens of karma. Don't be afraid! From a spiritual and growing point of view, karma is kind. It only has your soul's best interests at heart. Swinging like grand scales in the direction of our present-day choices, these scales move slowly, deliberately, and eventually toward your future. Since karma holds the entire world's need to experience the whole of life in totality (not just your own need), this force is lovingly neutral. Karma doesn't punish with a "bad relationship" or a lack of love. When one direction gets out of whack (cause) for various reasons that may not be revealed to you, the karmic scales simply tip toward the other direction (effect) so you can experience and spiritually grow from what's been set into motion. Yes, we choose the future of our love life with the choices we do or do not make today. From a karmic point of view, there is no such thing as a casual relationship, there are only *causal* relationships!

We all get stuck. The reasons we stay in difficult relationship are complex. But there's no better reason to get unstuck, starting today, than keeping karma in mind. This means examining who you are right now. For example, the old you, the person who decided the relationship was right for you yesterday, may have outgrown the relationship today. If you want to remain a spiritually evolving human being who is totally satisfied and happy with her entire life, the fact remains that our intimate relationships must keep pace with who we are today, not who we were yesterday. Doing what it takes to inhabit your version of Planet Bliss is just a choice away. If you've reached an impasse and refuse to choose anew, you could be unnecessarily stuck for a very, very, very long time.

Soul Mate Secret
No. 6

*Your unexplored beliefs, fears, and
unworthiness push love away.
To break the cycle of difficult relationship karma,
you need to recognize your Saboteur and your Shadow.*

*T*he body is good at discerning the difference between diseased and healthy types of people. But it is your whole self, after all, who is attracted to someone bearing gifts of pain and difficulty, or perhaps attracted to no one at all. What's that about?

When the devil's got your (soul) mate, that demonic or challenging person may actually be an angel in disguise, giving you the opportunity to do some self-investigation. That person may be demonstrating a shadow trait or hidden superpower that you've refused, or been unable, to claim as yours. If you know how to explore this person for your gift, you might realize they may even be bringing you a step closer to your soul mate! After all, every person has something for you if you know how to recognize it. And if you're fortunate enough to not be attracting kook-balls into your love life, maybe you're not owning your own self-worth, causing you to project all the beauty and power you possess out onto people you think are smarter, prettier, or more loved than you. These are issues you may need to work on.

In a relationship, we project our stuff onto others all the time, so it can get real confusing, real quick. Add to this two specific universal archetypes that contain our ignorance, our unexplored powers, our wounds, and our fears. The Shadow archetype is responsible for the relationship that "never works out," the one that eludes, or the one that keeps hurting us in myriad ways. The Saboteur takes direct orders from insecurity when it should be relying on intuition. Thriving on minimal self-awareness and low self-esteem, together these archetypes are perfect partners in crimes of heartlessness. A victory for the Shadow and the Saboteur team is a loss of soulful relationship. In order to avoid that trap—that "relationship mistake" we make over and over again—we need to recognize what it is inside of us that pushes love away.

Soul Mate Secret
No. 7

Fall crazy in love with yourself
and people will fall for you.

*T*hanks to the imprinting of my female ancestral line, who equated "self-love" with "self-ish," I had to spend a few years discovering how to eat dessert first, shop till I dropped, draw my boundaries, figure out what I loved, and drop the guilt about doing it. During this time of self-love learning I also found it necessary to distinguish the difference between narcissism and healthy self-love (yes, there's a self in *selfish*, and that's a good thing!). Sometimes insecurity needs to be sacrificed on the altar of self-love. Hallelujah! You may need to do this for yourself.

None of us can ever get enough love—that's the innate truth of being human. When we find our soul mate relationship, we wonder: *Will our partner leave us? What happens when he or she dies?* The ego may like to distort our bottomless need for love with its own version (I'm a bottomless pit of love-want and I won't ever reach full or fixed), but that's just another distortion that conveniently resonates with low self-esteem and fear. The truth is, it seems we have no upper limit for the amount of love we need. By the way, those people who believe love is in limited supply will use your love to fill their insecurities. I also used to think self-esteem was a static state or a pinnacle of healed achievement; now I know that how we feel about ourselves changes from day to day, and sometimes from moment to moment. We all need more love than we think! And there's no reason we can't have it.

It's hard to deny that certain people are more good-looking than others. Yet attractive-ness is a state of being and a learned trait, which has nothing to do with how we look or the family we're born into. Those who have attract-ive power always share certain commonalities: they are courageous, they have positive self-regard, and they listen to their inner promptings by acting on them, to name a few. They also know, and work, their natural assets. Attractive-ness is not in your DNA: it is learned! And yes, a funny thing happens when you start loving yourself: other people love you, too. Love shows.

Soul Mate Secret
No. 8

To attract love, let go of your need for instant results.
Remain expectantly positive,
even in the face of mixed results.
Turn ALL results into positive synchronicities
and signs that a perfect love is coming.

*M*entally affirming, letting go, receiving, and learning to read signs and synchronicities are part and parcel to every answered prayer. So is faith. Faith requires that you let go of your need for an Insta-Soul-Mate (if you could get one of those, you'd have him already!). Faith involves a few tests too, and Cupid, cleverly disguised as faith, will throw a wildcard in your path, a person who isn't quite right for you. Sometimes that wildcard person is a test of your resolve to stay on course and hold out for what you really want. Other times their appearance suggests you may need to do a little more healing, tweak your wish, or choose another love spell. You will have almost-but-not-quite-right soul mate meetings, you can count on that. However, when you learn to read the positive signs surrounding the Universe's "incoming message," you'll realize every crossed signal or mismatch is another sign that someone far more perfect for you is on their way.

You don't need to bide your time waiting, though. You can develop a sixth sense for incoming soul mate messages. And you can figure out how to ride the waves of energy you set into motion. No matter how small these waves may seem to un-trained vision, each is filled with meaning. Attracting soulful love always reminds you to trust what you know. Since soul mate meetings always have varying degrees of magic, mystery, and synchronicity at work, you must know that your dreams, signs, imagination, and inner revelations are in soulful conspiracy with the universal energy field of Love. *Oui, oui*, yes, that perfect love is coming!

Soul Mate Secret

No. 9

Love is, and has always been, magical and mysterious.
Restore magic and Mystery to love through enchantment.

The modern dating dynamic seemed to only offer me two roles: the shark bait or the shark. Neither set the scene for love. Testosterone does not only *feel* predatory, it *is* predatory, and this can cause many of us to flee the singles scene altogether. And without the spiritual tools to discern between the veritable freak show of boys who come a-knocking and the really fabulous guys, I thought, *Why bother, anyhow?* There's a more elegant way to attract, and it doesn't involve competing with other girls, our own hang-ups, or putting ourselves so entirely "out there" that we forget who it is we're really looking for. It only involves working on our self, and a few magical spells.

Many people are put off by the use of the words *spell* and *magic* because they think this involves interfering with the will of another person or manipulating the natural order of things. This isn't that. Psychic intention is not at all forceful, it is "attract-ive" and gentle, like the magically mysterious aspect of falling in love. And the receptive magnetism of Venus power doesn't manipulate or seduce; instead, Venus power is about drawing others in with creative-spiritual energy.

Once you've worked through all the previous Secrets and you've identified your deepest desire, you can put that magnetic intention into form using everyday objects sacred to Venus in order to draw love toward you. We all want to do something to attract love, and those of us who enjoy working with tangible materials (and those of us who like the gratification of results!) will really enjoy enchanting. Just as the human body is a vessel for spirit, objects, love altars, and rituals are sacred vessels we can use to embody our desires.

What Is a Soul Mate?

Soul Mate Secret No. 2

A soul mate relationship is joyful. When a relationship skips the love and goes directly to wounding, it is a clear signal this relationship is for your healing resolution and not for ever-after.

Relationships are like Rome, difficult to start out, incredible during the prosperity of the "golden age," and unbearable during the fall. Then, a new kingdom will come along and the whole process will repeat itself until you come across a kingdom like Egypt . . . that thrives, and continues to flourish. This kingdom will become your best friend, your soul mate, and your love.

HELEN KELLER

ASK THE QUESTION, "WHAT IS a soul mate?" and just listen to what people say: a soul mate completes you. A soul mate lifts you to your highest potential. Soul mate love brings us from separation to oneness. Soul mate love heals and teaches lessons. A soul mate is . . . *Hallelujah! Finally!* The person we've been waiting for our entire life.

So. Really, who is this mythical soul mate person?

Almost everyone agrees that soul is the piece of the eternal in each and every one of us, that which is immortal and undying. The soul survives death and re-birth. Funny thing about soul: is it a noun, or an adjective? It's both. You might say, "She's got soul!" You might taste soul in food (soul food). We always recognize soul. Like the genre of soul music itself, listening to artists like John Coltrane or Erykah Badu, you can feel the smooth, creamy deliciousness of soul. Likewise, we can describe a person as soulful. Because we can describe soul, we can define soul in a feeling—a feeling of soulfulness. We recognize soulfulness when we encounter it. Soulfulness as a quality is distinct and recognizable, wise and compassionate, loving and kind. And finding that unfathomable, mysterious soul of life is a little like try-ing to find the secret ingredient in soul food: you may not be able to nail down the exact amounts and ratios of spices, but you know it when you taste it. It's got a lot of heart.

That's where soul and mate converge, in soulfulness of your heart. A soul mate rela-tionship is defined by its ability to heal, to reunite all the opposites and contradictions in yourself. Incidentally, that's what healing is, too: integrating opposites and reunit-ing to wholeness. Undoubtedly you've heard the expression "soul mate reunion." Re-unite, re-union, re-store to wholeness . . . healing shares the same purpose as the soul mate, and that's no coincidence. A soul mate reunites us with our eternal wholeness.

What does your soul mate look like? Your soul mate possesses a handful of universal qualities and a number of very personal ones specific to your growth, as well as the capacity to fulfill your dreams. If this is still too vague for you, good. You'll need to get specific on the specifics. Once you reach a certain point in your readiness, you are limited only by your imagination and your ability to call your soul mate to you. Chances are, you've already begun calling the soul mate to you by trial and error (it's called dating), where you've begun to learn how to discern who they might be from who they're definitely not. So you still want a formula, huh?

Well, attracting your soul mate is not instant; it's individual. But there is a sort of formula to it . . .

Ready?

First, there's your personal, spiritual, and life readiness, and the soul mate's readiness for you (yes, they've got personal business to grow through, too). Oh, and there's Mystery, so you need to read the signs when they appear, or you risk being too busy creating elaborate requirements for them (my real soul mate wouldn't wear Dockers, be a plumber, or have kids). Then, there's learning to tell the difference between a soul mate and a karmic mate. And there's working through your own false beliefs, such as thinking you're not worthy enough to attract the person of your dreams. Of course, if you're stuck in a half-hearted relationship or pining for a previous love, you're sending out a busy signal to the Universe. Don't forget about patience and timing . . .

Pulling your hair out yet? Yes, it's enough to make a girl call off the hunt for a soul mate.

And that's exactly what you need to do.

Finding soul mate love is not a race against your biological clock, your best friend's marriage, or the fact that you're turning thirty or fifty this year. Until you stop acting from desperation, from a lack of love, fun, joy, whatever it is you think you're missing, and start creating these things for yourself, you'll feel incomplete no matter who you're with. Finding your soul mate is more about patiently exploring the rich emotional stuff that comes up with the people you meet on the way to your reunion (all those fears, hopes, yesses and nos) than the final destination. You already have everything you need, inside you.

The only thing to do is to laugh at the absurdity of a soul mate mission, then take confidence in your self. Your search for love is not separate from living your daily life with purpose; it relies on it. Everything you've done up until now and everything you're doing right now, every thing, decision, and attitude, is playing a divinely fine hand in your soul mate connection. Likewise, every relationship you've had up until now has taught you a little more about what you absolutely must have (and what you don't want) in a soul mate connection. So you're already on your way there. This is just one more little box of tools to play with.

One more thing: desperation, fear, and uncertainty are the kiss of death for the goddess of love. Those emotions cramp her free-flowing style. So lighten up. Be playful. Be courageous. Abandon yourself. In the night sky, Venus is impossible to miss, sending a "come hither" pink twinkle to the surrounding stars and planets. Surround yourself with people who really appreciate you, and don't play small in the shadow of others. You have your own unique luster. Shine bright and have fun!

The (Quick) History of the Soul Mate

Twin flame, twin soul, soul mate . . . there are many names for the same timeless love. The soul mate is both ancient and a modern reinvention. And as with many cool things, like astrology, the backstory involves the Greeks.

In his masterpiece, *Symposium*, Plato described it (more or less) like this: this dude Zeus was atop his throne in Olympus observing his kingdom of men, women, and hermaphrodites (incidentally, the word *hermaphrodite* comes from the Greek god Hermes and goddess Aphrodite, who were originally joined together as one person!). On this particular day, Zeus and his Olympians overheard a conversation at the water cooler: the subjects were plotting a plan to climb up the fireman's pole to heaven and overthrow the kingdom. The gods were not pleased, so they immediately decided to destroy humankind. But Zeus, being the charitable opportunist he is, proposed a better idea: why not cut everyone in half? Not only would this double the number of human worshippers, it would weaken everyone's strength so they wouldn't be able to carry out their big plan to overthrow heaven! Cha-chingy-ching-ching!

So Zeus split everyone down the middle. The two halves, hopping around on one foot and trying to use one arm, were not only miserable, they were longing for their other half. Zeus, in a moment of charity, decided he would allow them to reproduce (again, he'd get more worshippers), and in meeting their mate, they would reunite with their other half.

There are many ways of looking at every myth. For this one, I personally favor the following angle: our twin soul will help us finagle a way up that fireman's pole at last, into the realm of the godliness or goddess-ness. That's what everyone was doing before they were split in two, anyhow. As the story implies, reaching heaven together isn't a long shot, and the soul mate relationship was designed to help us contemplate, if not reach, our own divinity. Your mutual longing for reunion is not only pheromone-ally fabulous, it's also a soulful craving to reach higher ground together.

Yes, talk of the soul mate has been hanging around for centuries, but if there ever was a super-hip soul mate revival, it happened in the 1960s. That's when the timeless search ramped up, people read Carl Jung and Edgar Cayce, and soul became groovy again. People began looking for their own soul in another warm body. As seekers grew more and more interested in becoming spiritually conscious human beings, it changed the contract and content of what a relationship was about. "A lifelong mate to start a family with" just wasn't cutting it anymore. Divorce rates skyrocketed; it became clear that people wanted more in a mate than a lifelong partner for card games, they wanted someone to grow and become more self-aware with. Clearly, the couple that stayed together, evolved together.

The 1960s soul mate comeback rode the wave of what we now call the "New Age" personal renaissance, as spiritual seekers sought their soul mate. "We met at church and fell in love . . ." became "We had this incredibly explosive heart-chakra connection I can't explain!" Or, "It was like my third eye opened when she walked in the room!" As people began expanding their definition of love to include their spirituality, meaningful connections between two people were no longer regarded as random; rather, they were ostensible spiritual synchronicities. Past lives were discussed, explored, and regressed ("We met in a sixteenth-century monastery and our love was forbidden, so we snuck out to the garden every night . . .").

The soul mate connection is timeless. It still remains a soulful and a spiritual reunion, and this meeting is imminent. That's the timeless promise of the soul. Perhaps you have traveled (or will travel) lifetimes to reunite. But unite you will! The universal takeaway is this: together, a soulful love expands everyone's consciousness upward . . . so "let's climb the fire pole to heaven together!"

What of the time apart? That's where we humans drive ourselves crazy in the search. We try on soul mates for size. We explore and find our self and discover what makes us tick, so we know how to recognize our other half. During the spiritual separation that precipitates the most fabulous reunion of our lives, we have the choice to spend our time in a variety of ways. In my experience, we can best prepare for our reunion by remembering who we are, by recalling our own divinity. Our twin flame is a mirror of us in all ways—strength, fabulousness, facility—but with a super bonus: they restore a piece of our missing soul back to us. Remembering who you really are is all-important in the job of attracting your soul mate. It's an innately spiritual pursuit, and that's the difference between finding any old life partner and finding your soul mate. Still, if there's one thing both soul mate experts and love experts agree on, it's this: if you can't see the lovable, brilliant, worth-getting-off-the-couch-for person in you, start there. You can always get busy on the job of loving, discovering, and appreciating yourself.

Your soul mate task is to attract someone who amplifies your light, like times a hundred. That means owning your own megawatt power so you can find someone equally fabulous. Urban mystic Stuart Wilde has said, "You don't need a slug for a soul mate. Many of you have tried that and it didn't work." You'd better find someone strong and *able* to do your soul work with. Soul mate love will bring romance, support, and everything you ever dreamed of, but your problems don't disappear just because you found your soul mate. They sort of . . . graduate. So you best choose wisely.

Recognizing Your Soul Mate Chakra Meditation

Soulful love not only opens your heart chakra (the energy center surrounding your heart space), it actually expands it. In the presence of soul, you feel like you have energy love tentacles connecting you to the divine heart wisdom of the world. A soulful connection restores you to your innate perfection, your own wisdom, to your very best self. Sound good? The good news is you've already experienced this love, way back before you were cut in half, so your soul remembers the feeling. You can pull in the presence of love with a current soul mate relationship, with a sibling, best friend, or teacher-guide. All soulful connections qualify as soul mate connections—those with compassion, wisdom, total acceptance, and deep abiding love. Or you can pull on the energy of a neutral but timeless image of love—like a flower, as this meditation does. My favorite is a rose or lotus.

Reserve about ten to fifteen minutes for this exercise. When I was actively attracting my soul mate, I did it right after morning sunrise yoga, during the time of day that inspires hope and generosity. Create your own setting by contemplating a sacred space—say, facing a garden or beautiful altar.

Sit quietly and let your consciousness settle gently around your heart chakra. Notice how you're feeling. Is your heart tight or constricted, empty or hardened? Don't label it as good or bad, just notice the feeling and breathe with it.

Now imagine a flower on top of your heart, a beautiful rose or lotus, pink, red, coral, or white—whichever color suits you right now. Breathe into your heart, and with every breath, see the flower waking up in your mind's eye, the color beaming more vibrantly and the petals more dewy.

With every exhale, notice the nuance and intricate beauty of the flower, the fold of a petal, the sweet scent, the delicate organic and feminine shape.

With each inhale, allow a petal to slowly begin unfolding, opening.

And when you're ready . . . with each exhale, begin to visualize the flower's stem soaking up nourishment from your bloodstream—the blood of life—pumping through your heart.

Continue breathing in and out, opening your petals ever so slightly, and nourishing your flower with your water-blood.

Now, breathing in and out with the flower, slowly feel your heart flower begin to expand in love. As you feel your attention and breath settle around your heart and the blood from your veins pump your *prana*, or life, force into your heart flower, allow yourself to become swept up in this magnificent movement of breath, blood, beauty, and unfolding . . . so you're no longer thinking about the individual instruments but soaking up the whole orchestra. It's all happening without your participation, just your appreciation. In tandem, you're opening to love. You don't even have to think about it. Your being is vitalizing your heart center.

No fear, only opening.

No contraction, only expansion.

No hardness, only softening.

No anxiety, only peace.

No insecurity, only safety.

You may slowly begin to feel a gentle release, followed by a peace, bliss, or neutral awareness. Stay in this space as long as you like. This is how you feel in the presence of your soul mate. This perfection is yours and it will complete you.

I recommend doing this meditation every day for at least a week to really begin to notice how it's working on your heart space. You may feel more open, more aware of your heart, and more aware of what it's saying. Cultivating this openness helps you "remember" love.

So from an energetic level you'll be able to better judge when you're in the presence of oneness, completion—and eventually The One.

Past Lives, Heart Memories, and Soul Mates

You've heard the stories of lovers reunited after lifetimes apart, both coming together with the memory of unrequited love. When they meet again in this lifetime, they may remember who they once were—two lovers separated by war, tragedy, or the condemnation of social or religious beliefs. Maybe they repeat the same scenario again in this lifetime in a different but metaphorically similar way. Maybe the cookie crumbles all over again; maybe it doesn't. Either way, their reunion is spectacularly fantastic and seems somehow fated.

I don't believe Hollywood makes up these love stories just to satisfy our romantic yearning for love, but you may. Many people believe that past-life relationships can and do exist in the present, but you may not be one of those people. Logically, it does make sense that those relationships with more emotional attachment, trauma, and heart memory would travel from the past into the future faster than Marty McFly, because those same people (or alternatively, different characters with a similar script) have an investment in completing their karmic script with you, too! After all, if our many lives are strung together in one long continuing story, who better to play the role of our current lover than our lover from a past life?

It kind of gives the old pick-up line "Do you come here often?" a new twist, huh? But, there's no scientific (verifiable and repeatable) proof about reincarnation and there may never be. The theory that people cross time to meet again relies on Mystery.

The majority of us don't have lucid and specific recall of our past lives. And why don't we remember? I like this Buddhist story about what happens between death and rebirth, which attempts to explain why we forget the details of our past. Between incarnations, there is a period of formlessness (while waiting for our new mommy and daddy to get it on, and our number to be called, perhaps?) where we just wander in the Bardo. Our soul wanders upon a river, the river of forgetfulness, and you drink away the details of your most recent life. Supposedly, if you're very thirsty and drink too much, you lose some of your earned wisdom, too, and may have to repeat important lessons all over again in your next life.

Sounds more like a weekend out in your early twenties that you'd rather forget, no? Well, similar to your college happy-hour daze, it's also a necessary forgetting.

Imagine how confusing it would be to have past-life memories clouding this one. Someone would ask you what you did yesterday, and you'd flash back to 1615 and recount a scuffle with a servant!

Likewise, spiritual evidence suggests that we may choose our new contracts with people in the space between lives—who we'll love and lose in this upcoming life, the circumstance of important life teachers . . . in other words, we may choose our destiny. And certain people, because they chose not to drink from the river of forgetfulness, have recalled time spent in that space between. They can remember uncanny details of their previous life and parse out the details of the next—"I will be a doctor. I will lose my first wife at a young age, because I will need to benefit from the growth that loss and renewal brings," etc. If this is true, the reason most of us don't remember becomes obvious. If we knew how our entire life would turn out, we'd likely be immobilized by the knowledge. We'd suffer from a sense of dreaded fatalism about our "fate." It's a necessary forgetting then, so that our consciousness can remain focused on the here and now. If our destiny is predetermined in choosing how to respond to that destiny, everything can change. As Doc told Marty, "No one should know too much about their destiny."

Heart memory is a different story. If our mind memory gets inebriated by the river of forgetfulness, the emotional memory of our previous births survives. In the study of astrology (studying the Moon's South Node, in particular) and through researching many charts, it quickly becomes obvious that the memories of the heart are strong enough to survive death and rebirth. The heart is a powerful guide that way, and it is the wisest of teachers. It makes sense, too, that these heart memories involve others, as we learn some of our deepest life lessons from relationships that are clothed in Mystery, many of which wear garments of love and attraction.

Heart memory is strong enough to attract the person who will help heal what needs to be healed in this lifetime. The heart memory knows all facets of love— where it has hurt before and where it must heal to be whole. The heart may attribute love or pain or both to an actual person (and this may explain why we're compelled to form relationships with the people we do). If we've had previous contracts

K.I.S.S.

LIFETIMES OF IT

Reincarnation. How many lifetimes are we working with here? It's hard to know and contemplating that question really puts a new spin on your personal history, expanding it far beyond yourself and outward into new dimensions of time and space. When I first began expanding my consciousness through the study of astrology, I was relieved to discover that my big deal of a life really was much bigger than little ol' me. At the time, my problems were catastrophic by anyone's measure, and overwhelming, too. But knowing I'd experienced lifetimes of crap made all the difference! Here was my birth chart on this piece of paper, a picture of me that symbolized possibly hundreds or thousands of years of accumulated karma! In that moment, I instantly became a bigger person. The knowledge of the great Mystery gave me spiritual levity and more than a little grace to handle what I'd been given.

with them, we may actually be "destined" to meet again.[1] Heart memory may explain the mysterious reason we're attracted to a particular experience or a particular spiritual lesson of love.

Memories survive as our current attitudes. Suspicion, distrust, love, adoration . . . maybe they're all mixed together for you! The heart doesn't need details and particulars to know that it's connected to someone. It remembers the feelings of familiarity, comfort, and love.

---

1 Various karmic and soul mate stories I've come across suggest that we don't always reunite with the ones we've loved before (their karma may require them to live in Poland in this life, while you're taking care of business in San Francisco); however, all of us will meet people with heart memories whose "story" fits into ours. Whether you believe in past lives or just the metaphorical feelings, we receive the juice to grow from anyone whose growth needs align with ours.

You don't have to believe in reincarnation; just knowing you're experiencing a timeless and profound connection, that the heart has clicked with this person, is all you need to know. Our heart memories quietly guide us toward connections we'd never dreamed of, in ways we'd only dared imagine. And no matter what the nature of the relationship is—be it healing, karmic, or soulful—the common denominator is a return to love. Guided by heart memories, we move through this life, following our heart.

So if you have any doubts that the love you find in this life will end when your heart stops beating, don't. You take your heart memories with you!

Mate, Give Me My Soul Back, Dammit!

When we're talking about soul, when it feels absent or missing in a relationship, demanding its return is a reasonable request. Your average juicy karmic relationship will make this need obvious—by first giving you a few important lessons replete with growing pains, then by gently (or not so gently) reminding you of what it is that you're still missing.

What's a karmic mate, you ask? The soul mate and karmic mate are two very different faces of love. In the case of karmic mates, two individuals' respective heart memories line up to finish karmic contracts with each other. Common karmic meetings revolve around transforming an old pattern, repaying a debt, healing an injury, resolving a conflict, and often all of these at once. But here's the clincher: those same qualities that initially attract us to our soul mate—feelings of familiarity, attraction, and even a level of comfort (the karmic mate is far more familiar than comfortable, though)—all belong to the karmic relationship, too! So how do you tell the difference between a mate who will give you a piece of your soul back, and the mate who has a score to settle and an expiration date?

The key indicator is that when the relationship's essence revolves around resolving old bonds for you or the other person, it eventually feels like old bondage. A predominance of suffering over joy is a sign you've outgrown the contract and remaining together no longer makes sense for either person. A soul mate relationship does not feel like prison, it feels joyful.

Some rare and remarkable karmic relationships will restore soul through a miraculous transformation by one or both partners. It's as though the locus of your karmic relationship revolves around resolving conflict and healing trials for a time, but handled with compassionate care, the relationship rises like a phoenix from the ashes of devastation into empowered soul mate love. This doesn't happen without tons of personal work and effort. It is rarer still that the relationship actually survives these karmic trials intact.

The most common type of relationship is karmic. Karmic mate bonds just need to run their course, burn through the love lessons, and die in the smoldering ashes. There's precious freedom in burning through that kind of bondage: after the fire, love heals and, finally, you both get to make a fresh start, alone. Your relationship served a purpose, and you've completed your contract with each other. But you don't complete each other. In fact, you will usually find out you're more powerful apart than you were together.

Does it sound like a bum deal, these karmic mates? Can't we just fast-forward directly to the soul mate part, you ask? No, we shouldn't ask for that! Karmic mates teach us tons about our self! They are around to help us complete a phase of development important for our personal evolutionary journey, or even that of a familial or cultural legacy. Karmic mates will make us better people if we let them teach us what they are here to teach. Karmic mates, albeit often circuitously, will help our destiny unfold. The key is recognizing when we're complete and then exiting as gracefully as possible. When the suffering grows bigger than the joy, we know we've entered the territory of generating more karma work for the future.

The fictional love story between Romeo and Juliet is a good example of a karmic mate story with soul mate undertones. Romeo and Juliet's story was far bigger than their fifteen-year-old selves, complicated beyond their ability to manage. Larger-than-life family feuding and social prejudices blocked their innocent love from blooming. They held a special attraction for each other, and coincidence and synchronicity conspired to bring them together (and also keep them apart) until the contract was completed. Unfortunately, the soul mate relationship of healing, integration, and reunion never took place in their brief lives; their love, amid so many complications, tragically ended their lives. Perhaps they healed rifts between

K.I.S.S.

THAT'S NOT MY SOUL MATE, THAT'S MY KARMIC MATE!

Seeing as how karmic mates are as easy to pick up as a gallon of milk at the 7-Eleven, the list of common-sense questions below may help us discern the difference between a soul mate and a karmic mate:

- Are you trying to analyze the person's strange behavior instead of listening to your heart's simple truth?

- Is the person no longer who you thought they were? Do you find yourself wanting to change them into a fantasy, or back into the person you thought they once were?

- As you've gotten to know this person, are their values, beliefs, character, and intentions incompatible with yours?

- Is their behavior wacky by the rest of the world's standards?

the Montagues and the Capulets, but the two young lovers were not destined to complete one another—at least not in that lifetime. But, Romeo and Juliet could meet again as soul mates in the next life—now *that* would make a fine sequel!

Alas, it's a mythic story, but there are tons of modern-day loves found and lost under sad circumstances. Some are completed in the death of the relationship, or in literal death. When a karmic relationship cannot continue in this lifetime, taking a larger, spiritual perspective can help us see the necessity of this kind of meeting and its inevitable parting. Sometimes contracts play out for mysterious reasons that are larger than our understanding, and in order to comprehend them, we've got to enlarge our concept of what this love and its demise might mean. Through their death, Romeo and Juliet's love story awakened the hearts of those who had prevented their love, and that's one way of receiving heart healing for the *Anima Mundi*, the World Soul.

Past Life, This Life

The past-life connection is awe-inspiring. It often resembles the very recent past, because it has or is playing out in this lifetime, but not always romantically. In my work with relationships that carry karmic or soul mate connections, the exclamation I most often hear is, "That wasn't a past life, it's this one!" That's what happened when my girlfriend Kelli sought me out for a past-life reading.

As I read the symbols, I painted an eerily familiar picture of a glamorous woman on the arm of a well-liked but dangerously powerful man, a Tony Soprano kind of guy. It turns out I was describing a role she had relived in her early life with both her father and her brother, whom I'd known nothing about until this story came to light. Although these relationships were primary and not exactly romantic, they were definitely karmic connections representing the core of her unfinished business and heart-healing in this lifetime.

For my friend Kelli, being "arm candy" for a powerful but deceptive and ultimately hurtful man felt familiar. It didn't get her what she wanted, which was to feel nurtured and protected by safe, unconditional love. In the world in which she grew up, love came with conditions, hard edges, and terrible requests. Love wasn't soft and warm and nurturing—it was every person for their self. So she did what many of us do with hurt hearts: she went to the opposite extreme. In an attempt to skip the healing work, Kelli tried to embody or become the love she never had. When things fell apart for others, she became a safe haven for them without having gotten that love for herself. I suggested that her preparatory soul mate work was to nurture unconditional love for her own self and to notice when people triggered her need to caretake or make up for a deficiency of soulful love. She had clear signposts to watch for: the bad boys in the crowd, for those were the ones that she felt attracted to. Many people with abusive parents are subtly attracted to their abuser. They have business to complete with those harmful people.

In my work, I've found that past-life connections always play out in this one, especially during the first twenty years of life. Sometimes events happen all over again in exactly the same way they did before, and other times the story picks up where it left off. Stories of wounds may leave us feeling like we have a phantom limb. And whether reliving a past-life story or a current one, if we feel vulnerable to being hurt by those who love us, it's because we are vulnerable. It's hard not to feel raw, and often we recognize it in the pain we feel around our heart chakra. This tenderness also makes recognizing a repeat story in the current life incredibly difficult to face.

If we're vulnerable to the confusion of falling into invisible patterns described by previous relationships, it's up to us to see through our own confusion, not blame the other (or our parents), and do our best to look into our own re-created role within the relationship. It's also important to keep forgiving ourselves when we "mess up" and slip into old patterns of falling for the partner who triggers painful experiences of love, particularly if a relationship has addictive components. In this case, forgiveness of self and others can work miracles on our hearts.

Soul Mate Reunions

There's a Turkish word, *kismet*, meaning one's destiny in life. Some consider their kismet and their soul mate to be one and the same. Your soul mate indeed may bring you closer to your destiny, or destiny can bring you closer to your soul mate, as in the case of a couple reunited after years (or lifetimes) of separation. That's where this love story about soul mate reunions comes in.

Shortly after my husband and I were married, I adopted my husband's then "cute" habit of reading the wedding page in the *New York Times* every Sunday. As I began reading these announcements, I realized that it's one of the few reliable news items guaranteed to entertain and warm the heart. Among the most remarkable love stories, I began noticing a pattern of separation and reunion. A pair would meet and feel a spark, and for whatever reason—a move across the country, graduation from college, or being involved in another relationship—were separated. Years would pass, sometimes even decades. Then they'd happen to see each other in the elevator of the same apartment building or at the event of a mutual friend and discover that the spark was still there, except this time, the road blocks no longer existed. They had finished their other business. Any leftover obstacles to love were no longer big enough to keep them apart.

Something similar happened for my aunt Elsa, with an angelic twist. Growing up, I always admired the beauty and independence of Elsa, who was my mother's stepsister. She was a flight attendant back in the day, when it was a glamorous life. Then she became an advertising executive in the 1980s, and I idolized her as the quintessential 1980s power woman. Successful, beautiful but also perpetually single was how I thought of Elsa. She would wait close to fifty years to reunite with her soul mate.

When Elsa was in high school, her stepbrother's best friend, Warren, was always hanging around the house. At the time, she had just joined my mother's family (her mother passed away just a few short years before her father remarried my mother's mother). Adjusting to a whole new family and still grieving for her mother, she didn't pay much attention to Warren but noted that he liked to joke around with and tease her.

Neither Elsa nor Warren ever married. Over the years, Warren stayed friends with Elsa's stepbrother (my uncle) and he would always inquire kindly about her. When my mother died at age fifty, both Warren and Elsa attended the funeral. I didn't know this at the time, but the funeral would prove to be their soul mate meeting! Elsa and Warren reconnected so instantly that they ended up spending day into evening at one another's side. (In fact, for years afterward, my sister and I wondered why Elsa hadn't attended the actual service. She had been cozied up with Warren in a corner of my grandmother's house!) These two married a year later, bought a farm house, and lived out a shared dream of rural country life.

Life is surprising. Cupid is rarely recognizable, sometimes wearing the somber clothes of devastation, loss, or death. Elsa's mother's death led to her first meeting with Warren, and my mother's death reunited them. The awareness that love is alive even amidst the deepest suffering is a profound spiritual truth. To expound on this, if we're able to do the courageous work of keeping our heart open, even amidst life's suffering and loss, miracles bloom. Love can triumph over loss.

In my aunt Elsa's story, an unexpected matchmaker, the angel of death, was a force of compassionate love. Elsa's dates with death (her mother's, then my mother's) didn't keep her from her soul contract. Perhaps it had already been arranged, meeting her soul mate at that place and time. Maybe two angels—her mother and my mother—held everyone to their appointment. Elsa's date with destiny was fulfilled.

Let this story be deeply reassuring. If you have a contract with a soul mate, from years ago or previous lifetimes, you are destined to meet. And meet you will. Nothing can keep you apart, including time and circumstance. The events surrounding your meeting may not be obvious to your rational mind or ego, but from the soul's perspective, it all makes perfect sense.

I remember once asking my grandmother why she was never remarried and she always said, "The timing wasn't right." It seemed sad to me at the time, but now I see her truth in that wisdom. For some people, like my grandma, the timing may never be right—because the spirit needs to be alone for evolutionary purposes. We must always listen to our truth.

Yet I do believe, if we are meant to meet our kismet, there will be a time when it is right. We can keep the faith. We can honor the Mystery that we simply don't know when.

You Have Many Soul Mates, You Have One

You think you have one soul mate? Think again. Chances are you've already been with several, someone who awakened your heart and connected you to the deep reservoir of love. The heart is always in the process of waking up, and a soul mate is anyone who expands our heart and deepens the Mystery of life. I'm going to tell you a story about meeting one of my soul mates, and I've italicized the signs of a soul mate connection.

Once I met a remarkable man when I was working as a waitress in a coffee shop. As I served him coffee, he commented on my hands, "You have the hands of a caretaker." This startled me because I was a caretaker, and hearing so at the time I was deeply grieving my mother's death was helpful. As I continued to serve him, I found out he was a healer. I immediately thought: *I need healing.* The conversation continued and *we had so much in common, that eerie feeling of awe began moving between us.* We were both born in Ohio, and our first California residence was a very small seaside town outside of Santa Cruz. Our interaction was infused with familiarity and "aha!" moments, and when he told me he was going to see a Prince concert in Oakland that next month, my jaw dropped. He was the only other person I knew who loved Prince as much as I did. We exchanged phone numbers, but when he left, I didn't know what to make of the relationship. Despite our amazing first meeting and all those connections, I wasn't at all sexually attracted to him!

I called my girlfriend, of course, who excitedly began quizzing me: Does he have a house? Where does he live? He sounds perfect for you, you're both into healing and it sounds like you enjoy the same things. Oh, he must make great money (she's a Taurus, so money matters) and you should definitely call him. She was right, we had so many connections, of course I would call him, and I did. But despite *an inner knowing that we were pieces of the same puzzle and we had finally found each other*, it still didn't feel romantic. She suggested that the romance would come in time. It didn't.

As our friendship deepened, it became clear that this was no chemical romance. I mused over the deeper nature of this relationship: the more we shared our dreams and goals, the more we were *excited and stimulated by one another*. How could we have so many things in common and not be life partners? I was an attractive, intelligent woman, and I felt the same about him as a man. Slowly, as he began to teach me what he knew about spirituality, healing, and generosity, the soul of our relationship became clearer. This wasn't a romantic connection; it was a spiritual one. Both of us felt we had a lot to learn from each other, and deep companionship was definitely a part of it. But more than this, I had never had a man in my life who loved me so generously, and for a long period of time, he was that man in my life.

No, he was not The One, but he was one of my soul mates. Many of us don't come together to do just the romance piece of love; we come together for a larger purpose revealed over the course of the relationship. Some of us need to grow up together, and we do this by getting married young and helping each other learn the ropes of life. Others of us need to grow spiritually before we're able to be romantically partnered. Others still need to find that person (and not necessarily a life partner) who helps them bring their life's work into the larger world. The reasons you and your soul mates join are as varied and complex as you are, but you can have more than one soul mate. Remember, *a soul mate relationship is recognizable by its soulful quality, the meaningful way it opens your heart.*

K.I.S.S.

YOU HAVE MANY SOUL MATES, YOU HAVE ONE

Some people will have many different partners in life. If this is you (and you probably know who you are!), consider the sanity-saving thought that not every relationship is meant to last forever. For you, there's simply too much to try, taste, and experience to roll into one single person. Consider that the sheer amount of "living" you have elected to experience in this lifetime would never allow it! Try this: Instead of turning every new date into The One (if only to save yourself from unnecessary emotional suffering), give yourself permission to experiment, be unconventional, and be irrepressibly curious. Allow yourself to be you! And when you make that leap of self-acceptance, a surprising thing may happen—you may just find someone as multi-faceted, unusual, diverse, and colorful as all get out. In short, you've found your quirky-as-you-are soul mate.

Romantic love is not required for a soulful relationship, but the romance part is like a really good hook—it snags our attention and reels us in for the deeper love work. We all want a grand, sweeping love affair, but there may be other attractions or reasons for being together. We may be attracted to the security of partnering up or the financial stability someone offers. We may be attracted to their worldview and that soul mate can show us a new way of looking at things, one we'd have never discovered without them. Any relationship that moves you to higher ground, expands your heart, and makes a deep impact on your life qualifies as a soul mate connection. So when you're looking for The One, understand that you have the power to find them—after all, you may have found a few already!

Summary: Recognizing Your Soul Mate

A soul mate connection has all of these qualities:

The feeling of your relationship is: this is comfortable.

You feel a compelling connection you can't rationally explain.

There's familiarity between you.

You just feel right in the presence of this person.

You bond over synchronous connections fairly immediately.

You're excited and stimulated by one another's presence.

They may play a recurring role in your life.

The overriding emotions you share on a daily basis are joy and love.

Looking for a Few Good Men

Soul Mate Secret No. 3

The energy of abundance attracts love. Lack is the opposite of love. Anytime you feel lack, do something that makes you feel abundant, opulent, and rich.

Where have all the cowboys gone?

PAULA COLE

You've hit the Internet dating sites, worked your social network, and fished the office dating pool, and you're done. You took a chance or two and never really found anyone worth risking your heart for. My search for a soul mate fell somewhere in between. I dated a little and came to the not-so-rapid conclusion, after some very long dry spells, that there were no available men. Correction: no available *good* men. Sure, there are plenty of players, daters, and haters, but no *good* men. It's a common complaint. But when I hear it now, it tugs at my heartstrings because I've lived with that misunderstanding.

There are many reasons we choose to believe this fallacy. Maybe we're ambivalent about being in a committed relationship to begin with, because we think we'll lose our freedom, or we think we won't have time and energy to focus on our career. Or maybe you've been burned before. And then there's the obvious—you just haven't met the right guy yet! The thing to remember is that when you become the right person, good men are everywhere. And if we think differently, the only one we're kidding is our self.

So how do we change our mindset? First, instead of focusing on the "not available" part, I want to redirect your attention to the "good" part, because it was that very word that first got me thinking about the power of intention.

When I was in my late twenties, I lived on the island of Maui for a brief time, where I worked as an art consultant in a trendy gallery. I had jumped from the frying pan into the fire, from a decision to leave a high-paying but high-burnout job to move to everyone's little slice of heaven, Hawaii. I was lured there by a man, of course, a Scorpio Svengali whom I deeply cared for but didn't love. I naively thought I could move in with a man three thousand miles away from home and keep our feelings for one another casual! After only a few weeks, the rose-colored glasses began to crack.

The gallery I worked in happened to be almost all women, several married, several unmarried. From these women, I learned that even on Fantasy Island, dating isn't easy. Everyone on the island knew everyone else, and although it was very cozy, the predicament presented a host of challenges. No one could date anyone's ex, for starters, because that would show poor taste and disloyalty. But of course everyone did, so there was that incestuous circle vibe. New hotties came in "fresh off the boat" every week to visit, great for a fling but not long-term love. As I listened to the inside skinny, I grew exhausted just thinking about the prospect of finding love. I was pretty much off the market anyhow, and in no position to look, considering I was all emotionally tied up with the Svengali.

One woman in the gallery, Lisa, was newly engaged. She was gorgeous, friendly, and outgoing, so I naturally thought, "Of course she's engaged, huh? She's the kind of woman who could wrap a man around her finger in a snap." But then she told me how much time she'd spent dating the wrong men, and that it really hadn't been easy finding her true love. That is, until she put her specific intention out there: simply, "Bring me a good man." Lisa wanted someone faithful and true, with a good heart. It was a simple, decent, heartfelt request. Yet the emotional energy behind that request was like rocket fuel, fired directly to Venus, goddess of love. And boy, did Venus deliver. Quite literally, a good man showed up—his last name was spelled G-o-o-d-m-a-n. She had met her Mr. Goodman.

And now this woman was engaged to be married. When she told me her story, I just about fell out of my chair. Had she been surprised? Did she ever think she would or could attract her fiancé like that? She had been just as surprised as I was by this miraculous parting of the heavens, which suddenly seemed, under the light of clarity, less miraculous and more, well, smart. Then I looked at her magical powers differently. She wasn't just another beautiful person in love, someone who had a secret special power (beauty, personality, charm) that I either didn't possess or couldn't find in myself. The only difference between her approach and mine was that she had used her brain. This woman had used her intelligence to find her soul mate. Hey, I could do that!

K.I.S.S.

RULE YOUR WORLD

Core beliefs rule your world. The problem is we don't realize how they sabotage us because we're too busy believing them. When I realized that I might be perpetuating my own demise, I changed my thoughts by immediately turning a negative into a positive.

When you get into your own "there are no good men" mental funk, or when your girlfriend groans that prayer of self-defeat, the only thing to do is negate it immediately. Flip it. It's simple and powerful. "I'll never find the love I'm looking for" becomes "I will find the love I'm looking for." Here's another: "I'm attracted to superficial men, not soulful, spiritual men" becomes "I'm attracted to soulful, spiritual men, not superficial men." You can flip any negative message into a positive one, and you literally retrain your mind to expect the positive.

The hardest part of this exercise is actually discovering your core beliefs. Negative core beliefs resist being found out—their very existence depends on our ignorance of them. We just let them run, and they rule our world. To get a good idea about what you're really thinking, I suggest regularly practicing meditation or automatic writing. The goal of both is to let your mind unfurl all your negative and positive thoughts without judgment. If you notice repeating patterns, bingo! You've discovered a belief. Over time, you can kick those beliefs out of your mind like the hairy, love-sabotaging monsters they are!

Intention. Was it really that simple? As I packed my bags three months later and returned to San Francisco, I took this new discovery with me. I started rebuilding my life in the City by the Bay all over again, and although it would take me years to begin the search for my soul mate, I began busily wrapping my head around what I'd learned in Maui. I began threading artful intention into every job and housing situation, and into every search for funds when needed. Each and every time,

I found that using one firmly planted intention was so elegant and took far less energy than pounding the pavement. Doing so allowed me to eliminate the noise by holding out for my heart's truth. Over time, I learned so much more about my ability to elegantly attract what I wanted instead of thinking I had to go "make it happen." Back in Maui, the future Mrs. Goodman had used her intention like a yardstick to measure every man she met. Those who weren't truly good for her, men who didn't measure up, wouldn't get past the front door. I decided I would do the same from then on.

The Scarcity Myth

We don't see things as they are. We see them as we are.
—Anais Nin

After hanging out with that group of women on the lushly feminine island of Maui, all of whom had incredible magnetism, I learned that only a few of us were truly tapping our power to receive and attract. Instead, many of us were frustrated by love, and, getting caught up in frustration and a feeling of lack, we began reacting with our Mars, in this respect, the planet of fear and strife: Where have all the good men gone? There are no good men to be found, anywhere. When we're living in misunderstanding, it's impossible to attract love. We begin to think like hunters on the prowl, full of jaded discouragement, or we give up and curl into a fetal position of passive apathy. Either choice sends out a man-repellant attitude.

Let me tell you right now: scarcity is a myth! Every city tells the tale—different city, same story. San Francisco, Maui, or L.A., I can imagine a group of girlfriends sitting around right now kvetching about no good men. It goes like this: San Francisco: "All the men and women are gay!" Maui: "They come to the island; six months later, they leave." L.A.: "Everyone here is so superficial. I need to move to Alaska to find a man who values me for me." Oh, and Alaska, supposedly with the highest number of single men per capita in the United States: "There are no good women!" You have no business perpetuating this myth; it will only hurt your search for love. Love is abundance, not scarcity.

And any lack in your life can hold up your search for love. Many times our less-than ideas about ourselves are merely scarcity beliefs that can be dissolved by investigating our thinking.

For example, as I write this, the world economy has officially entered a recession, which means inflation is high, the values of certain world currencies are tanking, and people say there isn't enough money to go around. Does such a thing even exist? In a scandalously man-objectifying but belief-busting experiment, let's compares apples to oranges, men to dollars. Money (men) never disappears; it (they) is somewhere else. Things may lose their value, but money doesn't disappear; it's just held somewhere else. Likewise, love may hide for a while, but it's never gone. It's only carousing, multiplying, dividing, and in all likelihood, making love, creating more of itself. Ha!

We get so used to automatic scarcity-thinking that we don't even notice it's running our life. I have a client who came to me saying she'd been single for years. I was pleased to tell her love energies are entering the picture soon. Then I asked if anyone had been wooing her lately? She firmly responded no, yet fifteen minutes and another topic later, she remembered that, yes, someone had been hotly pursuing her—and it really bothered her because she didn't like him at all.

My client "forgot" that said man was all over her like white on rice. I suggested she might be unconsciously running an old scarcity tape. The fact that she was being wooed, even if unmatched with her desire for a specific type of man, meant that the delightful woo-woo we're all looking for was absolutely in her auric field. How exciting! Yet as she listed all the ways she had been disappointed in the past, I wondered to myself: the stars say she's receiving a love infusion, but will she be available to receive it?

This happens more often than not in the search for the soul mate: we receive an influx of relationship energy but grow sick to our stomach about who we're not attracting. If we treat it as an opportunity, noticing this offers a real opportunity to move past old patterns. When we attract the people we don't want (or when the people we desire are unavailable), the reality is, we're stuck in a core conflict. The only reality is that it is we who are doing the attracting. We might refer to this conflict as "confusion" when we're talking about it with friends, and it is. We're confused by the difference between who our conscious mind tells us we want and who it is that actually shows up.

My client continued, illuminating a recurring pattern in her life. She told me that the attention from an "unwanted admirer" wasn't unfamiliar. She had ended a love affair with another man (a married man) who recently reappeared as a potential new employee at her workplace. The thought of seeing him there every day also filled her heart with dread, and that strain of negative attention was blocking the flow of "I'm available and interested" Venus energy.

Here's the deal: I'm absolutely sure she wanted to be available to love, and I'm just as sure her heart was preoccupied.

So. Within my means, how could I help my client woo the woo-woo of the Universe into her corner? I suggested that she write down who it is she did and didn't want (using the Dear Cupid Spell, see p. 279) through the eyes of her past relationships. I said the process could amplify some old wounds about other people who had hurt her and that she could respond by either following the signposts to some serious heart-healing, or stopping short. And she might stop here—doing the work to attract soulful love is not for the faint of heart! It requires our full soulful presence, that we show up in our life, for our own self. Asking for who we want and believing we deserve them can blow open all our trap doors, our self-betrayals, our pain at not having been loved the way we wanted, our justifications, denials, depression, our whys and our why-nots.

Incidentally, clearing up where we've been in misunderstanding is like required reading for the main course (which is sustaining a real love relationship). Tons of self-examination and objectivity are prep work for the real-deal soul mate relationship. You will discover how richly valuable this self-knowledge is when you're finally in that soulful relationship and love disarms you, robbing you of all your excuses and all your "stuff." Love sees through all that jazz!

There's nothing like having a load of relationship energy thrown right at where you're stuck to illuminate those areas that have been blocked for too long. Living the scarcity myth is a lot like looking in the mirror and selectively seeing only what it is you're missing. What you've been missing is the rest of the story. Through uncovering our scarcity myths, justifications, and excuses, and exploring our attraction for less than who we deserve, we have an opportunity for self-knowing, possibility, and joy. In other words, by exploring the other side of scarcity, we finally discover abundance.

Exercise: Two Sides of The Same Coin

Myths, like the scarcity myth, are simply stories. When we view them from a symbolic perspective, myths show meaning and soulfulness. When we don't look at them as metaphors for our interior, they resemble highly exaggerated versions of an inner reality, one we can't see because either it's too painful or we haven't learned how to "see" that way. So we say he's a jerk or he's unavailable, when we're the one who is unavailable and we're the one treating our self poorly.

Every relationship has a gift for us, even the ones we're struggling with! To discover the gift in a problematic partnership, re-frame the problem they're handing you as though it were your problem. In the case of an unavailable partner, some questions you might want to ask are: Am I truly available for what and who it is I desire? Do I consistently settle for less than I deserve? Have I gotten too used to limitation? If we're attracting less than we deserve, it's up to us to discover the abundance lurking in the lack. It's painful to really accept that it's not that they are what's wrong and that you are what's wrong, but accept it we must.

Companion Spell: DEAR CUPID SPELL

Divine Timing

People write to me asking, "When will I meet my soul mate?" It can be difficult to tell my clients that they won't be meeting The One this year, but I owe it to them and to my craft to be honest. That doesn't mean, however, we should hang out just waiting. In my experience, the best thing we can do to attract a soul mate is take the next step in our own life. To accept where we are right now as a phase in a larger journey to love.

In the hands of the right practitioner, the magical arts speak real truth, but even if he or she can describe the shape, color, and size of what your heart wants, no astrologer or magician knows your level of readiness. The attitudes, choices, and self-awareness you have today shape what's coming next. Only you are in control of your destiny, and you are always just beginning. If you can be honest with yourself about where you are in the journey, and that you may have some different work to do between now and then, you'll arrive at your desired destination a lot quicker.

I'm thinking of a friend I've known for years and admire deeply, a Vedic astrologer named Grant, who relayed the following story to me.

Grant had a young twenty-something client who came to him with the concern that her love life was doomed by the stars. She had been told as much by another astrologer, and Grant didn't disagree! No matter how much he wanted to say it wasn't so, when he looked at the charts, he saw tremendous difficulties. Bound by his profession to deliver the truth as described by this ancient and very precise predictive tradition, he did just that. He said to her, "You will have no problem meeting men and finding dates but as far as finding a compatible lifelong match, that won't happen until you're fifty."

Many of us might have a very hard time hearing this, especially in our twenties. Yet when he relayed this information, she was blasé and totally unfazed by his prediction. She said he had only confirmed what she knew to be true, and to be honest, it relieved her to hear it from him because now she could go about the business of getting on with her life!

In our right mind (not our love-starved one), we understand that to everything there really is a season. We all have an inner knowledge about who and what we're ready for. When we look for the truth on the path of our soul, the truth really does set us free.

So if you're wondering "When will . . . ?" the answer you seek is inside of you. And you can find it! When I was in my late twenties on a walk one day, I had the sudden intuition that I wouldn't be with my soul mate until I was thirty-four (in reality, I got married when I was thirty-three). Later that day, I shared this inner knowing with a friend, who gazed off into the distance as though he were momentarily contemplating the direction of the wind or a flight of birds and said, "Yes, that sounds about right to me, too." I do believe there's truth to be found inside of us, if we ask. Whether it's two years or twenty years, you'll recognize the truth because it feels right.

Of course, this knowledge didn't stop me from keeping my options open to all the connections I encountered. After all, my intuition didn't tell me when I would meet my soul mate, just when I would be with him! But by asking the deeper question, "Well, what next?" instead of becoming like the goddess Andromeda chained to an island of rocks waiting, I knew it would happen in divine time. And so my energy became liberated to do other things.

There are many forks in the road in life. If you feel the soul mate is your destination, then living your life is the path that will get you there. How you meet a challenge or desire, or how you respond to your next spiritual task, in this moment, is a step in the right direction. When that moment is going to happen is less important than everything leading up to that moment. Every wrong turn you make right, every special conversation you have, every heart prompting you follow, and every intuition you heed will prepare you to receive the soul mate blessings that are in store for you.

❧

Exercise: Soul Mate Meditation
When Will My Soul Mate Arrive?

You have the answers you need. I know, it sounds deceptively simple to ask—but often asking, with an open mind and heart, is the one thing we neglect to do. Before doing this exercise, try to arrive at a place of harmony and non-attachment to any outcome at all (I suggest reading the section on the seventh chakra first, see p. 165). When my answer was revealed to me, I was on a long walk in nature and very attuned to my own silent stillness, and the answer hit "out of the blue." In fact, it's much easier to receive answers from your higher self when you're relaxed, at ease, and in emotional-mental-spiritual harmony. Do your meditation, walking, tai-chi, yoga, etc., before this exercise.

Go to a place physically, and psychically, where you won't be disturbed. Close your eyes. Visualize yourself sitting here in this room. Now step out of the picture, so you're an observer watching yourself breathe, noticing the details of the room. You are pure consciousness, just noticing the quality of light on the wall, the color of the floor, the pictures on the walls. Notice how you can float around the room and still see yourself clearly sitting here, in this moment. We'll call this your special awareness.

Take your special awareness up through the roof, so now you're seeing the house in which you live, from above. You can see your neighborhood, the cars on the street. Looking in one direction, you notice the mountain range, the sea—whatever is your natural environment. Direct your energy higher and zoom into the clouds. Now you can see the city in which you live—an aerial view from above. And a little higher, your home state. And even higher, now you can see your continent, and then the planet Earth. Now your awareness is merged with the cosmos, you look around and see a black, starry atmosphere. You're surrounded by planets and stars.

Imagine a time line appears, a "wrinkle" or fold in time resembling your lifeline for this life. Perhaps it looks like a silver or white glowing sliver against the sky. At one end is your birth and at the other, your death. You may experience memories and begin to visually place those on the time line. As you watch memories populate your time line, you have a clear sense of where you are currently, and can "see" where you are in your life. Put a year, or age, next to that image of you, as though your lifeline were a ruler of time, measurable in increments. Now, if you haven't already asked, ask for your soul mate to step into the time line. You may sense a presence or see a glowing light somewhere on the time line, or the outline of a person. Trust exactly where this image lands. An age or a year may immediately pop out for you. If not, use your past memories' distance from current time

K.I.S.S.

GOODBYE, CAT LADY

I used to be afraid of this one, and I have girlfriends who have this fear, too. I was afraid I would be the weird witch-y cat lady in the neighborhood, kept company by magical potions and her feline companions. As we grow in self-knowing, this fear, which relies on insecurity and self-doubt, vanishes. The beautiful older women I know who are building lives without a partner have had one (or several) soul mates for long periods of time and decided they'd rather be single. But as one friend has said, "I just enjoy spending my time on myself too much to share it." See, after several soul mate relationships, and with wisdom, you just get to know yourself. You stop using the cat lady fear as a weapon in your search for love. If you're alone, you'll know in your heart that you're meant to be alone because you simply enjoy this option more than the other. By the way, I resolved my cat lady fear by totally embracing it! I got two black sister cats . . . and then found out I was allergic and had to find them new homes. I did practice magic, however, and look what happened!

as a ruler, and use those increments of time as a measure for when your soul mate will arrive. Don't second guess your first thought or image. Your first thought is the best thought. Trust the answer you receive.

Now thank your soul mate for appearing and begin to descend back to Earth. Through the stars you see Earth again. As the planet grows more visible with land masses and ocean, you're pulled down into your continent, then your state, your city, neighborhood, and room. Then allow your special awareness to enter back into your body through the top of your skull. Breathe slowly for several minutes. Ground yourself.

Companion Spell: AFFIRMING FOR LOVE

Courting Fortuna

You've heard of the phrase "lucky in love." You've probably known people who live by this phrase, too. They have tons of opportunities to be in a relationship, but they have no idea who or how to be in that relationship. Hmm, is being lucky in love a blessing or a curse? What good is being lucky in love if you're not prepared to accept its blessings?

People have asked that of the Roman goddess Fortuna for years. Fortuna's name is synonymous with both blessed and cursed luck, and in artistic renderings, she's often depicted as blind (just like the goddess of justice). We might think Lady Luck is blind, that luck is happenstance, something we stumble upon, or that we're born lucky. The real blindness surrounding Lady Luck is our own. We think luck is random. We often don't realize that we can court luck. Ask a gambler who takes home big winnings and you'll discover that every decision he made and every intuition he followed (or didn't) bears down on that one moment of heavenly opening. We think, "Ooooh, they just got lucky!" It's so not true.

Fortuna is not random. She actually works a lot like karma or the goddess of justice, but with a flirty twist—with Fortuna, sudden bounty appears for no apparent reason. Your own life is full of examples of how her "blind luck" works: think about how many times a window of opportunity opened, when suddenly "everything came together." That job you'd been slogging away at for years was actually giving you the exact skills you needed—who knew learning that obscure computer program would make you a hot commodity? That "lucky coincidence" gave you the skill to jump confidently into a wonderful opportunity called your destiny. Another example: maybe all the heart healing and growth you'd done in a previous relationship has allowed you to move light years ahead in this one. We often can't see where we're headed, but we can court Fortuna and plant seeds for our own luck. How? One word: preparation. For luck to find you, preparation is everything.

There's a card in tarot called the Wheel of Fortune that offers even more insight into the phenomenon of "luck." The Wheel of Fortune spins around and around, never stopping. Round and round you go, and when you're at the top, you're the tops (though by virtue of being at the top you'll eventually be at the bottom, too)! The Wheel of Fortune brings opportunity to get out of jail, move five steps forward, and collect $200 as "lucky" occurrences. Throughout life, everyone has the opportunity (actually, many opportunities) to take a spin and have their turn on top.

When you're at the top of the Wheel of Fortune, everything you touch has the potential to turn to gold. However, there's that pesky problem of fool's gold here, too. It's the old all-that-glitters-is-not-gold conundrum, and the decision of how to handle fortune is our own. We may reach for something (or someone) false or flashy, a substitute for the more substantial gem that we happened to miss while we were being wined and dined by Mr. All That Glitters. But if we make the wrong choice, we later realize we're dating a fool—or worse, that *we* are playing the fool.

It's as if sometimes opportunity knocks, but its got the wrong address—and it's usually because you gave it the wrong address. You kept putting off following your heart—your dream of moving to Spain—and thus you didn't sign up for that Spanish class and you missed your meeting with a soul mate named Julio. Or maybe you deserve better than you're getting, but once again, you've settled for less. Let's say you were hanging out at a bar, and you got all excited when Mr. Hot Shot came in. While across town at that exact moment Mr. Soul Mate was waiting for a 5:30 appointment with his therapist—who also happened to be the therapist a friend referred you to several weeks ago. Of course, you would've run into him after your 4:30 appointment had you decided to invest in yourself and make the appointment! Don't buy into the illusion of fortune by thinking that others are simply luckier than you. It's not always easy to see, but this is how "good fortune" really works.

You can start courting Fortuna now by asking, "How have I been underestimating myself?" The way to receive the bounty that's in store for you is to keep asking that one question, and then listen for the highest answer. You can also court Fortuna by staying focused on your destiny, by following your own heart, not following someone else's as though their heart had the answers yours doesn't.

When Fortuna smiles at you, you've reached a real self-defining moment. Will you be insecure, checking your teeth for remnants of lunch in the mirror, or will you wink back knowingly? Because Fortuna will smile on you from time to time, but she doesn't come along every day. We may not know when she will arrive (unless you consult an astrologer!), but if you keep your eye on the prize and keep walking toward your dreams, when she does, you'll be poised to make a big evolutionary leap forward. You'll simply be poised to take advantage of an opportunity—and experience what people typically call wicked good luck.

Leave "blind luck" to those who think they were "born lucky." Good fortune is actually a combination of preparation and patience. To capture Fortuna's attention, be supremely ready. And good luck!

The Truth is the Hardest Part

Gosh, this section title sounds like a country song refrain! Well we've all been guilty of doing it. Of turning someone into soul mate material when they're just not. Of course, he did tell us he had a girlfriend/was only casual dating/was only looking for sex, but the truth is we were too stubborn, blind, lonely, dependent to face it.

Well, don't beat yourself up about it, it's hardly uncommon. Indeed it's almost socially acceptable these days to lie to ourselves, or to lie about the true state of our relationships. After all, if the other person is not meeting our needs, it conveniently, always, somehow seems to be their fault.

I had this epiphany while listening to Eckhart Tolle and Oprah (in their webinar for *A New Earth*) advise a woman who wanted a commitment from a man. A man who was letting her know he was unavailable in so many ways. Tolle suggested quietly, and matter of factly: "Why not ask for it? Give yourself a time frame and if he doesn't meet your needs by then—leave." To which Oprah, in her off-the-cuff Sagittarian Moon style, replied: "Well, that's bold!" I was struck by her exclamation. To me, Tolle's advice was simply good common sense. Advice columnists make tons of money doling out this sort of grounded realism. It isn't brain surgery. But the woman seemed unmoved on any point, preferring to stay stuck on the same tired note she came in on. Why was that?

I thought about it and realized that if you're afraid to ask directly for what you want, it's because there's a chance you may not get it. Who wants to hear that they won't get what they want? Hearing that answer would mean surrendering the fantasy of eventual change, because the answer might be no. As Kate Winslet, in the provocative wake-up movie *Revolutionary Road* said, "You know what's so good about the truth? Everyone knows what it is however long they've lived without it. No one forgets the truth—they just get better at lying." The lie is preferable when the truth hurts too much.

How does a relationship between two good people grow deceptive? The truth, in black and white, begins on the simplest of pretenses—we want a mate who is available. Then, we meet someone who isn't available. There's nothing wrong with wanting what we want, and there's nothing wrong with being unavailable. Hopefully, they're honest about it (and when their mouth isn't, their behavior always is). But when we refuse to accept the truth as they've shown it to us and instead continue moving forward into a dead-end involvement, we start lying to our heart. We tell ourself we can change either them or ourself to make this relationship work. Maybe we use their unavailability to justify our low self-esteem or our inability to ask for what we really want. Or maybe we'd rather be unhappy with someone than happy alone.

Whatever the reason, what does believing this lie cost us? A real shot at happiness? A meeting with our soul mate? When we build the foundation of our relationship on unmet expectations and desires, the truth really is scary. The whole bottom—who we want them to be instead of who they actually are—will drop out. That's not setting the foundation for soulful love, that's a recipe for disaster.

I once dated a man who didn't treat me how I wanted to be treated. I told him as much and that's when he finally got real with me. He said he had been married, he wasn't actually divorced yet and was gun-shy about getting involved with anyone. Ah, that's why he was acting so strange! He showed me his ugly warts and to be honest, I didn't like him any more or less than before. My honesty had given him permission to be more real, which made me think that maybe he had a decent reason to act the way he did with me. Maybe other people had reasons for their actions, too!

Most of the time, honesty is given freely. I realized the more honest I was with the people I was dating, the more honest they were able to be with me, and what a relief that was. I didn't necessarily see my soul mate in front of me, but with cool honesty running between us, I could finally see my heart clearly. Hey, this truth-telling could quite plausibly bring about a love revolution!

But there's another benefit to honesty: as this person shows you who they really are, you'll also finally see what they're really capable of offering you. This is infinitely valuable, because not every person is meant to be your soul mate. There's great freedom

K.I.S.S.

KNOW YOUR NO'S TO FIND YOUR YES!

We have lots of judgments floating around up there in our mind, screening our heart through a perceptual filter. Some of these judgments are good and necessary because (as you'll learn in the next chapter) mastering the art of discernment—not just saying yes to anyone—will help us choose the right mate. Yet, in the search for a soul mate, our judgment, clouded by past wounds or natural tendencies, can cause us to miss that beautiful person right in front of us. Maybe we have a hefty amount of suspicion or distrust surrounding responsibility, so when someone is late to pick us up on a date, we think, "Yeah, you're late, I've heard that excuse before," and that thought frames the evening. When we can't separate someone's actions from our habitual response, we miss out on an opportunity to explore a perfectly fine person. Sometimes we need to contemplate why we judge people the way we do in order to discover the beauty in front of us.

in this knowledge, because when you really notice the actual person sitting in front of you, not just the one you want to see, who knows what beauty you might discover. A great friendship? A new expert on nineteenth-century romantic poets? A professional ally? They may be limited about what they have to offer you. So what?! They might just finally tell you who they are. And if clarity of heart is the only gift a person can offer you, that's valuable in itself.

As you are generous with your truth, the truth will be generous with you. The truth will always set you free and your happiness depends on it. But don't take my word for it—just ask anyone in a relationship with someone who has "lots of potential, really he does" just how much fun they're actually having.

Companion Spell: THE COMMON SENSE SUTRA

Exercise: Love the Ones You're With

Just like working a muscle that learns to respond and take action when we get on the treadmill, love is a learned response and action. If we want to exercise our love muscles, we will need plenty of practice with all walks of life. "Love the one you're with" is a great adage to work with because it helps you build up your love muscles and grow attract-ively stronger. From the homeless beggar to the co-worker who drives you nuts to the partner you're having difficulty understanding, once you let them into your heart they'll help you understand your heart a little better, and you'll grow in love! This isn't an exercise in tolerating someone else's insanity (which I don't advise), but one of making space for all the different forms of love. Sometimes it's those one-step-removed relationships, say our relationship with a local shopkeeper, that tap love's spiritual generosity and show us what's possible in love. Who hasn't had a random act of kindness open their heart? So practice responding with heart to everyone you meet. Notice what closes your heart. You won't want or be able to meet everyone's needs, and that's a heart lesson in itself!

Love is Imagining Someone Different

In real love, you want the other person's good.
In romantic love, you want the other person.
—Margaret Anderson, editor and Official Woman of Discernment

On the whole, our culture of romantic love, the idea that "there's someone ultimate for me and, oh, when will I find him?" carries a lot of baggage—and it's not a cute little Louis Vuitton set, either. Collectively, the air has grown so heavy with expecta-tions, desperation, and neediness for a soul mate that it's a miracle anyone's finding anyone these days. When a girlfriend pins her hopes on the pretty new guy at work or a friend of a friend hooks up with "Do you complete me?" "Are you The One?"

thinking, it's darn near impossible to allow her natural loveliness to shine through the sheer noise of desperation. Yet the bright planet herself, the goddess of love Venus, hasn't grown dimmer, despite the fact that it's gotten thick out there.

There is an emotional tractor beam of love that, when pointed at a dream, can manifest miracle love. But that same beam can drive love away when we pin all our neediness, dependencies, and hopes onto every Tom, Dick, or Harry (or Rasheed, Miguel, or Julian) we meet. It's a slippery slope. Neediness can fake out our best hopes and intentions for an unconditional love by putting conditions on everyone we meet. Love crumbles under that pressure. And when we're sizing up everyone we meet with so many conditions and expectations, experimentation and playfulness die a tragic death.

To differentiate between the romance of true love and romantic love, we need to really see the person in front of us for who they are, not who we want them to be. Otherwise, our unacknowledged differences prevent love from blooming. Relationships that never get to the level of commitment we desire often begin with one partner wanting to change the other partner. We may fall in love only to discover the other has a legitimate need that we simply cannot or do not want to meet: a man wants to have children, the woman doesn't; I'm available, you're not; he likes curvy women, and she's skinny. It's no big deal. At this level, nothing's personal. But then again, that's not romantic love; that's just surface attraction.

Romantic love lives on hope. Boy is that a fantasy-fraught place to start a relationship! It thrives on unconscious promises and unspoken and/or unrealistic expectations for the other. Romantic love never stands up to honest inquiry, because that would be the death of the fantasy. Compare this to soul mate love, which sees the best in the other, yet accepts the whole person, warts and all. Soul mate love has truth in it, yet does not surrender the romance part—indeed, it's the romance of true love.

That said, romantic love is an easy sell, but you don't have to buy it, hook, line and sinker. If you're in a romantic relationship with conditional promises, expectations with indeterminate time frames, or the promise of eventual change, your love affair may be arduous. People can and do change, but it won't be smooth or easy. After all, most people don't magically wake up one day to realize that what you've been telling them all along was right! If they were going to change, they would have done it by now. Dramatic shifts of consciousness are more often accompanied by tremendous personal upheaval than by peace, love, and happiness. If you're in love with someone you want to change, the best advice I can offer you is this: accept them for who they are. By accepting that they may never change and by relinquishing your attachment to that change, there'll be a lot less suffering for all involved.

It's not easy to detach so completely from wanting someone to be different, especially when we have legitimate wants and needs they're not meeting. Maybe you're going to earn the title for sainthood—and if this describes you, I'll nominate you!

It's entirely common to "fall in love" with one person, only to discover that they're someone else completely. Sometimes it's because they're carrying a piece of us, carrying our Shadow or have a healing lesson (see Secret No. 6). Other times, it's because we sprang for romantic love, the culturally conditioned fantasy, instead of soul mate love. Romantic love wears rose-colored glasses, and the more attached we are to an ideal, the harder they are to take off. That's the problem with romantic love, and that's the baggage I spoke of.

Holding out for the hope that someone will change takes a toll on the heart and soul of love. There's a more elegant solution. You can start imagining someone different, someone just right for you, by using your spiritual consciousness, and your imagination. You *can* imagine someone different! That's what the next section will teach you.

Think With Your Venus

Soul Mate Secret No. 4

To pull love toward you, tap your Venus magnetism.
We can attract the person we desire most by holding
a mental picture of who we want and imagining them
into existence.

Venus names our capacity to be promiscuous with all of life, to enjoy it, surrender to it, play with it, and create from it.

DANA GERHARDT

THINK WITH YOUR *what*? THE feminine archetype is known by many names in numerous traditions, but we know her as the goddess of love—Venus. A woman of contradiction, she is just as maternal as she is perpetually single, as flirty as spiritual, as wholesome as winsome. She is every woman, and we often see her as the goddess of youth and beauty, a tantalizing temptress. Well, she certainly creates desire like no other, and while desire can whip up wars and jealous rivalries, it's her captivating, mesmerizing, and attract-ive powers that ally her with every law of attraction ever written.

I never participated in *The Secret* craze, yet I do know the secret behind it: all laws of attraction—from the power of attraction to "opposites attract," from "like attracts like" to "give and ye shall receive"—belong to and originate from Venus. Such are the ways Venus works her otherworldly magic on us humans. Understand her laws and you can know the secret to attracting, too.

Venus is a resonant force of femininity, but Venus is also the spiritual principle of magnetic desire. She's constantly at play in the Universe and is used by both genders to relate and connect with what and who we love. Yes, everyone has a Venus! When I discovered the earliest teachings of Venus all the way back to ancient Sumeria, it was like finding a hidden treasure. I discovered that Venusian femininity is magnetic desire embodied, and her goals are timeless: love, peace, and happiness. Sounds simple, right? But there's been so much misunderstanding about how to achieve these goals that the record needs to be set straight. For years, Venus' sublime sparkle has been covered with superficial slime—but I endeavored to restore the magic to the misunderstood muse! As with any power, Venus' magnetism is in the way you use it.

To take my attract-ive powers to the next level, I needed to clear up all the misunderstandings between being attractive (good-looking) and being attract-ive (able to attract). There's a difference. A well-heeled woman with money can become instantly gorgeous, but it takes intelligence to become an attract-ive individual. Oprah has successfully navigated the pitfalls of Venus (vanity) while retaining total Venus beauty rights. She's hasn't confused her power to attract with her appearance. Clever lady.

Nonetheless, in modern times, Venusian types are often seen as artificial, distracting, or ditzy. Cooperation or passive femininity gets manhandled into submission; desirability is turned into sexual manipulation; appearance-consciousness is associated with frivolity and excess. You name a Venus attribute, and I'll show you its ugly stepsister. When the things, people, and ways we naturally love and enjoy are shamed, distorted, or one-dimensional, the same goddess that leads us by the hand to love also leads us to confusion. No wonder so many women are baffled about the real source of their attract-ive powers!

It took astrology's view of the goddess of love, beauty, and happiness to distinguish the divine dish from pop-tart propaganda. In astrology, Venus isn't just about surface beauty but also soul beauty, enjoyment, and pleasure. The more I got to know what made me truly and organically happy, the more magnetically receptive I became. I asked myself: What do I enjoy? What makes life worth living? What turns me off and on? What gives me, wild, orgiastic unlimited pleasure? What curls my toes and excites my heart? And who did I imagine coming to me at night in my dreams, meeting me as my soul mate?

Because a state of imagination, relaxation, and joy for life precipitates all attract-ive power, armed with a newfound enthusiasm for all things love-ly I asked myself, What gets me in the mood?

Only then could I imagine my soul mate into existence. It was a daring move. Was that too big of a leap to make, from thinking about what makes me smile to landing a soul mate? It's a leap of imagination! Understanding your attract-ive power goes way beyond the promise of otherworldy romance or sexy shoes and into the realm of spiritual connection and transcendent soul mate love. Understanding how to think with my Venus elevated my attract-ive powers to a whole new level of expression.

I used to think that the goddess of love was unrelated to the rest of my life. Now I know she is relatedness itself. She is *eros*, the passionate and sensual connection to what and who we love. I now know Venus isn't just the sugar-coated frosting on the cake—as the world will happily tell us, she (read: love) holds the entire cake together! She ties everything together with love. And what's more important than that?

Throughout history, men have underestimated women. That's symbolic of how everyone (male and female alike) often underestimates the power of the feminine. Yes, throughout history, the foolish have underestimated her powers, but the wise think with their Venus.

All About Venus

The descriptors of Venus are: magnetic, elegant, attractive, receptive, fulfilled, pleasure-loving, playful, happy, emotionally content, beloved, muse, admirable, goddessly, at ease, relaxed, peaceful, sensible, sensual, feminine, abundant, loving, fun, joyful, passionate, sexually potent, sociable, beautiful, flirtatious, charming, strategic, spiritual, creative, saucy, sexy, tender, sassy, sensitive, idealistic, intelligent, superficial, soulful, gracious, graceful, clever, warm, likable, pleasant.

Hmmm, what's Venus? She is multifaceted, and she is many things at once. Just like a woman! She is also individual, just like you. In astrology, Venus is the archetype of feminine receptivity. As the universal symbol for womanhood, her glyph (♀) resembles a handheld mirror, a reflective surface. When we look in the mirror, she shows us the style, artistry, and flair that we use to attract. When we reflect on our internal responses of pleasure or displeasure, happiness or unhappiness, she shows us who and what we like, and who and what we do not like.

She's also an advertisement for the perfect partner, our soul mate. Her sign reads: Only the Sensitive (Cancer), Soulful (Pisces), Adventurous (Sagittarius and Aries), Kooky (Aquarius), Stable (Taurus), Introspective (Virgo), Emotionally Mature (Capricorn), Witty (Gemini), or Bold (Leo) Need Apply. Your adjectives will be different, as every person is different, but the goal is common: happiness. We each have a pretty specific set of cue cards for the person or people we're going to be comfortable and happy around. Just as our Venus sign answers a lot of questions about the nature of our soul mate—who we're attracted to and why—she advertises our own attract-ive attributes and a way to attract our soul mate. We'll learn about your Venus sign soon, but first it's important to know Venus holistically. She has many more faces than you might think.

First, there's her creative face. Our creative efforts won't go unnoticed by Venus, the artist and muse. The heartfelt harmony and connection she inspires—from the realm of cultivating love and beauty among humankind to the artistry of refining more harmonious relationships among all things, people, objects, and ideas—affect our ability to pull people toward us. Yes, to *attract* them. Your favorite designers share the aesthetic intelligence of Venus and have a special sensibility for harmoniously connecting opposite and/or contrasting moods, textures, shapes, and colors to di-vine effect. You may successfully put wild Uncle Bob and your mother-in-law in the same room and accomplish a Venusian feat of harmony, too! There are many ways to achieve feats of oppositional balance. While the means of "pulling complements together" may be different, the end effect always fosters a sense of inner balance and harmony for all. When we're creating with Venus, the feelings are of proportion, bal-ance, harmony, and contentment. In other words, we're vibe-ing on peace, love, and happiness!

Venus is also infinitely joyful and positive. Imagine a cocktail hostess with a hor-rid attitude and you'll understand why a negative state of mind generally repels good people. The love goddess' goal is bringing harmony, and nothing does this like a positive attitude. Is she superficial? Well, sometimes. We've all known people who seem to have a smile plastered on their face 24/7, and they generally make people happy, so no harm done there. One of Venus' laws is that like attracts like, so joy and positivity will attract more of the same. Of course, no one can pull off being super-positive and joyful all the time, and that's why it's in perfectly good taste to invoke the goddess when you need her. Being joyful and positive is attract-ive.

She's also just plain attractive. As the goddess behind every major cosmetic cam-paign, Venus is used by us women to kick up our charm and intrigue several notches by making ourselves appear stunningly alluring and available (without looking com-pletely available, which is the real trick). New shoes, great hair, and the right makeup can make us more attractive, and they often do. But the other half of the equation is the mood of contentment and fulfillment that activity or desire inspires. A trip to Tiffany's or to India (depending on your Venus sign) can do wonders for a girl's mood, as joy is the secret to inner glow and beauty. And we all know how men feel about women who are confident, happy, and passionate—they're crazy about them! A sense of personal style and taking pride in your unique features and everything you do to bring beauty and balance into your life makes you Venusian.

And don't forget Venus' receptivity! Creating artifice and manufacturing allure to attract men was one of the mythological Venus' more popular pastimes. Here's where we can get stuck on the matter side of the equation, instead of the purposeful meaning behind all this focus on physical attraction, which is receptivity. If making ourselves more appealing, and thus making others more receptive to us, isn't the real art of attraction, what is?

Many of us have already covered this side of Venus: we've bought the physical formulas for beauty, along with partnerships that left us feeling as empty as a used-up jar of $100 La Mer face cream. We think having better clothes, higher-priced face cream, tighter jeans, and more money will make others more receptive to us. This isn't untrue—it's just only partially true. When we focus our attention on our material and sexual attractiveness, we'll get partners interested in only—you guessed it— the joy of sex and the sensual pleasure of owning things (oh, and don't forget looking eternally youthful)! There's nothing wrong with sexual pleasures, but you're probably reading this book to land a soul mate and that's a whole different animal, indeed.

Okay, so Venus is creative, positive, pretty, and receptive. All the creams and Jimmy Choo's may help, but if receptivity is what we're aiming for, it's a state of mind—actually, it's a very attract-ive state of mind. When we're in a Venus, or attract-ive, state of mind, we're positive, warm, receptive, and therefore sending out "I'm ready for love" vibes. Venus' attitude is hopeful, positively expectant, and socially smart as a whip. She knows that maintaining an expectant and positive attitude toward love is one of the most powerful forces of attraction.

When we're responsive to others, people respond to us. That's a Venus law. When we're receptive, we're open to considering others' points of view and what they can do for us. We've opened the door for a relationship; an un-receptive mind is like a closed door. A receptive frame of mind will help with all your relationships.

K.I.S.S.

THE BICYCLING FISH

Gloria Steinem once said, "A woman needs a man like a fish needs a bicycle," and growing up with a feminist mother, I inherited that unspoken belief. I believe, in this way, feminism has done women and men a grave disservice. Many women equate being strong and independent with being independent of a man. What effect do you think that has on a man, who is genetically programmed to provide for the woman he loves?

I know, I know, many women like providing, and some men enjoy being provided for! But when we give off that "I can take care of myself, don't help me" vibe, we can unintenionally push people away. We may refuse their offer to be generous with us. If I'm receptive, I may consider that someone might have something to offer me that I don't have, and so give that person the opportunity to give it. Everyone has something to offer, and they're just waiting to give it to you! If you're communicating that you've got all your needs covered, thank you very much, they may not even stick around long enough to get to know the real you. The whole fish and the bicycle thing just doesn't hold water.

Venus is also multitalented and imaginative. Now that we've set the record straight about who she is and who she is not, Venus can really do her thing. Just as she pulls together colors, designs, and people, we can use that same intelligence to create and hold a cohesive mental picture of our perfect life partner. That's because it all begins in the imagination, and imagination is the supernatural talent of Venus available to everyone, because everyone (both men and women) has a Venus. It's your innate goddess-given power to attract exactly who and what you want. As the universal feminine archetype, this go-to girl is available to anyone, at any time. It's so simple. Well, if it's so simple, why isn't everyone doing it, you ask? That's a damn good question. The answer is in the symbols.

Reading the Signs in the Symbol

Think about that handheld mirror I mentioned earlier, the orb atop a cross, which is also the astrological symbol for the planet Venus (♀). Every culture recognizes a circle or ring as a symbol of commitment and also the eternal circle of life—the timeless wedding band is symbolic of the committed union of marriage! Now visualize the cross, the handle part, located under the mirror. In all world religions, a cross is innately spiritual. Putting a circle-ring and a cross together, we get: the ring of commitment resting on a foundation of spirituality. Are you having an a-ha moment right about now? I hope so.

So it seems that for the goddess of happiness to bless us with an eternity of utter bliss and fulfillment, our commitments to one another (i.e., our relationships) must be linked to our spirituality. For eternity . . . like, forever. Whichever you prefer.

Now this idea really takes that superficial ditz called Venus to a whole new level, doesn't it?

Spirituality and love. They used to go hand in hand—right down the church aisle. I do believe that by focusing all our attention and energy on the handheld mirror, that is, on the art of physical and sexual attraction in attracting a mate, we've focused on the beauty reflection and neglected the life of our spirit. Spirituality is the missing ingredient in many of our relationships. In fact, I'm boldly suggesting that by not bringing spirituality into all your relationships, you've remained single! I know—it's bold. But someone had to say it, and it may as well be me.

There's more to understand about Venus, and again, I'm turning to astrology to do so. We all have a personal set of spiritual values that we use as a yardstick in our relationships. Yet before they can be enacted, our spiritual values need to be tested against our reality and experiences. For example, Venus in Pisces people are generally very good at what we call unconditional, accepting love. That's a spiritual value anyone can idealize as positive, but it doesn't always serve a gal's search for love. Maybe she finds out that giving her love unconditionally hurts her sometimes (she trusted the wrong person), or clouds her judgment. The saying goes that the ocean refuses no river and neither does a person with Venus in Pisces! The spiritual impulse is to be that receptive ocean, to accept anyone and anything; so imagine how difficult it might be to discern which is the right "river" or lover to accept. One of

Venus' teachings is learning to say no; not everyone should be invited into our inner sanctum.

No matter how much we want to, most of us can't perform a spiritual bypass. We can't be spiritual before resolving our inner conflicts, those seemingly opposing tugs on our heart. We may intellectually "know" our spiritual values, yet we can't bypass the Venus work of defining our nos, taking responsibility for our yesses, and making choices based on self-esteem in order to get to the right relationship. Venus work stands at the threshold of true love, and before we can reach our highest aspirations for a relationship, we will each meet Venus as the goddess of discernment and Venus as the goddess of self-esteem. We will make relationship choices (Libra) out of our self-esteem (Taurus). In the process, we grow closer to our heart's wish for that one true love.

Because Venus is the ruling planet of the sign of Libra, the Scales, we will deliberate over who to give our heart to. Oh, it's agonizing isn't it? (If you've ever had a Libra friend, you get my drift!) Then we eventually make a choice. We say yes to the person we're attracted to and go for it. As we get involved, maybe we realize it was a superficial attraction. Maybe we realize we didn't have enough in common to really gel into forever. At this point, we might ask: Is this relationship compromising me? What am I willing or unwilling to settle for? Am I ambivalent about this person? If we're not coming from the same place, where are we coming from? Our consciously considered choices, at this point, have an incredible impact on our relationship success, as the choices we make in relationships begin to define us (often starting in our teen years)—from who to pursue romantically to what we have in common to who we "settle" for. We pay the consequences or reap the rewards for how successful those choices are.

Venus is also the ruling planet of Taurus, the sign associated with self-esteem, and you simply must have healthy self-esteem to make good choices. Bottom line. You need basic levels of confidence and positive self-regard and self-worth. If this is you already, consider yourself cosmically blessed! From the start of your soul mate search, you will make better choices about who you choose to love, and you will attract healthier people because you're coming from that place of ease in your own skin. You know you've got to love yourself to be loved the way you want, but at this stage, you may be still learning. And you're not alone. Many of us will attend the School of Hard Knocks and enroll in Love Lessons 101, so we can discover more about our self-esteem and learn to define our relationship values more clearly. Some of us just keep faking it till we make it, but we eventually graduate with a degree in self-worth. We always make better choices with healthy self-esteem.

Your conscious choices and your self-esteem affect your ability to be happy and to attract the partner you want. This two-part process helps us arrive at the next stage. You've figured out that your self-worth is not dependent on your cars, clothes, popularity, or looking youthful and beautiful—those are all disposable and material. You've started to define your values, through making choices and accepting the consequences for those choices. That's worth repeating: it's by making choices, good and bad, and taking responsibility for those choices that we discover our values. By experiencing the consequences of choices, we learn where we've been separated from the spiritual truth about who we really are.

Once you learn to make choices based on your self-esteem, mountains move out of your way. Having a foundation of healthy self-esteem goes a long way in helping you define your spiritual values. How? The most reliable values, ones you learned through those hard lessons, are the same values you can count on for continued happiness and self-worth. For example, kindness is my religion (it's also the Dalai Lama's spiritual value). After being treated unkindly by a guy I was dating, I realized that while I intellectually possessed this spiritual value, my life was out of synch with my spirit. Addressing my self-worth issues changed all that. Making a decision out of self-esteem creates congruence with your spiritual values. In this way, anyone can become more attract-ive or receptive to love. Nurturing the spiritual cross part of the symbol supports the love-ly circle on top.

There's another benefit to identifying your spiritual values: when you recognize what values like integrity, positive self-regard, compassion, helping others, and mutual respect feel and look like, you attract them in others and increase your attract-ive spiritual wattage. These realizations are far larger than you; these personal values aren't just nice thoughts, they actually energize the world! That's why visionaries, spiritual teachers, and yogis are magicians of the highest order, because they break down personal barriers (and humanity's barriers, too) by teaching spiritual values. Hence, you too can move mountains, through identifying and practicing your values.

And as you discover your values and make them central to your life and love philosophy, those once painfully conflicting or confusing relationship conundrums may become suddenly simple to you. That person you used to be fuzzy or uncertain about, well, now your feelings grow crystal clear. Try it and you'll see!

Exercise: Discovering My Spiritual Values

This is an exercise designed to help you understand how the consequences of your relationship choices have helped you form values. So dig out your love alchemist's notebook and have a talk with your spiritual side.

- What shared values do you consider most important to a relationship?

- Match your values to your current friend or love relationships. Do the people in your life reflect your spiritual values—or are they operating from a whole other set of values?

- Can you see how your past relationships helped to define and clarify your values? Often we will make a choice that will then form one of our values, as with the Venus in Pisces woman who formed a value about compassion and codependence.

- Do you hold certain values, yet allow the closest people in your life to treat you in a way that doesn't agree with those values?

- Have you defined the values that another person must absolutely share with you to keep you happy and in love for the rest of your life?

K.I.S.S.

PRACTICE WHAT YOU PREACH

Spiritual values are so tied into commitment that they're often included in wedding vows. Here are some common examples of spiritual values.

- Love thy neighbor as thy self (mutual respect).

- Do unto others as you would have done unto you (integrity).

- I will honor you by forsaking all others (honor).

- I am joined to you in sickness and health, for richer or poorer (compassion).

Put into practice:

- I can put myself in another person's shoes (empathy).

- I don't have to agree with another person's point of view to accept them (mutual respect).

- I refuse to be involved in an affair that might hurt another (integrity and honor).

- I do my best to help people in need (compassion).

Thinking Magically

Venus is no ditz, she's intelligent! Which brings us to the final facet of Venus to explore: disguised within the Venus circle of commitment is the semi-circle, the antenna-like horns of Mercury (☿). The Venus-Mercury connection goes deeper. In Roman myth, Venus and Mercury were lovers, and in soul mate myth, Mercury (who went by the Greek name Hermes) and Venus (Greek name Aphrodite) used to share the same body and a gender. Ever heard of Hermaphrodite? That's Hermes and Aphrodite, two lovers who shared one body!

Mercury was the divine messenger whose appointed task was shuttling messages or thoughts between the Divine and human realms. Mercury's role for you is the same. Mr. Winged Heels will shuttle your love wish upward to the heavens. He will also shuttle valuable synchronicity, coincidence, love messages, and event-worthy news right back to Earth—to you.

The half-circle of Mercury, so cleverly and secretly concealed in the circle of Venus, invites a divine third presence into thinking attract-ively. We can do this intentionally through receiving inspiration and thoughts (when in meditation) and through projecting thoughts and desires (as in prayer). When an inspired thought pops into your mental inbox, that's also Mercury's doing. When you send a prayer out for someone you love, Mercury delivers that message. Like Verizon, he's 24/7 and he never stops working for you.

Mental imaging is the starting point for your love work. Call it prayer, call it imagination, meditation, or affirmation, but whatever you do, don't call it mere wishful thinking! This is intentional love in the making. Bring your heart into your wish for love, too. Venus is the promise of emotional fulfillment; heart emotions always empower our prayer for love. When we're content and imaginatively stimulated, we're in Venus' pleasure palace. We can see this emotional happiness connection in the tarot, where Venus charges the suit of Cups. Cups represent our emotional capacity for fulfillment, abundance, opulence, and heart-contentment—those feelings and objects of success that make life full and rich. So when we infuse our desire for soulful love with the emotions of satisfaction, joy, bliss, and pleasure by communing with those emotions from our values and desires, we are thinking magically. If we can soulfully imagine it, we can create it.

Yes, acting on your deepest heartfelt desires, following your heart, and identifying your spiritual values all align you with Venus. Form intentional thoughts framed with an attitude of positive expectancy and imagination from this place of self-awareness, and you're *really* holding an attract-ive love vibration! You project a beam of light straight to Cupid's doorstep.

Finally, to bring Mercury into your love quest with smashing success, be sure you're keeping an eye out for signs, synchronicities, coincidences, and messages while you're at it! I know, altogether this may sound like a lot of work, but it's important. After all, imagine being the FedEx guy of the planets and having an important missive to deliver from the goddess of love, only to discover that your recipient is not listening. Oh, how Mercury hates being ignored. He just adores your attention and presence. The longer you hold your wish in mind, the more likely it will be to come true. Held in mind and heart, your heart's wish will be delivered!

<hr/>

Exercise: What's My Spirituality?

Love is spirituality. The two are inseparable. That's why it's essential to have a spirituality that touches your heart, because that experience will connect you to the heart of the Divine, the diverse and manifold experiences and teachings of love. It's a powerful practice to remind yourself that spirituality isn't separate from life; spirituality is all of life—it's everything. And the good news is you don't have to be religious to be spiritual, 'cause if you're a human being, you're a spiritual being, right? So what is your spirituality? Is it nature? Is it surf? Is it sunsets? Is it gardening? I like long walks in nature, where I can tune in to that reverent radio station of receptivity and grace. I receive messages there. For others, it might be meditation, Christian church services, a spiritual text, or a loving, nurturing community. My husband's original love is surfing, but lately I wonder if it's transforming into a nightly ritual of Sufi poetry readings before dinner. Spiritually stumped? Locate your spirituality wherever you commune with the Divine, and wherever the Divine communes through you. My suggestion is to go there regularly to recharge your love batteries.

Take it from me: you will need to love bigger to attract bigger love. To find a spiritual, all-encompassing love, to really reach divine love, I challenge you to make your concept of love bigger. There are so many different types of love in the world: the love a mother has for a child, maternal love; being a friend for a friend, friendly love; or a the love of hospice volunteer for a dying patient, compassionate love. Make a list of all the different types of love you've experienced and with whom (there's no right or wrong, and you can make up your own categories, too, like teaching love or familial love). Was there a spiritual lesson here for you?

Muzzle Your Mars: The Law of Anti-Attraction

I was having coffee with a male friend of mine when I mentioned that I was working on *A Love Alchemist's Notebook*. Oliver immediately grew intrigued, since he had recently encountered a woman who, during the course of a business meeting, complained about her unsuccessful search for a partner while launching her breasts like missiles in his direction. Oliver wondered if she thought she was being attractive, because she wasn't. It was an unsolicited perusal and he was giving her zero positive feedback (being open to feedback from others is one sign of thinking with your Venus).

He went on and I listened closely—I'd been granted a bird's-eye view of the male mind and I wasn't about to pass this up! Oliver asked, was it simply a difference in style? You should know my friend is a subtle and sensitive Libra man, so this gal was holding up big cue-card drawings of magic marker breasts shouting "notice me!" to the kind of guy who can read sexual innuendo from a mile away. Could be a matter of style, I told him, but my guess was if this was her actual go-getter style, it would've probably worked on someone by now. It sounded as if she had her radar permanently locked on target but she could never quite make that rocket fully operational.

No, I finally conceded, she was sabotaging herself and that was a problem. It sounded more like the law of anti-attraction to me.

Desire. It can pull things and people toward you and push those same things and people away. You know how it feels when you want something or someone really badly and you can't let it go. You'd do anything, maybe even sell your soul to get it. This kind of desire works well for winning a sports match, pitching a concept in a sales meeting, standing up for yourself, protecting yourself, or any time you need to be at the top of your game and nail it (whatever "it" is). Such desire is about digging in and holding on as though your life depended on it. This desire also runs counter to the law of attraction. The ability to let go precedes all laws of attraction, because release has the attract-ive power to answer prayers. In spiritual love magic, relaxed desire is a necessary ingredient. Holding on to a specific idea, person, or agenda with a grip so tight we'd need a crowbar to pry your fingers loose is not. The latter may work for saving a person's life, but in love, it's a formula for anti-attraction.

In astrology, digging-in desire is represented by Mars, and it's completely different from the go-with-the-flow goddess of love, Venus. The masculine principle (Mars) is naturally aligned with men, as is the feminine principle (Venus) with women, but neither are gender exclusive: men can use their Venus, and women can use their Mars. However, Venus and Mars are entirely different principles and behaviors, and each is appropriate for specific activities. Venus is used for attracting love, establishing rapport, and keeping relations copacetic, while Mars creates heroic missions like starting wars, standing up for yourself, and having sex.

In life, we move fluidly between both principles. Problems occur when we mix up the two. Mars' marching orders are: chase, capture, conquer, and rescue. Check this against Venus' beauty credo: the world is one big ice cream cone and it's coming my way, I'll be ready for it! It's a subtle yet wildly important difference in attitude. Mars is red alert and high intensity, while Venus is warmly expectant and receptive. There's a time and a place for both, but Venusian intelligence is especially attuned to the nuances of the dance of love. When you're thinking with your Venus, you're making subtle connections, being receptive, and reading feedback, like my friend Oliver did when confronted by the torpedo-temptress. When you're in Mars mode, you're off and running with your own independent agenda and little awareness of the other person's desires, or even of their reality. Relationships are about relatedness, whereas Mars is about "me." Clearly, there is a real discrepancy between the two.

Understanding these principles extends far beyond simple personality typing to knowing which archetype to pull on at which time. Winning a promotion, fighting an illness, and standing up for oneself are Mars activities. I use Mars to protect myself, fight for what I want, and generate the willpower and energy to make a change. When I'm using my Mars, I'm restless for change, which serves me infinitely well when I need to strike out into new territory and make an ambitious move. But in love, such restlessness can be problematic. Elizabeth Taylor's copious, fiery Mars-Aries energy has burned through seven marriages. So yes, some women (and obviously men) do move through the world in a Mars mode rather than a Venus fashion. The trick is not burning down the house in the process.

So . . . what if your style is more man-eater than coy coquette? There's room for all of us. But for you, it's about balance. There are many beautiful, seductive, in-command women who captivate attention by being ballsy and competitive and going after what they want. And some women bring that leadership and entrepreneurial quality to everything they do in life. I'm thinking of the many female celebrities who project sexy Mars power, like Victoria Beckham (a.k.a. Posh Spice), a Mars-ruled, Sun-in-Aries woman with a highly controlled self-image and hard-edged sexiness. Posh has undeniable appeal as a woman and she's notably Mars-edgy. She's even said, "I'm a gay man trapped in a woman's body." (Aw, I'm sure she's a soft little kitten with Becks.) Posh is more sexy (Mars) than feminine (Venus), but she obviously knows Venus: she's appearance-savvy, playing her feminine assets to her best advantage. When she's in a boardroom, Posh probably has her subtle receptors attuned toward finding common ground, distinguishing the right time to gain consensus, and boldly pushing her own agenda. You don't get where she is without using your Venus. Using Mars and Venus both, and consciously, is key.

Desire is delicious. Desire is holy. The prefix *de* means "of," and *sire* means a father, so *desire* can be taken to mean "of the father" (and father doesn't have to be a man, it can be of the God source, the Divine, or the Goddess within you). All of your desires are holy, but not all are meant to be followed; that's why a successful love strategy involves the willingness to wait, to receive feedback from another or

K.I.S.S.

THE ART OF REFUSAL

Tapping our innate magnetism, enhancing our natural beauty, and approaching love loosely and in a spirit of playfulness are wonderful invitations for love. But it's not so wonderful to be turned down, rejected, or dropped from someone's radar. The thing about Venus love is that an invitation is an invitation—you don't want to force or coerce others into loving you. Sure, you can make yourself irresistible and compelling, but as loveliness embodied, you must always give others the option to refuse. In the modern dating world, it seems we've forgotten the subtle skill of being gracious. So when you get peeved about someone not calling back, don't sweat it. There are a hundred reasons why a love match just doesn't work out—and 99.9 percent of the time, it's not about you. It's not personal. They don't even know you yet, so how could it be?! If someone's not responding to your Venus call, take it as a sign that someone more perfect for you is still out there.

the Universe, to know when to let go entirely or change up your strategy. Mars and Venus both rely on our ability to channel our desires with wisdom. Desire is sacred. And Venus is the focused and contained vessel, the space where we can gently, patiently hold our deepest desires with heart. How do desires sit with our heart? The best way for me to know if a desire is meant to be followed is to spiritually sit with the object of my affection for a time and pull it toward me on the spiritual plane. If it's meant for me, it will come; if it's not, eventually it will disappear and be replaced by a new desire, one that's more right for me. That's a Venusian formula for attraction.

Companion Spell: MEDITATE ON YOUR MAGNETISM SPELL

Sex and Soul Mates

Years ago, a scrappy young Pat Benatar fiercely told us that love was a battlefield. Oh Pat, tell it how it is, sister! There are bound to be misfires and not-quite-rights—love's battlefield leaves no one unscathed. When we're figuring out how our newest love interest fits into our life, we bring our insecurities, past hurts, and soulful requests to the bargaining table, not to mention our pheromones—the love chemicals that scientists have pointed out are even found in the brains of the clinically insane! If we feel vulnerable to a sort of madness around people we're attracted to, it's kind of because we are a little mad.

So, would you trust an insane person with your heart? And that person on the other side of the table with love and sex chemicals rushing through their system likely feels similarly unnerved by you. That makes two insane people! The excitement of sexy chemicals rushing around your systems can be like having an out-of-body experience, except it's happening in your body. And theirs. Kind of. Feeling confused yet? Makes it hard to be rational, doesn't it? Or even be authentic?

That's the sex part. And then there's intimacy—a whole other story. Opening our body and soul to another exposes our vulnerabilities. Being deeply intimate with another person is like ripping open your chest, handing them a gun, and saying, "Please don't shoot!" Our trust is at stake, maybe even our very life from the heart's perspective! We are putting our heart in their hands, hoping they'll handle it with care. And there's no money-back guarantee on that one, either.

Mars, the planet of intimacy-inducing sex, is also the god of war. Mars contains our sexual hotness, that chemical rush of "let's get it on!" And so the planet contains our battle wounds, our sex drive, our protective defenses, and our scars. Where do war and sex meet in Mars? In the murky and sometimes dangerously unconscious land of intimacy, loyalty, and trust. What strange life forms live there, you ask? Entities that go by the names of: Pain, Suspicion, Fear, Remembered Betrayal, Misunderstanding, and Unforgiven Injuries. The plot resembles your typical spy movie, one revolving around secrets, intelligent psychological mind games, violence, and of course, sex. Oodles of it. All to reach that elusive goal of intimacy.

I'm sure you've visited this land; maybe you've even hung out there for longer periods of time. Ever had a relationship based on sexy chemistry, or on just sex alone, only to have it end in disaster? Ever gotten in a huge fight and had the best sex ever afterward? Sex can pave the way for soulful intimacy, and sex without the foundation of trust and safety is precarious, even dangerous—especially if we've been hurt, betrayed, or lack the tools to process painful situations. Unhealed, these old situations can continue to hurt us, or even strike out at others unbidden. Yes, a sexual relationship will turn loose those ugly monsters we keep in our emotional closet, right along with the crazy resistance to their discovery!

Being physically intimate brings up all our "stuff," which can bring out the worst kind of unconscious reactions. Subjecting another person to your ugly monsters . . . man, it's a real test for intimacy, not for the faint of heart. The stakes are high, and if we fail, we move from planet love to planet war in sixty seconds flat—or, in about the same amount of time it takes for a person to say exactly the wrong thing at exactly the wrong moment. When love is a battlefield that may leave us defenseless and vulnerable in potentially hostile territory, it makes sense to be with someone we feel safe with and trust.

Of course, it's scary. In fact, the land of intimacy can be so full of land mines that it becomes too scary to "get real." So we defend ourself against closeness by shutting down, by inappropriately reacting out of past injuries, by being suspicious of another's attempts to get closer, or more simply, to give to us. How can generosity be threatening? If a person's been hurt before, perhaps by someone who was also generous, giving can hurt, too.

Sex can be another way of shutting down. Purely sexual relationships can cause a sort of soul-numbness, one in which we can't truly, genuinely share our self with another. A sexual relationship of this kind, one that moves forward without establishing the safety of trust and caring, can be like Scotchgard for the heart, causing precious opportunities for healing and soulful tenderness roll right off instead of sinking in. When sex defends us against real intimacy, we've lost ground with soul.

And if we're looking for a soul mate, not a sex mate, we've got to do more than just take off our clothes. We have to get revealing and be willing to get psychologically naked with them. Yes, to have a soulful relationship, we need to bare more than our bottom! We need to bare our heart and soul.

K.I.S.S.

FLOWERING IN LOVE

How do we work with difficult emotions and blocks to receiving love? There are many ways—examining our beliefs, keeping a positive attitude, prayer, and magic making, for example, but I particularly like flower essences! Flower essences are not only Venusian but they're fabulous at helping you release emotions. Flower essence homeopath retailers (like Bach, FAS, and others) bottle these flower essence extracts, which work on subtle emotional and heart energies. You can use these essences for healing any love-related emotional stagnation. Try honeysuckle for letting go of nostalgia for love, bleeding heart to help you let go of a past relationship, or walnut oak for removing fears to love. If you're looking for an expert resource for working with flower essences, I highly recommend *Flower Remedies Handbook* by Donna Cunningham, who is not only brilliant at describing the subtleties of emotion attributed to each flower but also at relaying flower remedies specific to your astrological chart and Sun sign!

Classically, the god of war, Mars, is the consort of the goddess of love, Venus. Naturally! Throughout mythical history, they chased each other, hooking up on lovers' trysts, as lovers will do. Their ongoing union suggests that when we open our heart to love, we're also opening our self to warfare. There will be battles, and there will be scars. And at some point we each learn this truth: those same people who love us and whom we love are also capable of hurting us. That's the risk we take.

We can take heart in knowing this, though: we may have been hurt before, but it's not cause for defense, for suiting up our heart with armor, for reacting from old fears, or for having sex mates instead of soul mates. However, it *is* cause for selectively choosing someone to trust with our heart and soul. And *that's* the right partner to get naked with!

Companion Spell: MOURN THE LITTLE LOSSES SPELL

Finding Feminine Allure

While traveling in Europe, I noticed the women there have a definitively sexy style—one conveying both feminine receptivity and magnetic power. It's subtle and hardly noticeable . . . if you're a brick! Or if you're predisposed to only register the in-your-face sexiness of, say, Hollywood.

European women are rarely over the top, but they truly earn the title of being the more mysterious sex. It's not anything they wear but the attitude with which they wear it. The handbag, the hair, the shoes . . . these do not create the feminine power these women know they wield, but just enhance their natural elegance and class. As put-together and confident as they look, what you can't quite put your finger on is a more invisible allure. That allure is Mystery, a powerfully compelling enigma. And that aura of Mystery makes their man appear a mere accessory on their arm, a puppy on their leash. You get the impression that, were a European woman to say to her man, "Roll over, Gerald," he'd assume the Dead Bug yoga pose in no time flat.

What is the mysterious allure of the feminine? A pair of hot pants or tight jeans can do wonder for your figure, but if that certain something is missing, it's a feeble and far too obvious attempt at allure. After sitting in a café watching gorgeous woman after gorgeous woman walk by, I deduced that the sexually self-possessed woman is a far less obvious kind of sexy, but she is undoubtedly the sexiest woman on Earth. She radiates that enchanting mixture of confidence, self-possession, passion, and sensuality. Qualities that will drive any man (or woman) wild.

Feminine allure is powerful. An alluring woman knows the power she holds over the opposite sex. She must also know that the larger part of attractive magnetism is reverently holding and honoring her Mystery—that invisible and secret vibration that connects her to the timeless erotic beauty of the Divine Feminine, a facet of Venus. She is mysterious, enchanting, ancient, and timeless. Meanwhile, mortals try to manipulate, control, repress, project, or possess sexuality (and youth) but from watching the European woman (and seeing the way my husband grew spellbound in their presence), I got a glimpse into why Venus wants to be worshipped—it's the proper way to honor Mystery.

In America, I believe we have yet to master the art of subtle intrigue, and instead are bombarded with sexuality, even when we don't want it. In a country that

K.I.S.S.

YOU'VE COME A LONG WAY, BABY

Once it seemed the only socially acceptable way for a woman to use Venus power was to land a man . . . and then to ever so slowly forego her wants and desires; to serve her husband, family, and community; and accept her status as a second-class citizen. Nowadays we can keep our Venus.

We no longer need to give up the single-girl things that make our life fun and fabulous—our art classes, our hobbies, our girlfriends—for a relationship with a man. We no longer have to play hide and seek with our femininity, either: being culturally coerced into not speaking our mind, or becoming misled by "it's not polite to call a man" dating etiquette. No, our mothers' issues are (hopefully) no longer an issue. We can embody enchantment. We can wear the pants, and the delicate lingerie underneath. It's a glorious time to be a woman—we can finally be it all: sexy, smart, and empowered by our femininity! Once describing sexuality only, even the word "attraction" doesn't mean the same thing it did ten years ago—now it's a law! The law of attraction allows us to attract without lifting a finger. That's definitely thinking with your Venus. Hallelujah! You have come a long way, baby.

is pumped up on Mars-y, aggressive-sexual energy, sometimes being invisible feels "safer" than being magnetically alluring—much safer than being leered at walking down the street, hit on at the gas station, or judged on our looks alone. Conversely, we women can "arm" ourselves with warrior makeup and choose to convey an image of sexual strength over sexual subtlety, because we're not comfortable with showing vulnerable femininity.

It's no wonder some of us forego erotic power altogether, although that cost is also high. You lose a little bit of your attract-ive power in the process, which has manifold uses in both attracting a mate and in the professional world. To fit into the corporate world, some women think we've got to downplay our beautiful assets to be respected and admired for our mind. Doing so means we lose the social intelligence and magnetic receptivity of Venus!

Here's what I learned about feminine allure in Europe: true feminine attract-ive power thrives on Mystery. It is not obvious, like makeup or too-tight jeans. It's hard to put your finger on. It draws you in, but you never really know why or how. The reason feminine allure remains an indefinable mystery is that things stay more powerful by remaining hidden. The more subtle Mystery of femininity is not worn on the outside—but on the inside.

Hey Baby, What's Your Sign?

Now, for the cherry on top: your Venus sign!

We've explored the shared attributes of Venus, the goddess of love, and discovered she's inextricably bound to our imagination, our spirituality, our self-esteem, our power of choice, and to our attract-ability. Yes, we each have a Venus, which depends on when we were born (use appendix B to find yours). Venus is only one piece of your astrology chart, and thus, your life, but she's a biggie for love and relationships.

We each have preferences and desires in our search for love and that's the bright, intelligent attractor beam of Venus, sending signals "out there" to others. When someone is attracted to us, we becoming enchanting; when we're attracted to someone, our chemistry communicates, "I really, really like you!" But what does that actually mean—aside from an intuitive knowing about who we like, and what we don't like? And what does it really mean to think with your Venus?

Working on behalf of love, sending out subtle cues that contain all the information we've been missing about our attract-ability, Venus answers.

When you know your Venus sign, it's easier to get clued in to what you need in a soul mate. She identifies the type of person you want in a mate. Of course, each of us has unique preferences for our soul mate—and in a cool twist, our soul mate will also have these, too!

Owning your Venus sign is invaluable for inviting your inner temptress out to play. Her sign reinforces the positive attributes, talents, and gifts you have that will enhance your self-esteem. She will also help you avoid that manhole o' love you fall into when you're not thinking with your Venus.

Working your Venus sign amplifies your attract-ive and receptive powers, like a hundred times! Through discovering your own specific power for attraction (the way you charm and attract others), you amplify your ability to attract.

Your Venus sign answers can tell you this, and more. Yeah, baby!

Venus in Aries

The first sign of the zodiac is a fire-starter. You arrive on the scene like the first blush of spring. Your very being shouts and sings, "Look at how exciting, sexy, and fun your life would be with me!" You like the novel and new in everything—clothes, people, and styles—because they make you feel alive.

Your Love Charm: your brassy confidence. If you wear nothing else, wear confidence.

Your Soul Mate: could be sweet as a sweet pea, but they will bring out the fire in you, helping you express courage, willpower, and anger as healthy essentials for your relationship.

Your Attract-ive Power: the power of courage. You'd try, admit, and do things others won't. Courage is an ally you can tap—be it getting over an ex (you do so very quickly) and calling up a new love interest, or having the emotional courage to delve into your own heart and honestly look at your self.

Your Shadow: the old dilemma immortalized by The Clash: should I stay or should I go? You bring a spirit of adventure to relationships, which also makes you restless when you're in one. Creative or physical outlets offer serenity to your partnerships, albeit indirectly.

Your Venus Archetype: the daredevil, desert rose, lone ranger, heroine, femme fatale, rock star, warrior/amazon princess, provocateur, flirt, slut, seductress, competitive girlfriend.

Think With Your Venus Mantra: I am worthy and lovable just as I am. I share my passion with everyone I meet, and in so doing, inspire them. I am in charge of my love life: today is another day to choose healthy partners.

Venus in Taurus

Earthy, sensual, and warm but slow to heat up, love blossoms for you when you approach it at a natural, easy pace. You know when to stop and smell the roses, and you appreciate the simple luxuries that comprise real happiness. Thus, you find it.

Your Love Charm: your confident ease, comfort in your own skin, that *je ne sais quoi*, causing others to feel totally secure in your presence.

Your Soul Mate: a loyal, easygoing, and highly reliable soul mate. There's no guess work involved with this person—they make you feel safe, secure, and comfortable. No one-night stands for you; you play for keeps.

Your Attract-ive Power: the power of tranquility. Sit on a hilltop, stop and smell the flowers, have a sip of tea. However you do it, just calm down. Be still and love's riddles become clear.

Your Shadow: choosing the safe and secure partnership over one that challenges you to move out of your comfort zone and grow.

Your Venus Archetype: the caretaker, sweet pea, Eve (of Adam and Eve), Aphrodite, pin-up, beauty queen, trophy wife, silent screen actress, banker's daughter, millionaire heiress, Earth mama, nature lover, queen, matriarch.

Think With Your Venus Mantra: I am a living, breathing, walking, talking goddess with a bootylicious bod to boot. This doesn't make me a doll; I have real talents. I am resourceful with my talents.

Venus in Gemini

A mutable air sign, you enjoy being caught up in a constant whirlwind of parties, travels, discussions, and diversions. Flirtatious, experimental, and curious, you may find your self torn between two directions, interests, or lovers.

Your Love Charm: your mind. Copiously gifted in the arts of courtship and wooing, you dazzle others with your conversation and storytelling.

Your Soul Mate: interesting and interested. You need a sociable mate with a variety of interests, one who wants to hear what's on your mind. They may be multilingual, well-educated, and well-spoken; they must be absolutely fascinating.

Your Attract-ive Power: love magic. You enthrall them with your liveliness, vibrance, and shape-shifting powers. You're like a butterfly, refusing to be held or caught, forever changing, changing—how alluring!

Your Shadow: the dilemma of twos. Being restless with one love or lover, when you're just plain un-stimulated or bored. *Boredom* is just another word for "let's try something new."

Your Venus Archetype: the art salon-hostess, flirt, intellectual, magical fairy, elf or sprite, Cleopatra, Puella (eternal little girl who won't grow up), storyteller, provocateur, trickster, shape-shifter, actress, networker, muse.

Think With Your Venus Mantra: I was born to get into all kinds of playfully precariously situations in love, and I have a blast exploring the possibilities. I reserve the right to change my mind and change it back again. My twin flame does the same. When we meet, we'll have so much to share and talk about—in fact, we probably won't shut up.

Venus in Cancer

A gentle and heartfelt water sign, you're the first to notice when a person needs help, and you're the first to come to their aid. You embody unconditional love and dispense it practically—be it through a good meal, emotional nourishment, or spiritual support.

Your Love Charm: your creative imagination. Compassionate and sensitive, you illuminate soul dilemmas for others with your understanding. Lost souls and mystics find your gentle presence especially comforting.

Your Soul Mate: someone who wants to build a home together, though this extends beyond the four walls of place. Your spiritual companion is someone who also aligns you with your true north.

Your Attract-ive Power: the power of intuition. You empathically pick up on feelings and nuances others miss.

Your Shadow: your penchant for care-taking can pull in a mate looking for a mother. You can't be good for others if you're not good to yourself first. Sometimes that means saying no, and practicing tough love.

Your Venus Archetype: the mother, love poet, mommy's little girl, orphan, a lush orchid, incurable romantic, oyster and pearl, a lighthouse, safe haven, statue of liberty, shells on the ocean floor, buried treasure, Dorothy (of *The Wizard of Oz*).

Think With Your Venus Mantra: I am innately and extremely soulful—so this whole soul mate thing will be a cinch. I'll trust my first instinct and never second-guess my intuition. All I have to do is open my heart and remember that compassion doesn't have to spell *sucker*.

Venus in Leo

As a fixed fire sign, you want to be appreciated for your uniqueness, your creative expressiveness, and your loyalty. Your need for appreciation can come off as controlling or insecure, at times, but it will also draw people toward you. You honestly bare your heart in love—people always know where they stand with you.

Your Love Charm: your confident charisma. This dynamic Venus sign advertises playfulness, creativity, and fabulousness in everything you do.

Your Soul Mate: gives you that "falling in love" feeling all the time. They make waking up next to them feel like Christmas morning every morning.

Your Attract-ive Power: the power of appreciation. Give and ye shall receive, Venus in Leo! Regard their special beauty, talent, and power as awe-inspiring and you'll have them eating out of your hand.

Your Shadow: calling all the shots, making all the decisions in the relationship. You are a queen, yes, but if you want your king to feel like a king and not a court page, stop commanding and ordering him around.

Your Venus Archetype: the artist, ingenue, creator, attention-getter, clown, showgirl, diva, queen, actress, flame tulips, Beauty (of *Beauty and the Beast*), popular one, lover, enchantress.

Think With Your Venus Mantra: I spontaneously share my sense of joy and delight, because joy and delight are the best aphrodisiacs! I praise and adore others, knowing I am surrounded by fans who truly love and appreciate me. When I share my unique talents with the world, my gifts shine like sunbeams, encompassing others in a warm aura of happiness.

Venus in Virgo

Virgo is an earth sign ruled by smart-as-a-whip Mercury, and you're deeply sensitive, rapturously observant, and graciously appreciative. Modest by nature and far more experimental than you let on, you happen to possess the sensual and sexual skills that would make a nun blush.

Your Love Charm: competence and craftiness. You impress others with how competent, elegant, and efficient you are.

Your Soul Mate: an introspective soul who takes pleasure in exploring the interiors of the body, heart, and mind. You need a soul mate who enjoys whiling away the afternoons instructively exploring what needs improvement in the world—including your relationship!

Your Attract-ive Power: the power of discernment. You've got excellent boundaries and realistic insights on the motivations and behaviors of others.

Your Shadow: "fixer-upper" relationships, for you enjoy fixing others. Sometimes you overcompensate for feelings of unworthiness and self-doubt with über-helpfulness and ultra-efficiency. Then you get mad when no one appreciates you!

Your Venus Archetype: the servant, rescuer, Cinderella, sexual priestess, Virgin Mary, madonna/whore, angel, helpful one, enchantress, Garden of Eden, invisible one, prostitute, expert, critic, nag, codependent, masochist, love slave.

Think With Your Venus Mantra: I completely and totally accept myself, even when they're wrong and I'm right, and when I'm wrong and they're right. Today I choose not to sweat the small stuff and to remain happy instead. I offer the best of myself and look for the best in others.

Venus in Libra

A cardinal air sign, your Venus sign is motivated by finding great success in relationship, and to accomplish this, you've been gifted with intelligence, glamour, and good social graces. Love for you is a ballet of give and take—you'll work effortlessly, tirelessly, and judiciously to achieve the overall balance of your happily-ever-after vision.

Your Love Charm: charm itself. Blessed with worldly sophistication, guided by an innate sense of right and wrong, you attract others who are fair and sensitive to saying the right thing at the right time—just like you.

Your Soul Mate: your matched other, equal half. You impress your soul mate with how similar you are, and how great your life could be together.

Your Attract-ive Power: the power of rapport. You make others feel comfortable by inquiring, listening, and matching their behavior/words. You somehow make connections with people to whom you have no obvious connection.

Your Shadow: trying to make everyone happy all the time. Naturally concerned with others' well being, you'll easily accommodate their wishes (great!), unless you feel they aren't returning your kindness and you start keeping score (not so great).

Your Venus Archetype: the diamond, social butterfly, judge, scales, red rose, lead ballerina, director, ultimate hostess, one-half of a power couple, tightrope walker, negotiator, peace-lover, mediator, sensitive, "lover not a fighter."

Think With Your Venus Mantra: I am blessed with charm, dignity, and grace, and so is my other half. I don't have to change anyone to love them. I know my mate is already perfect and complete.

Venus in Scorpio

A mesmerizing fixed water sign, you exude the mystery and attractive charisma of a Bond Girl, or 007 himself. You fear losing control, and you also like surrendering control, which can create power struggles. You experience life-transforming intimacy with the people you love.

Your Love Charm: intensity and honesty. In your presence, other people feel quite thrillingly alive.

Your Soul Mate: capable of great psychological depth and fearlessness. Your soul mate is not a purely sexual relationship or someone who is psychologically unaware or emotionally unavailable.

Your Attract-ive Power: the power of magnetism. Your sexuality, even if not overtly expressed, is a smoldering, seductive promise that draws others to you. Your second chakra, or kundalini, energy is off the hook. Be careful how you use it!

Your Shadow: wanting who or what you can't have. You wrestle with your desires and your attachments toward people who may not be available to you, and who, if you attained, you may not actually want.

Your Venus Archetype: the black widow, prostitute, phoenix, thorny red rose, belly dancer, erotic dancer, smoldering ashes, scorpion, seductress, celibate, psychologist, jealous one, a fortress, betrayer/betrayed, vampiress, alchemist, shaman, spy.

Think With Your Venus Mantra: I am erotically alive. I honor my own emotional depth, sexual intensity, and honesty. I attract an empowering relationship formed on mutual trust, helping me to surrender my fears, let down my guard, and experience deep healing. This is the person I trust with my soul.

Venus in Sagittarius

Taking off at a moment's notice, heading out on an epic adventure comes easy for the fiery Sagittarius Venus sign, who takes great pleasure in exploring, learning about others, and accumulating those "once in a lifetime" love experiences. Your love passport is bi-coastal, reading "have bags, will travel."

Your Love Charm: you're up for it. When you're disappointed by love, you optimistically re-shuffle the deck and diversify your options.

Your Soul Mate: is up for it. The keynote of your soul mate relationship is continuous expansion and personal exploration. They share your freedom-loving spontaneity and appreciate the sensual exploits and learning possibilities you offer.

Your Attract-ive Power: the power of adventure. Is it possible to taste, touch, and experience everything? You'll try. Then you'll teach your lovers what you've learned.

Your Shadow: fear of losing your freedom to love. Are love and freedom really mutually exclusive? Really? Your love task is to experience freedom through love (although this may mean having a nontraditional relationship).

Your Venus Archetype: the gypsy-wanderer, seeker, nomadic princess, explorer, safari guide, mapmaker, fortune-teller, student, high priestess, exotic foreigner, philosopher, temptress, Puella (eternal little girl who won't grow up).

Think With Your Venus Mantra: I honor my need for spontaneity and sensual exploration in relationships. Every day is a new opportunity to try, taste, or experience something radically different than the day before. I revel in the dazzling perspectives and possibilities that my partnership offers me.

Venus in Capricorn

The ringed-planet Saturn rules Capricorn, giving you strong personal boundaries and a high degree of self-sufficiency and self-reliance. This can make you appear unobtainable or distant to others who want to get close to you, but also glamorous and worthy of respect.

Your Love Charm: your maturity. You're an ultra-realist when it comes to love. Your Venus sign advertises "I'm available for a real adult relationship. Only people with goals and ambitions need apply."

Your Soul Mate: mature and authoritative, or a wise elder in the community. They leave a mark of personal integrity and authority in everything they do.

Your Attract-ive Power: the power of dedication and commitment. Once you've decided what or who it is that makes you happy, you'll do what it takes to get and keep them.

Your Shadow: choosing a "safe bet" person for all the wrong reasons, like social status, power, or wealth. You may enjoy the security of a materially comfortable and stable partnership, but not at the cost of emotional warmth and companionship.

Your Venus Archetype: the adult, provider, ice queen, prostitute, power suit, role model, status-seeker, daddy's little girl, woman in a man's world, boss woman, single lady, wise woman, wizard, hermit, experienced one.

Think With Your Venus Mantra: I expect only success from love. I form goals, and build and reach dreams together with my partner. I am blessed with dedication and commitment to pull in the love I want. I know all things are possible.

Venus in Aquarius

As a fixed air Aquarius Venus sign, you are friendly and tolerant of others. Your Venus sign also needs to break a social convention (or two . . . or ten) in love. You refuse to be stereotyped in relationship, to be put in any box which stymies your true self. The need for the freedom to choose who, what, and how you love is exceptionally strong for you.

Your Love Charm: uniqueness. The more unusual and original you are in style, taste, opinions, and self-expression, the more attract-ive you become to others.

Your Soul Mate: an original. Your soul mate will probably defy the expectations of your culture, family, or society. They will wear signatures of an experimental, progressive, highly independent, and unusual character.

Your Attract-ive Power: the power to live and let live. Your inclusive ability to embrace others' differences and to accept them for who they are makes others feel truly accepted and loved.

Your Shadow: your need to have all your uncertainties and insecurities eliminated before risking falling in love with that one special person. You may prefer to spread your love thin across many friends or remain uninvolved rather than experience special love with one partner.

Your Venus Archetype: the sexual rebel, outsider, glamorous one, trend-setter, untouchable beauty, truth-teller, caged bird/free bird, prisoner of love, free-spirit, peace-lover, idealist, visionary, friend, humanitarian.

Think With Your Venus Mantra: I bring radical authenticity to the table of relationships, and the one who is still sitting there when I'm done is the one I want to be with. I offer unconventionality and truthfulness to my partnerships. They love me for my irreverence and eccentricity.

Venus in Pisces

As a mutable, mystical water sign who lives to observe and learn, you make the emotional life of your love relationship into your life study. Malleable and sensitive to others' needs, it's easy for you to fit your self into others' projections, causing your relationship to resemble a hall of mirrors at times. Endowed with a rich fantasy life and imagination, you enjoy creating ecstatic experiences of love, and you do this well.

Your Love Charm: boundless love. Your love is spiritual and all-encompassing. Unimpressed by worldly trappings, you see the essence of others, making it easy for you to overlook human imperfections and fall in love with their spirit and soul.

Your Soul Mate: connected to your spirituality. They rightfully sense an other-worldly mystical connection has brought you two together, just as you do.

K.I.S.S.

I'M EVERY WOMAN

Angelina Jolie, one of the wildest and strongest female role models we have, has Venus in the astrological sign of Cancer, a sign often associated with traditional female roles, such as mothering, care giving, and having dependents to care for—which she does. At least now. But back in the day, B.B. (before Brad), this mesmerizing water siren used her water-y Venus sign to call men toward her. She makes it look so effortless . . . but is it? Harnessing the power of the mysterious ocean, she drew men to her as the Moon draws in the tide. While this attract-ive power cast a wide net, she had someone very specific in mind, at least from her Venus' point of view. She needed a soul mate with whom to build a life and raise a family. Venus in Cancer's definition of love always includes home, hearth, and family. This is one example of the way we use our Venus sign to attract. No longer only the Venusian temptress of her youth, Angie's matured into both a mother and an indomitable queen. Maybe that's because her Venus' ruling planet is the changeable Moon, the archetype of Woman.

Your Attract-ive Power: the power of enchanted play. Life with you is never mundane—you cook up the kind of dreamy diversions and mystical moments that offer others escape from the dreariness of everyday living.

Your Shadow: kissing frogs while asking for a prince! Sometimes it's hard for you to tell the difference, yet when you do, you may still try to "rescue" the frog. Work on establishing boundaries and using imagination to turn your dream prince into a reality.

Your Venus Archetype: the hopeless romantic, magical child, actress, illusionist, victim, martyr, compassionate healer, Mother Teresa, beloved, good samaritan, lost soul, soul mate, codependent, sadist, psychic, rescuer, guru, ocean, siren, devotee, dream weaver.

Think With Your Venus Mantra: My outlandish, magnificent, and soulful diversions are enchantments that inspire others to no end. I know that whatever I ask for from love, I receive. As I identify what I don't want from love, I put what I do want into my imagination and then the Divine Heart of Love obliges my every wish.

Avoiding the Karmic Pits

Soul Mate Secret No. 5

If you're in a difficult relationship, you may be experiencing the consequence of a choice you made yesterday. You are a different person today, and you can choose to have a new experience of love.

Don't hold to anger, hurt or pain. They steal your energy and keep you from love.

LEO BUSCAGLIA

HERE'S SOMETHING WE NEED TO understand about attracting Mr. Wrong: en route to our soul mate, we will encounter love interests that trip us up, who lurk in our blind spot or represent the pothole in our road to love, in every sense. The biggest mistake we make is refusing to recognize him as a pothole. Oops, I did it again. And yet we really want the pothole to go away. Why doesn't it just go away? If the pothole went away, we would then start attracting the right guy, right? Wrong. The pothole won't go away. Mr. Wrong will continue to linger, as the nerd around your desk at work, the dangerous-looking guy at the end of the bar, or the gay or married man you crush on but can never have. Or the fabulously popular pothole, the really nice, perfect-in-every-way-guy you're not sexually attracted to. The existential pothole will always be there, and we only overcome it by walking around it. It's a simple concept, but we forget to do it. We need to lose our taste for our Mr. Wrong. Why is that so difficult?

The heart memory is strong; it can survive lifetimes on the bread and water of love scraps. So we get out our pen and paper and make a list of everything we want in a man—which happens to be the exact opposite of what we've attracted up until now. Then a funny thing happens. Along comes Fred, who seems to have everything we think we want, and we're not sexually attracted to him. He's overweight, or he smokes, or he's too nice but has most of those qualifications on our list. He's not our type. Our heart is behaving like a love-starved animal, seeing only two choices: Mr. Wrong or Mr. Not Quite Right. Neither fit.

I have a girlfriend who has been single for years. As long as I've known Surya, she's yearned to be swept off her feet and romanced, yet in the same breath claims she has too much fun on her own to be tied up with a man. "It will take an exceptional man," she's exclaimed on more than one occasion, "for me to give up the pleasure of my independence, the free time I enjoy so much." And then she met this wonderful man. He's warm, compassionate, caring, and so incredibly in touch with his feminine side, unlike any man she's ever met. This was sounding good, except there's just one little problem. You're probably guessing I'm going to say he's gay, right? No, he's a little person, a midget. And although he's perfect in all other ways, she's not sexually attracted to him. I wanted to laugh. Not at him, but at the hilarity of the situation. We humans are so funny. When we're not getting through to ourselves, the heart has no choice but to attract extremes. Surya attracted an exceptional but "unsuitable" man, because she was sending out mixed messages. The world obliged her muddled request.

In psychological terms, this is called a polarity. Basically, we're choosing the voice of the ego over the voice of love. The ego refuses to believe we'll get what and who we want, and that's our fatal error. We've split our psyche in two. We attract two extreme examples and find both wanting. We split down the middle to learn the difference between who we think we want to attract and who we really are attracting.

The heart doesn't think—it knows. It knows your love hooks. And it knows when you've bypassed the spiritual work of sorting out your emotional love hooks (because it's just too terrifying, hopeless, or painful) and when you've headed straight for the flip side. The flip side isn't better because it's less painful; it's more painful because now your ego is being shown what it will never have. But for some of us, a compromise is a compromise—and living a life without love feels easier than facing the painful fact that we haven't figured out how to love ourselves enough to attract the love we dream of.

Here's the pothole theory, summarized: The pothole won't go away. The only way we'll avoid the predictable relationship pothole is by choosing to walk around it. Not giving in to our attraction to the pothole is one way to begin to lose our taste for the difficult relationship. Yet the heart memory is strong, and we need to get curious about the difficult partner we're attracting. This process takes awareness. While the first and necessary step is walking around the pothole—learning to recognize and avoid a destructive relationship—the second begins the work of healing. Until we learn how to recognize and work with the Saboteur and the Shadow (see

Secret No. 6), moving away from the old pain and into new pain may appear to be the only option.

Companion Spell: THE HAITIAN HAIR CURE

Balancing the Scales of Karma

*You were strong enough to hold something for someone
else and you allowed them to learn their lesson.*

—CAROLINE MYSS, ON KARMA IN RELATIONSHIPS

I'm going to introduce you to karma. While I want you to relish the fact that the Universe is full of Mystery with a capital *M*, we're subject to certain rules like the Law of Karma with a capital *K*. Karma is one of those universal and immutable laws, and it is kind. Why bring up karma? Contemplating karma is especially useful when we're trying to understand how we've attracted certain experiences or people into our life. Karma is only one possible explanation—there are also inherited family patterns, family legacies, and spiritual lessons, but even those are essentially karmic, too.

Seated between these forces of Mystery and the Law of Karma is this one truth: we always attract the lesson (in the form of a person or circumstance) we're ready to master next. Maybe we don't have entire control over our "destiny," but responding to the best of our ability always moves us to the next level. One of the cool paradoxes of karma is that we really don't have to know why any of it is happening to get off the merry-go-round. So if you think you're in a cycle of "bad karma," you might try giving up on understanding the *why* of it all. Then you may actually catch a glimpse of your own power in shaping your destiny—choice and action. If karma is the invisible wave breaking today, the choices and actions you take today are the invisible ripple effect cascading into tomorrow's reality.

Karma is the Eastern concept of cause and effect, the idea that our actions and choices have consequences. You've heard "you reap what you sow," and karma is the ultimate balance for our actions, both positive and negative. While it may sound punitive from a Western mindset (especially if you grew up thinking there was a punishing/rewarding man doling out cookies or lightning bolts, depending on what

K.I.S.S.

KARMIC LOVE LESSONS

I know every relationship is, essentially, karmic. That's to say—if we were all so enlightened not to have work to do with others, we'd be carrying a "karma free" pass and astral-traveling the galaxy with our other half! Every relationship has a healing edge, helping us grow and evolve toward a higher love. But when a relationship delivers more than you bargained for, as in a painful or abusive relationship, sometimes the thing to do is outgrow that person. Only you can distinguish between karmic love lessons and soul mate love lessons; yet I've found there is one essential question that always helps. Of every relationship, ask: Do I have something to give or teach this person? Do they have something to give or teach me? If you hear a resounding *yes!* that's a sign that this relationship has great spiritual growth potential! Trust your first answer, then approach your partner from this angle. By doing so, you'll work through your karmic mates more quickly. Although when you find your soul mate, you'll discover that answering this question is much more fun and a heck of a lot easier!

you've done), but it's not. Karma doesn't judge. This isn't punishment or "repayment" for past wrongs. Instead, karma balances. Actually, you can think of karma as a neutral and loving force—a system of checks and balances for the world. The natural law of the Universe is peace, harmony, love, and balance. In this way, karma acts like a cosmic scale, sometimes swinging wildly to keep the world from veering too far away from love.

The confusing thing about karma is that the full extent of our actions will play out, but we won't always see those results. This explains why some people seem to be on the karmic grace plan in this life, left over from past lives. Maybe that person has a poisonous attitude that scorches everyone within ten feet and doesn't seem to have a problem with it, or a person plays the victim and also manages to be taken care of by others. These people appear to "get away with murder," but karma will step in eventually. We may not see the consequences of their negative or positive actions in this lifetime, but they will. Eventually, they'll be on the receiving end and experience the other side of the coin because, like gravity, karma is the law.

"Instant karma" is in the mainstream vernacular because it's easy to see right away, though in actuality, it's only one kind of karma. There are many different forms of karma. According to Vedic teachers, a most rooted form is Sanchita Karma, or soul karma—the accumulation of past actions from previous lifetimes. Soul karma is stored in the soul and some portion of it releases into our physical body and into our energetic body in this life. We'll take another portion with us to our next lifetime. Whatever form of karma you choose to call it, our talents, abilities, habits, predispositions, and attractions for certain people—including our soul mate—all arise from karma.

So how does this understanding of karma apply to your soul mate search? All relationships involve rebalancing the karmic scales. We may attract a partner who needs what we have because, by virtue of our abilities, gifts, and our own karma, we're helping them master a spiritual lesson for their growth. And that partner, in turn, will help us master a lesson for our own growth. Soul mates have karma. Karmic mates have karma. The degree and qualities of it vary, but karma it is.

I imagine the first sexual-emotional-physical connection we have with another as though it were a sparkle-glitter glue stick—it's got real allure, shimmer, and romantic bonding. For stronger bonds to form, though—whether karmic bonds or soul mate bonds—we need more than the lure of glitter-y fabulous attraction to really get going. Karma is stronger than the glue stick of attraction; it's like love's superglue. We know we're here to "work it out" together and until we're done, we just won't let go.

With soul mate love, we have far more choices and freedom in our shared karma. This is the difference between karmic and soul mate connections. When we meet out soul mate, it's as if karma has tipped the scales to the positive side of the equation, allowing us to explore new horizons and potentials with each other. We can practically see the happy karmic ripples of our coupling spilling from our hearts and out into eternity.

Karma in Relationships

A wise person once said there's no faster way to accumulate karma, good or bad, than through relationships. I wish I could remember who that was, 'cause I'd give them a nod and a high five. Whether it's actions and decisions made today or crossed astral planes from previous lifetimes, our karma always involves other people. And, as my teacher Steven Forrest says, "Our especially tough karma always involves other people." Under that light, it's easy to feel the brevity and heaviness of relationships (maybe so-called commitment-phobes feel this weight more acutely than others!).

Sure, there are lifetimes of good stuff available through relationships, and in mutually supportive relationships, that good stuff could ostensibly supply lifetimes of love. But when two lives come together, everything is amplified—every action and reaction is times two. This shows up and is perpetuated by the emotional attitudes and responses we give others. Maybe a soul mate is carrying really heavy baggage and we're worn down, or maybe we're happy to help. Maybe that person is passionate about something we dislike. What attitude does your mate bring out in you on a daily basis? It's worth thinking about, because as we stare into their pretty face every single day, that attitude will affect us, too.

No one comes into a relationship with a clean slate. Rest assured, everyone carries their own baggage. Baggage is universal—everyone wrestles with the seemingly immovable and relentless taskmaster within. In a sense, when we find our soul mate, we must willingly take on their baggage, too. What a mission! After all, we already have our own, no? We really do have to love them enough to want to do it—wholeheartedly and without begrudging, regret, or any other negative emotion that silently chips away at love. Otherwise, instead of creating love and sending it into limitless time and space, we're creating suffering and sending that out into time and space. And that's just not good karma.

The buck stops here, with soul mate love.

When we make the decision to invite another person into our life as a soul mate, we're inviting in everything about them, too. There's nothing about them we don't love and appreciate. We're here to be their safe harbor, their reprieve—and we're here to claim the same for ourself with them.

To remain in integrity with each other, we truly must embrace the person they've been in the past and the person they want to become. When we move toward a soulful relationship, we're embracing their ambitions, talents, and beauty and also their personal history, addictions, and yes, their baggage. We must make room for their dreams, too, which may or may not match our own. Are we willing to support their dreams, even though they're different from our own? If we feel judgmental or dubious about those dreams now, how do we think we'll feel several years from now, after we've been financing their dream of becoming a rock star? Depending on your commitment level and desire for lifelong love, everything about your soul mate's world will eventually become part of your world, too. You can count on it.

My soul mate once told me a story about an artist he used to casually date. He thought she was a fabulous lady and after a few dates, she took him to her studio and showed him her art. Uh-oh. Instantly he realized he hated her art! And at that moment, he decided not to pursue the relationship. As a sensitive artist myself, my first instinct was "how judgmental of you!" but his reasoning was solid. He said he imagined sitting at the breakfast table years from that moment, she bringing in a freshly finished artwork for admiration and praise, and he having none. Being forced to lie through his teeth. No, my husband wasn't being judgmental—he was exercising good judgment. He knew he couldn't embrace and support her world in totality, and that advance knowledge saved them both from suffering.

Knowing our desires, preferences, and limits is invaluable in attracting a soul mate relationship. The self-knowledge will karmically free us and make us more available for a real relationship. We have to come to each other as individuals, intact, complete, and whole on our own, in order to successfully thrive as a couple. This is necessary, but not just from the perspective of healthy relationship. If their burdens are quite heavy, we need to have the strength to carry them. Because we will be asked to.

Hopefully we want to help our mate carry their weight. Maybe we are strong enough to carry their burdens for them—at least for a while. This request takes place in every relationship. In some relationships, it's the determining quality of it: I have friends who spend an inordinate amount of energy being helpful and generous, which is its own kind of karma, too, if that's what you're looking for. When the giving is rewarding for you, you're in the Universe's good graces!

Not that anyone's keeping score of who carries whose burden for how long and how often. The key is that the giving is done without hesitation, disguises of sainthood, or hidden costs to anyone—it just feels good to give. This usually can't go on forever, though. Balance and reciprocity is a universal law, and it's Venus' law as well. We need to feel the giving and receiving moving in both directions, in some form of equal measure. So if you're wondering whether their burden will break your back, better to ask sooner rather than later.

All this talk about karma throws a chink in the "casual" part of casual dating, huh? That's okay. If you're on a soul mate search, you don't want to treat your heart casually. On one level, we want to have fun and be playful, open, and experimental on our quest for soulful love; but on another level, we've got to remember the wise accountant in our heart. We've got to be discerning and accountable to our heart and our soul.

Karma is love's superglue. We will create karma in our relationships, but we can create positive karma by coming together as equals and independents, two people who are motivated by soulful love to carry the occasional burden for the other. There's no bigger bummer than to find yourselves with aching backs, unhappily stuck together—when you could have been so happy together if you'd examined your burdens and karma in the first place.

⁂

Exercise: Waiter . . . Check, Please!

When you're finally ready to finish up love's appetizers with karmic mates, you can get on to the main course and dessert—soul mate love. Steven Forrest turned me on to this fabulous exercise you can try on follow-up dates. So you recently met a great guy or gal, and you're seeing each other for the second, third, fourth time. The requirement for a heady chemical rush of sexual charge has been exceedingly met, and in a moment of humane objectivity (likely brought on by the spinach stuck in their teeth), you wonder if this relationship is heading someplace soulful, or if they are just someone with whom you have unfinished business to take care of. Try projecting yourself into the future with this person (you can do this in your head without them ever knowing). If you were together a year from now, what type of issues do you think you two would face? Are those similar to ones you've already faced with other people? Look at their character, what they've shown you. If this person is in a committed relationship, and they're betraying the integrity and trust of that relationship by being here with you, it stands to reason that they will betray you in the future, too. Let the pearls of wisdom from your previous relationships come to bear on this critical karmic mate analysis—after all, you're not getting any younger and you don't have to waste your time. If you cannot clearly see a future of soulful love with this person, do yourself (and them) and favor, and exit gracefully. When the waiter passes by, kindly ask for the check while excusing yourself from heading down a new road with yet another old karmic mate. When they ask why you're leaving you can simply reply, "I've got an appointment (with my soul mate), and I don't want to be late."[1]

Family and Inherited Legacies

I mentioned my friend Kelli earlier in the section "Past Life, This Life" (in "What Is a Soul Mate?"), and how she attracted the bad boy in every crowd. Kelli's heart healing was to resolve the difference between the love she got from her father and brother with the love she now craved. Kelli's got that naturally gorgeous and glamorous, all-American, girl-next-door look, and she's a deeply soulful, spiritual, light-filled being. I've always believed there's a downside to everything, including exceptional beauty. Her beauty and charisma are so bright, it's like trying to look directly into the sunshine; it's difficult to look beyond the superficial obvious. But not only does she have the problem of feeling that her good looks eclipse the real beauty she

---

1 This exercise is paraphrased from *Skymates* by Jodie Forrest and Steven Forrest.

has on the inside, she attracts men who are often involved in underworld activities, drugs, lifestyle excesses, and the like.

The attraction for this shady character isn't superficial; it's got deep hooks in her personal history. Her father was involved in illegal businesses when she was a young girl, and he often took her along on his "dirty work." She described the lifestyle as glamorous, as she was the beautiful daughter on the arm of a very powerful and popular man, a man who also exposed her to incredible danger. Her family story resembles something you'd see in the movies, one with lots of friends, glamour, dark secrets, and violence. And in my personal opinion, she's been doing the personal healing work of eight lifetimes in this one. Being a reflective person, of course she's noticed the similarity between her father and the men she attracts, and yet she still attracts them. Why? She's attracted to these men. The people we're attracted to and the people we attract are often one in the same, even if that's not what we know we should want.

There's no getting around the magnetism we have for a "type," because we remember him in our hearts. And the most powerful heart memory can involve our primary relationship with our parents. They are our first caregivers, the people who taught us how to love. If we're love-earners, we learn that daddy's little girl behaves a certain way to get the love she needs to survive. Or maybe love came with sharp edges and rigid demands. For a child, love is an all-consuming force, more important than air, food, or shelter. Love equals survival.

As adults, this truth lives on in our hearts. Even as we're focused on material living, the power of love guides us back to the heart memory, which in turn guides us to our invisible partner. It's hardly conscious. To avoid being caught between a rock and a hard place, and in order to find our soul mate, we need to ask our higher self (not our ego) for more awareness and clarity. Ah, *this* was the wonderful/difficult person who taught me what love is. Ah, *this* is the person I'm trying to attract/avoid.

The heart memory won't be erased; it can only be examined. And this is an especially painful process for women who have been abandoned, neglected, or abused by their father or another family member. Many victims of abuse by a relative or family friend can't help but be attracted to the abuser. These primary relationships have a strong hold. When you keep attracting the wrong man or turning the right man into the wrong man, it has everything to do with the men in your life up until now. That's something to look at, and that's where Shadow work comes in (we'll explore the Shadow more fully in Secret No. 6). An unconscious mold has been set and either someone will gladly fill it for you, or you'll project that same issue onto someone who could be right for you.

I've learned this from sitting with people who appear to repeat patterns from their family relationships in their adult relationships. Some people take the exact opposite route that their parents did, as though an inner reflex tells them that following in their parents' footsteps is too painful, so they need to do the opposite. Others avoid relationships altogether, because love comes with painful augurs of memory and betrayal. All responses arise from a memory of love, its distortion, and a need to return to love.

There are many reasons we don't find the love we want when we want it, and some of them are mysterious, like the mysterious Universe, and will be revealed in time. But we can always get in touch with our heart by asking the right questions. Examining our family relationships in the light of our past relationships and our current relationships or lack thereof, we can put ourselves in the best possible position to receive the love that's already on its way.

Tribal Chakra Exercise

The first chakra is related to basic survival. It's sometimes called the tribal chakra, and is located on our tail or "sit" bone connecting us to the ground. It is also sometimes called the root chakra, as it is the root of our energy.

This personal energy center is like an ancient tree planted in the ground of everything and everyone who supports our world. The tribal chakra contains our unique repository of inherited beliefs and judgments about how safe the world is and isn't; it is our inherited worldview. Early experience informs our sense of safety and our beliefs, many of which were formed out of necessity or self-protection. Like a self-fulfilling prophecy, we attract those people who support our beliefs, but our beliefs don't always support our search for soulful love. For example, when a mother holds the belief that "all men are bastards," on some level, her children believe her. The tribal chakra affects us in life and love, for better or worse.

The goal of this next exercise is to understand how our collection of inherited beliefs connects to our survival and to our search for the ultimate love. In the spirit of better understanding our heart, we will learn what beliefs we inherited from our tribe and whether these beliefs weaken or support us. Do they keep us in integrity or weaken us with doubt? Are there any beliefs we're ready to uproot?

What you will need: your love alchemist's notebook and a pen.

Put pen to paper and take a tribal chakra inventory. The following questions are from the book *Sacred Contracts* by Caroline Myss, a wonderful book to help you discover your soul's purpose in this lifetime:

1. What belief patterns about relationships did I inherit from my family?

2. Which of those belief patterns still have authority in my thinking? Are any of these no longer valid?

3. What superstitions do I have? Which have more authority over me than my reasoning ability?

4. Do I have a personal code of honor? What is it?

5. Have I ever compromised my sense of honor? If so, did I take steps to correct the breach?

6. Do I have any unfinished business with my family members? If so, list the things that prevent you from healing those family relationships.

7. List all the blessings you feel came from your family.

8. Describe tribal characteristics within yourself that you would like to strengthen and develop.

After you're done, reflect on healing steps you might take to facilitate the new awareness you discovered. Get creative. For example, if you discover that you've been holding an automatic assumption about relationships, you might investigate it by talking to family members, if that feels safe. If you discover your inner child is still holding on to what's no longer true for you, you might rewrite a new belief that feels more right for the person you are now.

Being Present to Choice

Every week I hear from people who find themselves in love triangles, are with cheating spouses, or are habitually attracting partners who lie or are abusive. I feel deeply compassionate for these predicaments. I don't believe anyone truly wants to be in a difficult relationship. Yet I always find myself moving back to choice. At some point, our very self made a choice, consciously or unconsciously, to learn something about a most fascinating subject: you.

There are many ways to learn about ourselves, to locate and master our strengths, and one of those ways is being in a difficult relationship. Yet a soul lesson of mastery can be demoted from graduate level work down to elementary education when we stay in a past choice—that is, when we keep responding to today from the position of a past choice.

I have a client who was in love with her childhood sweetheart. They fell in love, had a child, and moved to the United States. But when they arrived here, life became difficult, and her husband became physically abusive toward her. He never was abusive toward their young son, although the boy soon became fearful and angry toward his father. The woman broke off the relationship, and he decided to leave the states and move back home. When she went back home over Christmas, she saw her ex again and noticed old feelings returning, good ones. When I last saw her, she was feeling lonely as a single mother in a country far from her home, trying to work out how to be with her ex again.

Only the soul knows how long it needs to stay in a karmic relationship to learn the lesson, to receive the healing. Despite our rational mind's logic that "I know better than this," or the protest of family members and friends, the heart holds on until it's done. Some of us need to follow the trail of tears to the healing end; maybe we attracted this broken relationship in order to learn about the ways in which we're broken. We'll stay exactly where we need to be, in the relationship, until we're done.

And in the midst of that harmful relationship, we don't always understand our self or the lesson that's trying to be learned. For people who come to see me with this kind of conflict, the only way out is through. We need to accept that we're in the trenches and that slogging through the emotional muck is exactly what we need to be doing. That's where the ceiling on our mind finally lifts. Until we are done healing our own self and telling our story of pain, we're not done. We need to hear ourselves telling and retelling a tale of confusion until we "get" what needs to be gotten from this painful spot.

I know we can only take responsibility for our self at the level at which we understand a situation. The word *responsibility* literally means "ability to respond." Sometimes we're not able to respond without some extra support. A guide can give us ears to hear; so can art-making, writing, exploring spirituality, or talking to a confidant. By gently exploring our disillusionment over the difference between where we want to be and where we actually are, the thing blocking our growth is worn away by our tears, like water ebbing at a cliff.

There are many ways to move out of a past choice, or a karmic relationship, and into a new choice, and they all require our presence. The present is the most powerful place to be. It's the place where brand-new choices take root and fresh new beginnings will blossom.

Try this affirmation: As I understand this situation and my role in it, I hold myself responsible for my actions and choices. I don't turn my back on what I see. I can always respond from a place of presence. I make the choice to do so today.

Exercise: Breaking the Karmic Chain

This exercise is a meditation on being present to everyday choices and how those choices shape our future. Everything in your life today is a direct result of yesterday's choices. The choices you make today build tomorrow's reality. Be empowered by this knowledge and be responsible for it. Remember, you're bound to live out your choices, but if they're no longer working for you, you're not bound by them. You can always choose differently today.

To break the karma of staying in a relationship pattern you no longer choose, take an inventory of your choices. Write down the choices you've made in the past that affected your life in a big way (and be sure to include the choices that were made for you, which you either turned around or contributed to, through your own actions). List your major life events—a decision to move or go back to school, for example. Then write down your spontaneous responses to the following:

- From your wiser, more experienced perspective, would you make the same choices?

- Sometimes we make uncomfortable choices because we must. Forgive yourself for those now, in writing or silently.

- If you would've made a different choice, how do you imagine your future might look today? Would it be different?

- Identify one new choice that you'd like to set into motion today. Make it happen.

With every new choice you make starting today, begin asking: Is the choice I'm making moving me closer to the reality of my dreams, or farther away from it?

End this exercise by affirming: I am a different person today, and today I can choose differently.

Relationships from Hell

Are you in a relationship from hell? Well, say hell-o to your new best friend, Persephone, the goddess of almost-doomed relationships. She earned that title by getting married to the Underworld demon himself, Mr. Hades. It was truly a match made in hell. There are many versions of the myth, depending on who's telling it. In her mother's version, Persephone was unwillingly abducted into the Underworld by Hades while on a walk through a field of lily-white flowers. In a Jungian analyst's version, the lily-white Persephone may have "asked for it," because she needed to learn from the darkness. Perhaps the only way to free herself from mama's apron strings was to be abducted by this dark god.

If you've been in a partnership where you've felt victimized, disempowered, manipulated, lied to, taken advantage of, or abused in any way, you've played the role of Persephone. She represents the stolen innocence in all of us. In her naivete, her innocence was stolen. This isn't a victim role, however; losing innocence is a virtual rite of passage for most women, and very few of us make it to adulthood without having survived at least one, if not several, relationships from hell.

The danger of hanging out with Persephone for too long is insistently living on the light side when our relationships reflect far darker forces at work. Maybe we're with a jealous, possessive, or abusive partner. Surrounded by darkness, we may cling to the light version of truth, like Persephone did, unable to see our role in it. It takes a special kind of seeing, a willingness to see in the dark, to acknowledge that there is something about our self and our role in this relationship that we're not seeing. If you're in a relationship from hell, only brutal honesty can save you. And that's damn hard. It's hard to admit, for instance, that if we're sticking around with users and abusers, we're probably using them for something too—could it be fear of our own power?

Power is always an issue in relationships from hell; someone else seems to possess all of it. Persephone eventually made the choice to take her power back. She eventually chose to live with Hades (she ate six pomegranate seeds) for six months of the year, and with her mother the other six. Her mum Demeter, goddess of harvest, agreed to this arrangement, which is why we have seasons of light in spring and summer and seasons of dark in autumn and winter. The only way to get your power back from a real soul-stomping is to claim your choice to be there and be ruthlessly honest with yourself about your role in the relationship.

Persephone's story is no endorsement to live with a dark lover. I like to think that she transformed her relationship to her own power and thus found her ability to negotiate power in relationship. Maybe (with the help of a good psychologist!) she discovered her power of choice, and chose to both stay and leave. Relationships from hell present opportunities for real empowerment. When we're in one, there's only one choice to make: integrate the dark and the light within our very self.

A relationship from hell has any, or all, of these qualities:

- compelling and invisible magnetism (it's as though you can't break away)

- subtle or overt abuse, and power trips

- obsessive attachment, irrational jealousy, sexual addiction, or controlling behavior that dominates the relationship

- your gut feeling tells you that this isn't what you dreamed love would be . . . but you can't seem to leave

If you're in a relationship from hell, you might try:

- admitting you're in the dark about the relationship

- expressing your unacknowledged helplessness, fear, rage, grief, or anger to a trusted friend; these are all are natural and healthy parts of being human; own your dark side; your anger is your anger—own it so your mate doesn't have to express it for you

- learning to see in the dark; the Underworld is the symbolic "unconscious" containing motives, needs, and wounds we may not be aware of; explore your family history and any traumas you've suffered

- mining your relationship for gold; psychologists are Persephone's best friend— they mine the depths (pain) for answers that yield precious meaningful gold (wisdom)

- leaving, if you need to; get support to do this

- looking at your relationship with your father; it was Zeus, Persephone's father, who arranged for this Underworld abduction to take place, without her consent—has your father ever betrayed your confidence or trust? How has this lack of fatherly protection contributed to your painful situation?

- looking at your bond with your mother; face it, moms are all good intentions and love, but sometimes they're too clingy and too close for comfort—her well-meaning advice can actually sabotage our personal life; if we're too busy taking care of mom at the expense of our own individual needs this can cause problems in our intimate relationships

Finally, there will be people in life who love us and whom we love back, but who aren't always good or healthy for us. These people will teach us about our own boundaries. They will also teach us about our Saboteur and our Shadow—which we'll explore fully in the next chapter!

Companion Spell: SEXUAL POWER: THE POMEGRANATE SPELL

Making Friends Out of Enemies: Your Saboteur and Shadow

Soul Mate Secret No. 6

Your unexplored beliefs, fears, and unworthiness push love away. To break the cycle of difficult relationship karma, you need to recognize your Saboteur and your Shadow.

There are many more people trying to meet the right person than become the right person.

GLORIA STEINEM

My girlfriend's sister married a man she clearly didn't love. She was just ready to settle down and have a baby, and he was a good friend. Hey, they got along and she wasn't having luck with anyone else. She's the kind of girl who wanted a ring, and since she wanted one, she got one. When they started trying to conceive, nothing happened. A fertility specialist confirmed his sperm count was low and they'd have to spend a good amount of money and time on fertility treatments, and she began to realize that she didn't love him enough to enter these trials with him. This new awareness that she didn't love her husband gave her new resolve . . . to begin an affair with her yoga instructor. She eventually left her husband, but not for the yoga instructor, though she wanted to. He was in the midst of a messy divorce with kids and said the added stress of a new relationship was too much for him. The last I heard, she was living at her parents' house.

When I hear stories that start off on the wrong foot from the very beginning, my heart groans. Why do my sisters get themselves into these terribly difficult situations? Don't they understand that entering into a relationship with anything less than stars in their eyes and a song in their heart will cause suffering? In a nutshell: no, they don't understand at all.

Sometimes it takes total unhappiness to get us to step outside of our beliefs about the way things should be and consider other (far more effective) alternatives. When our perception is cleansed of limiting beliefs and misunderstandings, we're far more free to create what our heart knows to be true. Sometimes we simply don't yet have the tools to do differently than we've done in the past. When this is the case, we may need to find an example of the type of love we're looking for in order to discover a new paradigm for a loving relationship. And sometimes throwing out everything we thought we knew about love is a very good thing.

In order to begin the healing work of a relationship that's tearing you up inside, you've got to do something dramatically and radically different than what you're doing now. This doesn't necessarily entail ending a previously loving relationship—that's your call and it's not an easy one to make. To do anything dramatically differently with success and confidence (such as moving on), an inner transformation must take place. We've got to recognize where we go wrong, how we shoot ourselves in the foot.

Meet Your Saboteur

Let me introduce the concept of the archetype. Archetypes are ancient energy patterns that run throughout all of human consciousness. There are hundreds, maybe thousands, of archetypes alive in the world. I first encountered the concept through astrology, where the planets and asteroids embody just about all of the archetypes in the world.

Archetypes were introduced by the super-cool psychoanalyst Carl Jung. Archetypes are universal energy patterns and are especially easy (and fun) to spot in movies—the sick patient, the hopeless romantic, the fumbling villain, the funny sidekick, the hero. Their energy sustains individual and collective life by creating a common, shared thread that connects all of humanity. Archetypes are pure energy; they are just as personal as the energy running through your body right now. They're embodied in the roles of our lives. Like stock actors and actresses, when archetypes are recognized, they follow a fairly predictable pattern of the human experience.

No one person resembles only one archetype—we're multi-dimensional people—but movie roles generalize archetypes nicely. Think of the last movie you watched. Romantic comedy? Class nerd (the underdog) wins the cheerleader's heart (princess). Drama? The courageous main character (the hero) changed an impossible situation, inspiring you to do so in your life. There are many archetypes. Once you get going, you can intuitively spot and label them.

I've found two archetypes particularly useful in my soul mate work: the Saboteur and the Shadow. We'll get to the Shadow in a bit, but if I were to imagine the Saboteur in a movie, she would be the one who keeps falling in the existential love pothole because she just can't see it (and the audience groans). She's the girl who keeps going for the same brand of loser over and over again.

Drum roll please.

Introducing . . . your Saboteur.

> The Saboteur archetype is made up of the fears and issues related to low self-esteem that cause you to make choices in life that block your own empowerment and success.
>
> You need to face this powerful archetype that we all possess and make it an ally. When you do, you will find that it calls your attention to situations in which you are in danger of being sabotaged, or of sabotaging yourself.
>
> Once you are comfortable with the Saboteur, you learn to hear and heed these warnings, saving yourself untold grief from making the same mistakes over and over. Ignore it, and the shadow Saboteur will manifest in the form of self-destructive behavior or the desire to undermine others.
>
> —Caroline Myss, *Sacred Contracts*

The Saboteur specializes in shooting you in the foot. Your chance for power, confidence, and love—poof! It's gone. The Saboteur steps in when you decide to exit a highly promising relationship because it would be too painful to be that vulnerable. This Saboteur is fairly common. The Saboteur lurks in the shadows when you decide to date only men you don't really care about (and who don't care about you) because you're afraid of being abandoned. Hey, that was just my own Saboteur, but it might be yours, too!

When we see this sabotaging pattern in another person, we might wonder how he or she can be so blind. Well, what's obvious to the audience or to a friend isn't so obvious from the driver's seat.

You should understand that the Saboteur can be tricky. It may not want to be found out. Ignorance is how the vise grip of low self-esteem stays in power! For instance, the Saboteur can hide the little girl inside the woman who makes the choice to marry someone she doesn't love out of fear that she'll never get married. The Saboteur can be your alter ego drama queen who creates enough "big deals" to chase a man away. The Saboteur shows up as the married man or little person (as we learned in the story of Surya and her exceptional man) because a woman is afraid to ask for more. The Saboteur can shape-shift into a responsible adult who makes all the right choices for all the wrong reasons, like staying in a marriage "for the sake of the kids" and feeling diminished by it every day.

The Saboteur can even appear as betrayer. The life of exotic dancer and convicted spy Mata Hari (as seen in the movie *Mata Hari*) is a case study in the Saboteur archetype at its most destructive. Mata Hari started her young life in an abusive marriage, but through studying ancient Indonesian dance, she forged a career as a dancer and elevated erotic dancing to previously uncharted artistic heights. While working as a courtesan, she was accused of (though never admitted to) passing classified information for Germany during World War I and was sentenced to death. After a hard-earned rise to fame, Mata Hari blocked her own empowerment. By betraying the trust of others, and herself, Mata Hari became her own worst enemy—the ultimate definition of self-sabotage.

Yet the Saboteur is no enemy. Its goal is to empower your awareness about the ways you keep yourself from being successful, empowered, and happy. So why does it behave like an enemy? At the core, the Saboteur takes its direct orders from fear. Fear that there's not enough love to go around, fear of the unknown, fear that we'll be ignored, fear that if we change, we'll screw everything up.

The Saboteur can "screw up" a relationship by turning it into a power struggle, for instance. The Saboteur can keep us from taking the risk on starting a new relationship or following up on a new business idea because we're so deeply afraid. If Fear and Insecurity are like the Saboteur's frenemies, egging it on to do really dumb things, the Saboteur's allies are Choice and Intuition. Intuition is the voice alerting you to a red-flag situation where you might easily mess things up. And when we stop taking orders from fear, we take responsibility for the changes our empowered choices set in motion.

Making Friends Out of Enemies

Awareness of your Saboteur deepens your relationship to your own self, having the potential to transform your relationship to your self and to others. Sometimes my Saboteur comes out to play when I'm lonely or feeling neglected or invisible to my mate. We all have our triggers. For me, stress and being too busy come on strong, and I'll feel overlooked. When the person inside me doesn't believe I'm fully appreciated and loved, my Saboteur can settle into uneasy neglect, and drama often ensues.

The Saboteur can also play dirty. It can show up as someone who has authority or power over us, and because we fear they will take our power away, we (read: our Saboteur) might undermine them. But the thing to recognize is that the Saboteur has those same old predictable triggers—low self-esteem and fear. You can't teach this old dog a new trick, either, no siree. The only trick you can get away with is to recognize the Saboteur as your own right in the middle of a familiar drama, then listen to your intuition.

Listening to intuition disarms the Saboteur. Of course you've got to be able to recognize when you're responding to a person or situation out of fear or low self-esteem. Intuition calls often, but it's soft as a whisper. I had a friend who used to call his intuition exactly that—a whisper. He'd say, "I heard a whisper to call you, so I did." Of course, this friend was so fabulous at heeding his intuition that he'd call exactly when I needed, with important information for me. Listening to and acting on your whispers takes energy away from the negative Saboteur, and it makes your Saboteur your friend. Then your friendly Saboteur can alert you to the types of situations and people who cause that unfortunate downward spiral of self-destruction.

There are other ways to recognize the negative Saboteur and pull it into the light (see the exercise below). When we come to honest terms with how we sabotage our success and empowerment, the heavens part. Just think of all the energy bound up in your Saboteur, waiting to be used to your benefit!

Companion Spell: VENUS ALCHEMY SPELL

Exercise: I.D. Your Saboteur

The Saboteur specializes in reacting out of fear. Feeling needy, neglected, ignored, afraid, unloved, or unworthy will give the Saboteur opportunity to use these feelings and attitudes to reinforce a cycle of undermining behavior and poor decision making. Once you identify your Saboteur, you gain real power.

- At one time or another we will make decisions out of fear and those are the decisions we pay most dearly for. What fears do you give authority in your life? Name at least three of those fears.
  - What happens when fear takes over in my life? Do I lose my voice? Do I freeze up?
  - Have I let opportunities I was excited about or wanted to act on pass me by out of fear?

- Have there been any times, circumstances, or relationships in which you've suspected you might be self-sabotaging? Can you identify more than one instance here? Can you see a pattern?
  - Can I see my Saboteur's role with a person that I haven't been able to forgive or a relationship I haven't been able to move on from?
  - Do I recognize the Saboteur in myself?

- Sometimes our Saboteur shows up most apparently as a person who appears intent on undermining us. Consider that this person might be a reflection of your fears and low self-esteem (see the next section on Shadow).

- Intuition and healthy self-esteem can save us from making disempowering or self-destructive choices. Can you identify times when you ignored your intuition to your detriment, when acting on it might've helped? Intuition is only useful when we act on it.

- What emotional and situational triggers lead me into pointless, repetitive, or self-destructive behavior?

• Can I see the Saboteur in others? If I can see how they're blocking their personal success, could I offer them any advice on their Saboteur? What would that advice be?

Meet Your Shadow

With experience and with relentless self-honesty, we may realize the same relationship themes recur over and over throughout our life. The relationship we had with our father repeats. The same story about being betrayed or abandoned or disrespected repeats. The theme of feeling victimized or heartbroken or disillusioned repeats.

This is very personal stuff, but the themes are universal. The Shadow is an archetype just like the Saboteur, so it's a universal energy field that belongs to everyone. Remember the comic book character, the Shadow? The Shadow cloaks itself in darkness; the Shadow is made up of unconscious stuff, good and bad, dark and light, and until we examine it, it's mostly misunderstood because it's unconscious. Basically, we're in the dark about what we won't look at or can't see.

The Shadow is often present when blame is invoked, similar to the Saboteur. When it comes to recognizing our Shadow, everyone else is wrong—but not us. It's easy to blame someone else for our misfortune or misery because "they" did it to me. Blame is the Shadow's original culprit, and just like a murder mystery, when the Shadow appears, so do its accomplices, Suspicion and Distrust. And for good reason—we are suspicious of what we don't know in ourself.

The only way to have healthy, self-aware relationships is to own our Shadow. But how do we own what appears to be clearly someone else's fault? How do we own what we're not conscious of? By taking total responsibility for everything! Sounds easy, right? To your ego, it probably sounds like a painfully bad idea. Yet the only way to bypass the pain of continually relinquishing your personal power is to make the radical decision to take responsibility for all of the past mistakes and start there. That's right, all of it.

This is especially hard to stomach when we "attract" someone abusive, or when we have been betrayed, which begs the question, How could I have caused this? That question plugs right into feelings of victimization and low self-worth that we may already have. There's a subtle difference between "taking responsibility for" and "causing" a painful situation, and it's a good distinction to make. One involves self-blame, the other involves self-empowerment to take charge of our life. Looking at the entire enchilada as though it's happening because there's something we're not seeing or haven't acknowledged is like occupying the power seat with the Shadow. We acknowledge that there's a message here: "If I'm experiencing this strong dynamic coming from the Other, they probably have something I've been missing. They probably carry a quality that's ready to be integrated into my self."

Taking responsibility for the Shadow is a lifelong process, one requiring your diligence and tender compassion. Why is it so tough? The Shadow isn't easy to see, it lives in the darkness and contains our most raw wounds and pains. Try not to let the complexity and the darkness of the Shadow oppress you. Instead, let its complexity deepen your understanding and ultimately liberate you.

Bringing the Shadow to Light

Everyone carries a shadow and the less it is embodied
in the individual's conscious life, the blacker and denser it is.
At all counts, it forms an unconscious snag, thwarting our
most well-meant intentions.

—Carl G. Jung

"I can't stand drama queens" or "Homeless people should just get jobs." People with certain qualities bug us. They get under our skin, drive us crazy, even repulse us. We avoid them, we can't stand being around them. In a dark twist, maybe we dislike people who walk around blind to their Shadow, always blaming circumstances and others for their misfortune, not taking responsibility for their behavior. Yikes, I have that Shadow!

We all have our version of the Shadow. No one is exempt. We all have buttons that can be pushed. The guy who doesn't take responsibility is a perfect "hook" for me, and over and over I've attracted this Shadow quality in lovers and friends. I've played out this rerun so many times, I think it went into syndication! But it's *me* who is doing the attracting. Not until I examined how I was "hooked" on their energy and supported it by being super responsible, did I understand that my Shadow was drawn toward people who refused to do for themselves. Once I had choice and awareness about what I was doing, I became liberated.

That's when I discovered the golden side of my Shadow, where energy, power, and beauty lives. It had been previously trapped, gagged, and bound by maintaining unconscious relationship contracts like this one. By recognizing the positive intention behind the Shadow, the Shadow moves into light. When the Shadow is recognized, sometimes it disappears completely! In fact, Jung said our entire Shadow is 90 percent light.

The golden shadow also helps us fall in love. Have you ever been smitten by a romantic interest, friend, or mentor who you think possesses special qualities which you do not? You've fallen for the light side of your Shadow—and everything they represent is actually who you are deep down. That's the beauty of falling in love with someone we admire: what we adore in the other already exists in us, we just haven't claimed it yet!

We don't always fall in love with our Shadow. Sometimes we simply covet another's talent, beauty, or special-ness and project it outside our self. When we're envious or jealous of another's golden quality, our torture is a misunderstood longing to experience what we've disowned in our own self.

When we're looking for our other half, we usually discover our own missing pieces along the way. The Shadow deserves the positive credit it's due—it exists primarily to make us whole people who possess both dark and light. Take a Shadow Inventory (see next page) to discover your Shadow. If you've been bound to the Shadow for most of your relationship history, setting your Shadow free can feel sweet, indeed!

You've contacted your Shadow when:

- someone pushes your buttons or repulses you

- you fall for someone who is "too good for you," i.e., who carries all the light qualities of yourself that you cannot or refuse to see

- you're super critical of someone's character or values

- you polarize your relationships: you say your partner, co-worker, or friend is one way (angry and unloving) and you claim to be exactly the opposite (peaceful and loving)

- someone tells you something about yourself, and you have a strong emotional response against it: "I'm not like that"

- you say or do something out of character, like making a Freudian slip

- you lapse into strange behavior that you later regret, and you don't understand where it came from

Exercise: Shadow Inventory

The Shadow contains power we can use for good, not evil; happiness, not blame. Taking a Shadow Inventory can help you understand yourself better and get to the bottom of why you attract exactly who you don't want. This understanding can change your relationship to others, and to yourself.

Make a list of what drives you nuts about some people. What bugs you? What makes you want to just call the whole thing off in a relationship? A know-it-all? Nitpickiness? Immaturity? Cockiness? Superficiality? Hotheadedness? Anger? Maybe they remind you of your mother or your father. What is it in others that you absolutely cannot stand?

Now consider that these people are in your life to teach you about that quality in yourself that you may have disowned, left undeveloped, or per-

K.I.S.S.

INVITE YOUR FRENEMY TO TEA

Serve tea to your enemy? Can Nicole Richie and onetime enemy Paris Hilton be friends again? Yes they can! I learned about this concept in Buddhism, the idea that by inviting your enemy as a guest to tea—in essence serving a cup of tea and sympathy or understanding—they would cease to be an enemy. Kill 'em with kindness right? Well this has mystical and politically practical uses. A similar tea ritual was practiced by the Japanese to build consensus and promote peace among warring factions. The ritual tea was held in a room designated as an official neutral meeting place, at the outskirts of war territory. At ritual tea, Samurai warriors from opposing factions would leave their weapons at the door and enter the tea ritual in a spirit of nonviolence. The tea space held sacred and beautiful objects, mirroring the sacred inner space, and the whole experience was an aesthetic delight. You can perform your own tea ritual alone by imagining you're taking tea with your enemy, or with anyone who will bravely play the part of your "enemy." Ask yourself: Can we find common humanity and shared common ground?

haps rejected because it makes you uncomfortable. If someone's too authoritative or "trying to be the boss of you," are you looking for your authority? If your Shadow is someone with a temper, how are you with expressing your own anger? If your Shadow is flaky, lazy people, how often do you allow yourself to just go with the flow?

Now that you've identified your Shadow, look at the positive side of that annoying behavior, quality, or character trait. It's like flipping the coin to the other side. Come on, there must be something! Write down the positive motive behind the uncouth behavior of your Shadow figures. For example, being bossy could simply mean being able to exercise authority over others, a good thing. Maybe you're missing that. Getting angry is attempting to have one's boundaries honored. That's honorable. How are you at sticking up for yourself? A lazy person has trust that things will take care of themselves. Trusting the greater powers at work is a virtue.

Can you imagine how good it might feel to walk in your Shadow's shoes for a while? I bet you can!

Narcissists and Bad Boys

Most of us have encountered our own version of the narcissistic bad boy. These guys are easy to spot, and yet we still lie to ourselves. We recognize the signs that this relationship is wrong for us early on but choose to ignore the nagging voice warning us, "He's a little too interested, he's coming on strong, he's telling a lie." Yikes!

We're so desperate for love that the ego chooses the lie instead of truth. It's as though we're love junkies being offered a hit of love-crack. We know we're going to crash, our system depleted of all that's healthy and good, and we'll eventually find ourself balled up in a corner, feeling used. But at the moment . . . we're buying into a feeling, and that feeling is hard to pass up. Maybe we want to feel irresistible, to know that we could have that kind of power over someone. Ah, to be loved, the greatest power in the Universe! We want to be loved! So we look into someone else's eyes to see if we are worthy of love. If only we would believe ourselves worthy without needing validation.

Why do we buy the illusion of love? Empty promises and cotton-candy romance are the equivalent of a sugar high, and sometimes, they're all we think we deserve because we haven't tasted the real thing in so long. We're suckers for the quick fix because we don't yet have a nourishing, loving relationship with our own heart, with our own self. And if after one of these cataclysmic roller-coaster style relationships, we berate ourselves for being so blind, stupid, or gullible, then we've truly neglected to get to the heart of the problem: our heart is so susceptible to these bad boys because we're desperate for love. We want to believe we deserve love, and we do deserve it. But the ego, well, the ego is too desperate to really believe. The ego doubts real love is possible because the ego speaks the language of desperation.

Good Goddess, the attraction phase in a relationship is a heady rush, especially after a long dry spell! While it does simulate the anticipatory excitement of a deeper soulful relationship, the rush is not that same chemical cocktail that gets us so ecstatically high when we're in the presence of our soul mate.

So why do we consistently confuse superficial attraction with love? I think it's because either we've forgotten the heart-chakra fireworks of true love, or we've never experienced it. Once you know the difference, you never go back. But some people never seem to cross over from beginning a relationship to commitment. Stuck in the falling-in-love phase, they may never penetrate down to the soul of love. They dance there, making far-out promises, living in a perpetual state of hope . . . until it gets real. Till someone wants a commitment. Then they bolt, make up an excuse, start seeing someone else, whatever. They know how to "fall in love" but lack the tools and self-awareness to stay there and move into real intimacy.

Marianne Williamson says people stuck in this perpetual state are addicted to the attraction phase of relationship. This phase is of course equal opportunity; women get hooked just as easily as men. They leave the relationship for a superficial reason, and they may never tell you why—her feet were too big, she had this funny thing with her nose, she laughs too loud, etc. Jerry Seinfeld's fault-finding character on *Seinfeld* is a classic example of this type; there's always something not quite right with his date. You can be a hottie with tons going on but there's that one fatal flaw he just can't get over. He'll tell you you're not perfect enough, at least in his mind. Rest assured, *no one* is perfect enough for this Narcissus, the mythical man who fell in love with his own reflection. He can't penetrate into the heart of intimacy because he isn't done gazing adoringly at his own reflection. He may never be done.

The only thing you need to remember about the narcissistic bad boy is that you don't have to allow him to torture you. It's all within your control.

Healing Relationships

I'm fairly certain that when we attract the pain part of love before the love part of love, there's a homeopathic principle at work. Homeopathy is the principle of like curing like, and when a disease appears, this branch of medicine responds by administering a little prick of poison, the disease itself, as the cure. Like the vaccine theory, the homeopathic reasoning is that a smidgen of poison will cause the immune system to kick in and defeat the hostile invaders. Quite often, immunity kicks in after just one exposure. When it does—poof! Disease gone, patient healed. And when it doesn't—a lot of poison is, well, just plain poisonous for all involved. It's toxic, and staying in that relationship (or attracting a similar one) can make you really sick, especially when it drags on for some time or turns into a pattern. That's where healing relationships come in: those painful pricks of poison help us recognize and heal wounds and inoculate us against future exposures.

Companion Spell: LOSE THIS MAN: A SPELL OF PERSONAL PROTECTION

Especially after you get serious about finding your soul mate, you may begin attracting relationships like this, ones in which you're tested to find new solutions to old patterns, to gain new healing or insight, and the tester is none other than yourself. As one girlfriend recently told me, "I've had a string of bad relationships and the only common denominator is ME!" That's a powerful place of realization. That's where you get down to the nitty-gritty truth of clearing up the layers of past debris, hurt, and misunderstanding. When you look at your relationships as though no one other than you set them up, you have the potential to change deep patterns that prevent you from finding love.

Companion Spell: BLUEBEARD'S BOOTY SPELL

This happened for me. Once, shortly after I had started using some of the spells and magic in this book, I met a man we'll call "V" in a bookstore. V was an aspiring actor who struck up a casual conversation with me and seemingly became enthralled. I wasn't attracted to him, but boy was I curious to see where it went, especially seeing as how I'd just started working on attracting my soul mate. Doing soul mate spells really starts moving energy your way. The Universe will start playing Cupid, attempt to match us up, but we also may not yet be clear about what's blocking us. We may meet someone who has several of the qualities we're looking for, or one fantastic one, but who are not exactly what we need. We still have more homework to do!

I once read that after the initial five minutes of meeting someone, you've gathered enough intuitive information to know whether this person is right for you. This explains the popularity and success of speed dating! However, I discovered, that you also need to be able to hear and then act on your intuition. And during those first five minutes of conversation with our aspiring actor at the bookstore, I'd received (and ignored) three clear signals that he wasn't for me.

First, despite being a seemingly open and attractive guy, his energy felt off to me. He actually felt more repelling than attractive. This had nothing to do with how he looked or what he was showing me in words and actions. Second, he was vague about certain important personal questions, like what he did for a living. He said he was an actor, but aside from attending an acting class, how did he spend his time? He evaded the question. Third, and maybe as a result of the aforementioned shiftiness, I didn't trust him.

So why oh why did I give V my phone number and agree to meet up?

I let the chemical excitement of "He likes me! Oh, I'm finally desirable to someone!" override my intuition. It'd been such a long dry spell, and I wanted to play. I ingested the chemical drug of attraction the first chance I could. I rationalized with myself, justifying suspicion and distrust by thinking I knew myself well enough to bail when the waters got rough, which happened almost immediately.

From date one, he was hot and cold on me. Warm and flirtatious one moment and practically defiant the next, V was playing me. When he morphed into a child before my eyes and put me in the role of playing mean mommy as this actor acted out, I thought, "Well isn't that interesting?"

Then, instead of ending it right then, I decided to do a little experiment. I decided I would go out with him again, with the intent of getting to the bottom of why I was wasting my time on him. So we went out for sushi. I had the experience of watching him and myself as though I were seeing a movie, from a witnessing position. The witnessing position could be described as your higher self, or the presence of Spirit (read Secret No. 7 for more on this). That's when he openly flirted with our waitress on our date—asking for her phone number right in front of me. A part of me was in shock at his inconsideration and blatant disrespect, while another part of me just watched. As I sat there observing V, just wondering what would happen next, he justified his actions by saying we weren't committed, expressing his impatience to "get his drink on" and continue the night. True, we weren't committed. And I was so not committed to continuing that evening with him.

Companion Spell: COMMAND YOUR SPIRIT BACK SPELL

It was a strange experiment, but it wasn't new. He had been "re-cast" in a repeat performance of my love life. He played a character I'd met in my early twenties who had been careless with me, although I didn't have the spiritual awareness to put it all together at the time. As if made from the same mold, it was the same situation all over again—I had been disrespected and demoralized by someone I could barely even tolerate, let alone like. And when he hurt me, he didn't really hurt me because I didn't really care about him. It was a defense mechanism against pain and against love, one I hadn't recognized until I relived it there in the restaurant. I had believed that if I didn't let someone in, they couldn't ever really hurt me. My heart had been shut down all this time and I hadn't even realized it!

I also began to understand why I had dated so many guys in my teens but never experienced real emotional connection and intimacy. I had been covering up the emotional abandonment of my father by trying to get the attention of young men. I had been injured, and the injuries extended all the way back to my relationship with my father. What allowed me to have this revelation, now? It was that same "prick" of poison that did it, and for that, I silently thanked V and parted with no hard feelings. I'd encountered this character before, but this time was different: I had my intuitive third eye "open." I had invoked the spiritual presence of my higher self. I was also carrying an intention for real love.

I had learned about another spiritual tool, too: my intuition (which I had at first ignored). My intuition was strong when I'd sized up V and I ignored the signs during that very first conversation in the bookstore. Intuition is like a muscle—it gets stronger the more you use it. Kim Basinger said, "I feel there are two people inside me, me and my intuition. If I go against her, she'll screw me every time, and if I follow her, we get along quite nicely." I realized that the blithe voice that overrode my intuition saying, "What's the harm?" was actually my ego egging me on, not my heart.

Now I see that the real value of a relationship pattern that seems to be stuck on repeat. With spiritual awareness, dilemmas with a karmic mate, soul mate, relative, or friend can turn into healing opportunities. It was as though the heavens put this person in my path to show me exactly how I sabotaged my own search for love. I had met my Saboteur—and she was me. I had felt the "prick" of poison and realized I had a deep wound there. But by feeling that old poison, I could prevent it from happening again. If had been "set up" by our little betrayal in the sushi restaurant, it wasn't by him, or even by the waitress (who indeed flirted back). It was a setup from the Divine. The love goddess herself was conspiring for my healing and happiness.

Companion Spell: BURN THOSE SHEETS! RITUAL

❧

Exercise: Invite Your Spirituality On a Date

If you feel stuck and unable to move on from a certain "type," you can choose not to play a role you've played before. A Third presence is available to you at any time. Instead of reacting from your typical position of defensiveness or blame (even if it's totally justified!) try viewing this person and/or situation through the wide angle lens of figuring out what you have to learn from the situation. Take a witness position and objectively ask your higher self: What is it that I'm not getting here? Why am I attracting this situation or person (again)?

You may be surprised at what you discover!

You Are Loved

Soul Mate Secret No. 7

Fall crazy in love with yourself and people will fall for you.

Later that day I got to thinking about relationships. There are those that open you up to something new and exotic, those that are old and familiar, those that bring up lots of questions, those that bring you somewhere unexpected, those that bring you far from where you started, and those that bring you back. But the most exciting, challenging, and significant relationship of all is the one you have with yourself. And if you can find someone to love the you you love, well, that's just fabulous!

CARRIE BRADSHAW, *Sex and the City*

WHO BETTER TO TALK ABOUT love than the diva of love, Carrie Bradshaw? Let's start this chapter with an exercise. Read this next sentence and listen to your first internal response (hint: it'll be the loudest one).

YOU ARE LOVED.

How does it feel to read this? You might try saying it aloud: I AM LOVED. What does your head say? What about your heart? How do you feel in your body?

There's no right or wrong answer here. Your response is yours alone, and even if your response is "yeah, right, prove it," it's still valid feedback. Listen to your heart and it will tell you just how much attention and loving commitment you need to be investing in the most important relationship of your life—the one you have with yourself.

When I read these words, I'm always greeted with a shocking agreement: yes, that's right! The impact that reading these words has on me is like an electric current that suddenly triggers my heart chakra and stops me in my tracks. Sometimes I feel an inward smile creep across my solar plexus, a smile that often moves on to my mouth.

Maybe you're already there: you feel your heart open immediately as it recognizes in gratitude, "Yes, I am loved. Thank you." All kinds of thoughts may circulate in your mind: "No, I'm not." Or, "If I'm so loved, then why am I still single?" Or maybe you do feel loved but in an impersonal or nonromantic way—the love we feel from a pet, or a person who has made a profound impact on our life. "Okay, I am loved, but by whom? Who's doing the loving here, anyhow?"

That's a good question. That last question could be the be-all and end-all that finally silences the small voice that continues to doubt love. Who is doing the loving here? I believe it's a force far greater than any of us. I believe it is love from the Divine.

I don't assign love to one particular person or thing. People and things come and go, and saying love is only present in the presence of one particular special person would be courting loss. Death happens to everyone sooner or later. We will all eventually lose people we love. Instead, I see love as my birthright and the essence of my very identity, and I trust that others will recognize and respond to that in me. Knowing that I am love is all part of cultivating a greater relationship between love and myself.

Spirituality works together with love. In my experience, it is impossible to separate the two. Love is the unifying force of life. You don't have to believe in any particular deity to experience your personal connection to a love bigger than you. Love is all-inclusive and nondenominational. You can believe what you believe, that God is love or Buddha is love, and it doesn't interfere with the truth: *You* are love. Your birth is living proof of this miraculous force: maybe your parents fell in love and gave birth to you, a child of love. So your very birth was a result of love! Or perhaps things between your parents weren't quite so great, but your creation did increase the love in both their hearts, their love for you. There is no higher power for you to tap than what already exists within you. Naturally we forget this sometimes, so here's a reminder: love is your birthright.

I know recasting love from the personal force of love to an omniscient and ever-present force of universal love is a huge paradigm shift. It's a leap of love. To discover this truth for yourself, you may need to develop a special relationship with your own spirituality. But the rewards of this shift are immediate. First, you start to feel better! The loneliness you used to feel may morph into a sweet longing, and then into a feeling of connection. Once I realized that no matter who is or is not in my life at the moment, I never have to feel unloved again, I moved from loveless and lonely to carrying love on the inside. So what if there's no strapping buck wrapping his arms around me tonight? I have the confidence of knowing that love is not dependent on having another person available to me.

Because love does appear to occasionally disappear (it doesn't really, but sometimes circumstances and emotions can temporarily divert our love resources), at those times, all we have to go on is faith. That's a facet of love, too; love faithfully teaches us that it will return, no matter what. When I had no one to turn to, it was up to me to do the loving I was missing. It was up to me not to shut down, to continue reaching out to others, and to remember to nourish my heart. It took courage, commitment, compassion, and confidence to keep love alive on the inside (the four C's are the cornerstone of this chapter). And when I had a terrible day and I was too hurt, tired, depressed, or beaten down do the loving, I handed it over to a higher power. A higher power would do the loving for me. Set the foundation for love by practicing courage, compassion, commitment, and confidence, then surrender it up to a higher power.

There's something wiser and bigger than you at work in the world. My higher self tells me it is called Love, but you can call that loving force God, the Goddess, angels, Gaia, Compassion, Buddha, All That Is, The One, or The Creator. All are heartening sources of spiritual power we can tap when we're feeling unloved.

Consider that it might not matter who (your family, your self, your friends) is doing the loving, but that a higher force always holds you in love. Just as there are a million faces of love, they're all a part of the unified energy field. This unnameable, untouchable, invisible field of love is your divine love essence. By remembering that your essence is love, you tap a greater love—a loving force that's strong and capable. If you tap this greater love (or Love with a capital *L*) and allow it to inform the relationship you have with your self, it will hold you through darkness and light, loneliness and reunion. Love is your birthright!

The Crown Chakra

Dreams come to us from a divine source. If we follow them, they lead us back to a divine source. When we work toward our dreams, we are working toward our God. Our dreams are not futile.
—Julia Cameron, author of *The Artist's Way*

You've probably already noticed that imagination, devotional faith, inspiration, spirituality, and inner guidance are the qualities we need to strengthen and develop in our search for soul mate love. These are all also attributes of the crown chakra. Thus, the seventh chakra is aligned with love magic. If you think it would be great to have more of these qualities in your life, you're on the right track. So how can you "open" this chakra, in other words, help keep it happily spinning around?

First, let's define *chakra*. Chakras are energy centers, kind of like little battery packs that look like beautiful flowers! Chakras form our spiritual spine. The energy that "plugs in" at the crown of our head, comes through the seventh, or crown, chakra. It cascades downward into chakras six through one, where we have personal experiences and form perceptions about those experiences. So if there were an energetic entry point on the body where the universal life force becomes personal, it would be here at the seventh chakra, the chakra of the Divine. Yes, it's not "as if" our life is inspired by the Divine, but that *we* are Divine!

Maybe you've heard of "opening chakras" and wondered what to it was all about. When a chakra is "open," or energetically super-charged, it's happily, blissfully humming along. We experience our seventh chakra open-ness in a variety of ways, which I'll get to in a minute, but we can always recognize when we're in this chakra by the way we feel—we have no separation between body and Spirit, and we experience no separation between self and others. We feel connected to all of life. In this chakra, we recognize the truth that All Is One. Here, we also realize, that yes, we really are spiritual beings having a human experience!

The seventh chakra's bumper sticker (if it had one) would read "Be Here Now." The present moment is so powerful because the present moment is all there is! Have you ever noticed that no matter how much planning we do, nothing ever happens "in the future"? By the time anything occurs, it's the present! By living in the present moment, we locate the grace to see a situation, person, or circumstance clearly, and we experience moments of real awakening. By being in the present, we also become excellent listeners of the Universe. We can't hear the Divine if we're too busy running around distracted to even listen. When we plug into the seventh chakra, we "hear" with different ears and "see" with different eyes. We start to view our place in the world, the circumstances, the people and problems we encounter in it, symbolically and meaningfully. Time slows down. We wake up.

So how do we wake up our awareness? You don't have to meditate in a cave, though that may help. We have far more ordinary seventh chakra "mystical experiences" all the time. Ever had an epiphany? Ever been inspired? Inspiration is the "divine stirring" that empowers the imagination to create. Nothing in our world has been created without having been imagined, first! Makeup artist Bobbi Brown has said she was inspired by a certain pink on a trip to France, and that particular shade of pink fueled an entire collection. You might be inspired by this book to do a love spell, stimulating your seventh chakra imagination about what's possible for you in love. Through inspiration and possibility, the seventh chakra speaks. When we listen, it connects our most cherished dreams to their reality. These inspired stirrings, including our dream for love, are divine ones, so they're definitely possible. The seventh chakra's second bumper sticker (if it had one!) would read "Anything's Possible."

By being here now and expanding our conscious awareness, we become available to "hear," "see," or "witness" the highest potential of whatever lesson we're encountering or whatever question we have. When we take "be here now" to heart, we can even shift problematic paradigms that have been vexing us. I did this when I invited my seventh chakra out on a date (see Secret No. 6, Healing Relationships). No, I didn't drop into meditation at the dinner table, I simply detached from the situation and sent out a prayer for guidance—which is one way of contacting the seventh chakra. In soliciting the gods and goddesses for the spiritual lesson about this problematic person, I opened to the illumination of a larger spiritual perspective. I finally "got it"—the spiritual lesson in a repeating relationship dilemma that had bothered me for years.

There's also a place for humility here. When we recognize that we don't have all the answers, we also realize that we may not know our self as well as we think we do. Our perceptions about life and our responses to our experiences are largely based on assumptions, beliefs, memories, family inheritances, and various karmas, the whys and hows of which we may never fully understand. Making friends with the seventh chakra is learning to stop asking why (by the way, to keep asking why is a good way to stay stuck) and instead consider the question, What does my Spirit want to learn here? Paradoxically, it's when we surrender to the Divine what we don't know and don't yet understand that the answer is miraculously provided. It may not be the answer we thought we wanted, but it's the answer we most need at this time!

I like to think of the seventh chakra as the chakra for becoming a "spiritual grown-up," because through it, we gain spiritual perspective on the most difficult life problems—the ones that keep us feeling small and disempowered and seem to hold us back from living up to our full potential. Dreaming, imagining, visioning, inspiring, and opening the mind to possibility are all states of being that come easily for children. Hey, maybe a child's open and fresh perspective is the missing ingredient for becoming a spiritual "grown-up." It's certainly a seventh chakra perspective.

Making contact with our seventh chakra is contacting our "Higher Self" or asking it for an answer. Likewise, hanging out in the seventh chakra always elevates our consciousness to varying degrees—it's like we each already have a balcony seat in the mind of the Divine with a big Reserved sign on it. We can drop in and be present anytime. Doing so has myriad benefits, from receiving inspiration to imagining a different reality to resolving old patterns. When we hang out in higher consciousness and possibility, our awareness enlarges and expands. And sometimes, our consciousness grows so much bigger that the problems we used to have actually disappear.

❧

Exercise: Receiving Divine Insight

From the seventh chakra's point of view, everything and anything is possible! Just entertaining this thought or repeating it like a mantra opens the energy center of this glorious violet-white lotus flower. Inspiration comes through this portal, as does grace and humility and our ability to see things differently. We can strengthen our "higher self" seventh chakra ability by asking:[1]

- What spiritual lesson does this relationship or circumstance have for me?

- What remains a mystery about this person or situation?

- Is there a pattern between this problem and those I've encountered before?

---

1 Questions adapted from Caroline Myss, *Sacred Contracts*.

K.I.S.S.

HEAVEN IS A PLACE CALLED THE SEVENTH CHAKRA

Does Nirvana exist? If so, it's only a state of consciousness away. The seventh chakra has been long recognized as the center of "the mystical experience." Mystics experiencing the transcendent seventh chakra (usually during meditation or prayer) describe an influx of "spiritual consciousness" that overwhelms the physical body, personality, and mind. Some refer to this as receiving "cosmic consciousness" and some mystical souls have downloaded massive amounts of spiritual information here. Visionaries such as Gandhi, Albert Einstein, and the Dalai Lama received visions through their seventh chakra.

- Are there more possibilities here than I'm currently seeing?
- Does this relationship, activity, or goal serve my highest potential?

Love Is Abundance

We each have unique luster and strength, beauty and talent, confidence and creativity—but what's so easy to see in other people, isn't so easy to see in ourself. Well, you may fall out of your seat, but I'm going to suggest that the only person you've been waiting for your whole life is . . . you! While you're busy looking in the direction of someone else's abundance, not-so-secretly hoping your soul mate will come along, who is mining your own abundance? Not you. You're too busy wishing for what you don't have. Consider that others' abundance only exists to show you what's possible for you. Allow what you admire in them to fuel the search for your own abundant beauty, strength, and possibility.

There's an Islamic saying I love: "I was a buried treasure, waiting to be known." You are the buried treasure, and you are waiting to be discovered. No one else will do the job of searching for and excavating you. That's your job and yours alone. Once you find your inner treasures, though, you're definitely free to share. Your soul mate will admire and elevate your abundance, and even take it to a whole new level. But no one will find the glorious abundance you possess for you. Your quest for your soul mate will never replace the personal abundance that's yours to discover first.

Who I am, and what can I do? In my life, I know I've only touched the tip of the iceberg, and that's exciting. But to be honest, at times, it's hard for me to see this truth. I've confused my circumstances with who I am. It's a common misunderstanding, to mistake temporary conditions as a permanent reflection of our very essence. (For example, I'm overwhelmed and stressed right now, so I must be basically weak and incompetent.) We all get confused here. And we may think we are less than who we truly are, which is infinite.

The problem turns really hairy when the confusion between the abundant and loved you and your circumstances negatively impacts your self-image. You may think you've entered a permanent state of lack. In reality, we all will have life seasons—bountiful harvests and dry spells. This time of lack is probably more like a dry spell, but harvest will come again. Love will come again. It's important to remember this cyclical nature of love and life, because love automatically reciprocates our beliefs about it. If we think it's around, it shows up. If we think it's missing, it goes missing. Love isn't attracted by lack, it's attracted by abundance.

That explains why the single person who hits the bars every weekend and spends her spare time thinking about and looking for a man is perpetually single. She may say she's "putting it out there," but it would be better for her to change strategies, quick! By diverting her attention and resources outside of herself, she loses touch with how abundant she really is and she begins emitting vibes of lack and desperation.

You've probably heard coupled folks say, "When I finally stopped looking for love, love found me . . ." They surrendered desire, and in so doing, became able to receive. There's a point at which de-sire switches from a divine yearning "of God," to desperation. Choices made out of desperation usually end up as bad choices. How do you tell the difference? There are many ways of differentiating whether desire is coming from a place of unhealthy attachment or a place of healthy yearning,

K.I.S.S.

GET A LIFE

Pick up any *Cosmo* magazine and you'll see that men consistently say they like women who have interests, dreams, desires, and friends. It's almost cliché, and maybe you've thought this equated to another man looking for the perfect woman. But as clichés will, this one reveals a universal truth. Men like women who are strong, have opinions, are in control of their lives, and have a realistic grip on their assets and talents. Yeah, men are attracted to women who have a life. My husband says his first impression of me was, "She's got a lot going on." He still says this. And if I consistently take care of myself by paying attention to what it is I'm thinking about, who I need to spend time with this week, what talent I'm getting busy developing next by taking a class or reading a book, he always will. I do have a lot going on and I know it!

but the main one is your strong attachment to the result of getting it. *It* being anything or anyone. Pinning all your hopes on getting any one thing or person is a red flag. I certainly don't advocate surrendering your desire for love, just your unhealthy attachment about getting it. Surrender the desperate desires, then you'll discover the abundance you already possess.

Love does not want. 'Tis true. Love knows it already has everything it needs. Look around at this abundant Universe, this abundant planet—what, exactly, would Love have to want? Nothing. By far, the people who live the simplest lives are the happiest. Those who have learned the language of scarcity—greed, attachment, comparing self to others, and consumption—are in all likelihood the unhappiest. Now look within yourself, at the unlimited potential you have to solve problems and create just about anything. To speak the language of love, the language of abundance, you need only emulate the abundance within you.

No, love does not want. It has qualities of open-handedness, open-heartedness, and gentle flow. Love's only possession is easy generosity.

So if love does not want, what does it want from you? Love wants you to be discerning about what you desire. As we've learned through exploring Venus—what turns you on, what makes you happy, your preferences, and your likes and dislikes—depriving yourself of desire and pleasure is not attract-ive. Love wants you to go far bigger and bolder than wanting what consumption, attachment, jealousy, and hunger for the next big thing offer. Love wants you to make your life bigger. Make your dreams bigger. To embrace abundance, you need only look at the world through the eyes of love.

The Secret Power Everyone Wants: Confidence

I think that when we look for love courageously, it reveals itself, and we wind up attracting even more love. If one person really wants us, everyone does. But if we're alone, we become even more alone. Life is strange.

—Paulo Coelho, mystical lover

Have you ever noticed that the people who love themselves the most are the people we are most attracted to? I have a girlfriend who shines so brightly with confidence and self-appreciation that she can be in her sweat pants pumping gas and people of both sexes go out of their way to talk to her. Aside from being drawn to get to know her, I think the reason this happens is we secretly hope some of her fairy dust will rub off on us. And it often does. Like moths to a flame, we are attracted to people who are covered in love because most of us feel we don't have enough of it.

The people who are light-bringers, who bring this beauty and love into our world, making us feel like celebrities just for knowing them. I'm not talking about self-absorbed narcissists—their flame flickers and sputters after people discover their inability to truly show up for anyone but themselves. I'm talking about the woman with the self-esteem to walk tall, have opinions, and express her true feelings. She is at home in her body and has a beautiful sense of personal style, and she's the woman everyone wants to get to know and be around. A famous photographer once said, "The most attractive thing a woman can wear is confidence." Absolutely!

Yet, we women can learn to dampen our light. We have the glow of a dim light bulb, and that's on a good day, sending a weak attractor signal into the Universe. Some of us have learned to give our confidence away to others, who may deserve our admiration and affection, but not our power. We give it to those people who appear to have more than us. We think, "I'm not as outgoing, smart, pretty as she is." Don't go there! Otherwise we become the moth who gravitates toward the bright flame and then flies right in and gets burned. Instead, we can become the bright flame itself.

And when we believe it's the other, "beautiful" people who get all the love, their loudness will definitely drown out our strengths. If we are best at giving all the glory and confidence to ladies who live for the spotlight, how will we become our own best self?

Here's a secret: you don't need to be the brightest star in the solar system to shine boldly. Appreciate your own assets. Allow yourself to bask in the glow of a creative high of your own making. If you've finished a great art piece, or baked a cake for your neighbor, or given damn good advice to a friend, realize what you've just done. You've gifted someone with your loving attention. You listened. You created. You did something profound, something that only you could do. You turned your starlight on, and you shone. That "center of attention" beautiful woman is you!

Real love doesn't host popularity contests. Yet I think we're all a little vulnerable to the myth that popularity and beauty win love. There's a great line in the movie *The Jane Austen Book Club*. In a hissy-fit, Prudie accuses her husband of ogling a Valley Girl who long ago humiliated her in high school. When he tells her, "Baby, high school's over," Prudie replies, "High school is never over!" Somewhere inside of us (and maybe this is even more true when we're single), high school is never over. We're constantly comparing ourselves to others and deciding we don't measure up. It might be easier to replay every time we've been rejected or shown up by some other girl who has a certain *je ne sais quoi* than it is to name what we love about ourselves. It's time to change that. Because, from what I know about confidence, if it's vulnerable to anyone else's approval or one-up-woman-ship, it's not really confidence, it's low self-esteem.

Confidence isn't exclusive or snobbish. Confidence is equal opportunity, equalizing everyone who crosses its path. It's never an act, so it doesn't feel or look unnatural; rather, it is an expression of comfort in one's own authenticity and beingness. When another is truly confident, they don't steal our beauty or strength, they elevate and celebrate it. It's not that hard to recognize, either, for we feel better after being around them! The experience of being loved, seen, focused on, and heard as though we're the most important person in the room begins with living in your strengths. You can grow in confidence by giving that feeling of self-appreciation to others and by pursuing the activities and interests you enjoy. You can stop looking outside yourself for approval, and look inside instead.

Dive deeper into the subtleties of confidence, and there's usually an internalized storyline at work, something we believe about ourselves, which may or may not be true, but we are weaker for playing into that self-aggrandizement. This was happening to my girlfriend Kia. She said, "Some women have that special something. They go after a guy and get him. I've never been that woman. I'm more likely to pine for someone I can't have and end up with someone I'd least expected." She talked about how intimidated she became in the presence of a man she thought was really hot. And how, although she felt strong in other areas of her life, around certain men, she'd turn into a puddle of no-confidence-at-all.

I knew exactly what she was talking about. I used to feel the same for a time, and it's a huge projection. We put some admirable person so high on a pedestal that they become god-like and unreachable. We endow them with über sex appeal or MENSA intelligence or a better-paying job, or even greater confidence, and we then imagine they see us as inferior. Until we address the root source of our low self-esteem, this will remain a catch-22, sabotaging our relationships. By seeing someone else as infinitely love-attractive, we've become love-repellant.

Just as it was for Kia, the only real solution for me was to give up the struggle for Mr. Out of My Reach and move my focus from obsessing over my hang-ups onto becoming the right person for me. I reasoned that these unreachable men probably weren't as interesting as I thought they were. Guess what? I was usually right.

K.I.S.S.

DON'T HATE ME BECAUSE I'M BEAUTIFUL!

Even mythical, beautiful Aphrodite had problems. First, everyone was always falling helplessly in love with her. What a problem, I know, but not an uncommon one for Venus types! Because she was so desirable (and you know how threatening desire is to a man), Zeus married her off to the blacksmith of the gods, Hephaestus, who she happened to despise. No love lost here, though. He spent all his time working, allowing plenty of play time for Aphrodite—and he still felt he was the luckiest man on Earth! Aphrodite proceeded to pussyfoot around with his brother Ares (Mars) and notoriously meddle in the love lives of others. She promised the most beautiful woman in the world, Helen of Troy (who happened to already be married), to Paris, starting the Trojan War. Aphrodite was jealous, too. Goaded by a rival beauty, Psyche, she sent Eros with a poison arrow to Psyche so she'd fall in love with the ugliest man in the world, which backfired when Eros pricked himself with the arrow and fell in love with Psyche himself. No worries, Aphrodite always came up smelling like roses; she was given a place of honor at their wedding. Aphrodite was often grossly underestimated by others and at a high price. A socially intelligent woman, she used her people and networking skills and the power of persuasion to achieve her every desire. Even when she doesn't get what exactly what she wants, she always finds an angle that plays to her advantage. Maybe from reading the above you've identified an Aphrodite/Venusian type in your life. Or perhaps you are one!

Ironically, now that I'm married, it's raining men. Hallelujah! Some women say comfort in one's own skin—or as the French say, *bien dans sa peau*—comes with age, but I believe being in a committed relationship brings its own confidence. My inability to establish a comfort zone or safe harbor within myself was the root of my insecurity. It undermined my confidence and created internal conflict, which I projected onto others. Once I was secure in love, I no longer put up these imaginary barriers. However, my husband couldn't give this feeling to me until after I'd created it for myself.

So, when it comes to confidence, the world will gladly reinforce every fear you allow to seep into your life. If we think only extroverted magnanimous personalities with Sun signs in Leo and Scorpio succeed in winning friends and influencing people, the Universe will say "Okay, you're right," and send a handful of such people our way. The truth is, we are wonderful, and there's someone out there who will love your crooked nose or thin hair! They will love you in spite of your flaws, and sometimes they will love you more for them. Worries about your appearance or fears of being rejected for some tragic flaw? Your soul mate will see past all that jazz.

You already possess a unique inner light, and owning that will spark the right person's fire. So what if you don't light up a room with oodles of charisma or movie-star good looks? You will probably find someone else at the party looking for a creative, spiritual, or soulful type to hang with. And that person fits your soul mate profile better, anyhow.

Companion Spell: GLAMOUR SPELL

The Courage in Confidence

How do we esteem our self? With positive actions made on our own behalf, positive self-talk, and acts of love. According to the *Random House Dictionary*, to esteem is "to regard highly or favorably; regard with respect or admiration." Your actions need to generate self-admiration and self-respect. The people you choose to be in relationships with must regard you with respect and admiration. Missing either of these is a deal breaker.

I have a friend who is learning the ropes of life's ups and downs gracefully. When she's faced with a new stress, the ending of a job, a relationship blip, she vigilantly guards against feeling emotionally overwhelmed. Instead of withdrawing from the world or collapsing, she'll go on a walk, visit a new café, or go to an art gallery she's wanted to check out. Instead of flailing her arms and screaming "Help!" to the wind, she's created a support system of friends who are okay to call for help and encouragement.

My friend's actions demonstrate the best of courage. Through treating herself with positive regard and possessing a realistic respect for her limits, she finds equilibrium and an ability to cope. When we're in the emotional trenches, it's often hard to grasp what's real and what's not, and that's why support systems are so valuable. Maybe it's a person, a book filled with helpful insights, a therapist, or any new decision to respond differently. Ultimately, every step we take toward taking care of ourself during choppy emotional passages (or simply bad days) is a step in the right direction. We're stepping into more capable, confident shoes.

I admire every courageous step my friend takes away from an old pattern of self-defeat, and I endeavor to do the same for myself. Of course, she's not looking for my admiration or approval. But it's funny how loving yourself always generates admiration from others! It's a spiritual law, and it's downright paradoxical! Loving our own self is one of the hardest things we'll ever do, but when we're doing the hardest work in our lives, that's when we shine the brightest for others to see.

Discovering the courage to love yourself is an ongoing, everyday choice. You just keep making it. One day you think you've got the knack of it, and the next, it's like starting from scratch. Self-esteem fluctuates, too. I wonder if scientists have done research on self-esteem being tied to our hormones, because sometimes it's a roller-coaster that resembles PMS!

There's a difference between responding to our icky, not-so-confident feelings with old attitudes and patterns and responding to them with compassion and clarity. Sometimes the difference is between simply thinking about it and actually trying something new.

I like to envision courage in the everyday acts we each do as a string of paper hearts joined together, each supporting and building confidence on the next. How does this relate to love? Acts of courage always stimulate the heart, the center of love. The root word of *courage* is French: *cœur*, meaning "heart." The word *encouragement* actually means "to take heart." I love that! Courage has become so masculinized in our culture (hunting expeditions, war, public speaking, rescuing babies from burning buildings) but essentially, courage is all about the heart. The heart doesn't measure risk by size or proportion. Put simply, it takes heart to take a risk—any risk.

K.I.S.S.

RE-IMAGINING SELF-ESTEEM

Low self-esteem can be a source of shyness, but the two are not the same. Shyness is a quality of introversion. Low self-esteem may be caused or influenced by early conditioning, but we perpetuate it by the unconscious way we reinforce negative messages. The real trick to having great self-esteem is not figuring out all the reasons your parents didn't give you what you needed, but realizing what you're thinking about those old messages today. You can create a new response to those internalized beliefs that make you feel less than totally fabulous. And you are not your feelings. When faced with your own internal obstacles, it's your negative self-talk, not your feelings, that make up the core of your self-esteem. It's the voice in your head, not your feelings of being inferior, that perpetuates a negative self-image . . . or makes a radical new you. You can feel more confident and alive by acknowledging the voices in your head, and then choosing to think differently.

I completely endorse doable risks, and what I call "little acts of courage." Here's how I do it: I'm writing this from a foreign country, and today I'll risk having one new experience or meeting one new person. I know I'll also take the risk of sending an email to a client asking for upfront Euros for my services. This feels a little dangerous to me (it might not to you), but listening to my resistance and the voice inside my head that says, "Maybe I don't deserve to get paid for this work," means I can either ignore it or act on it. Everyone has a different threshold for courage, but it comes down to how much risk you are willing to take on a matter that's heart-important. If I don't heed the call of my heart, I fall into the abyss of low self-regard, which has serious repercussions. I think that, like a little tape recorder, my heart records all the times I backed down from courage, and the effect from those recorded instances is cumulative. For when I don't listen to my heart, I not only come to expect less from my self, I also expect less from the people in my life. Listening to and acting on my needs communicates self-respect to the heart; when I don't respect myself, the people in my life might not either.

We don't have to make big radical changes here, only small ones—signs that we're paying self-attention. Maybe we don't know how to respond to our own request, and that's part of courage, too—knowing when to take action on a need. We certainly don't have to do it all alone. Sometimes Googling "What can I do about xyz?" can really get a girl places. If self-love is a destination, advice, ideas, experience, and wisdom from others who have been there and done that are really valuable compasses. As is listening to your intuition, and just going for it!

Love may be grand, but it's not a huge production. It's a series of little things, strung together over time. That's how love works in your life. Think about the memory of your mom proudly beaming at your dance performance; the night a sweetheart cooked your favorite meal after an emotionally exhausting day; the way a friend really came through for you. When it comes to loving yourself, it's the little acts of courage you undertake that prove to your heart: See, someone inside here is paying attention! See how loved you are?!

Love is Compassion

When you begin to touch your heart or let your heart be
touched, you begin to discover that it's bottomless, that it doesn't
have any resolution, that this heart is huge, vast, and limitless.
You begin to discover how much warmth and gentleness is there,
as well as how much space.

—Pema Chodron

Thanks to the Dalai Lama and people like him, compassion has made a collective comeback. In some circles, it's become the answer to virtually every ill. So what is this spiritual panacea, and how will it further our search for soulful love?

Compassion is the open-hearted ability to relate to all facets of humanity (and yourself) as worthy, deserving, and good. Compassion is useful, and it is an essential part of relating to one another's basic humanity. Compassion, when practiced, always fosters feelings of understanding. That understanding plays a very large role in feeling connected to others and in being able to connect to them. In this way, relating to yourself and others with compassion can cross into a loving connection or even into a love connection. In this way, love is compassion.

But compassion is not love.

Compassion is only one facet of love. It's another spiritual paradox. First, we need to be compassionate toward others, toward all walks of life, to be kind and loving, so we can be open to that emotionally and spiritually fulfilling dimension of love. We also need to be compassionate toward our self, because when we unconditionally accept all parts of us, not just the good stuff, the people we attract will do the same. I'm pretty sure you want someone to love all of you, so why would you reject any part of your own self? That's a law of Venus and that's why compassion is useful in attracting the love you desire.

However, some of us have a very easy time being compassionate, which presents its own set of problems. We may feel the pain of someone else's predicament so easily that we take it on as our own. We may foster a relationship with a person whom we're compassionate toward but whom we don't really love. Maybe our compassion has an element of dependency in it—we think it's our role to be kind, nurturing, and forgiving at the expense of our own happiness. When it comes down to it, we're simply really good at being understanding and kind. But when our lovely and beautiful compassionate nature gets too soft and undiscerning, we may wind up keeping ourself from the passion, special-ness, and romance we deserve. Compassion should not be overly mushy, causing us to cave in to other people's need for us instead of honoring our need to be loved the way we want.

Compassion is one facet of love, but it is not the entire basis for personal love. And it is not meant to be so.

I have a for-instance here. A friend of mine, Rodha, has a neighbor with a disability who really needs her compassion, and she is able to help. They have a compassionate connection. They are friends, but he seems to want to be more than friends, or at least wants more from her than she wants to give. She acknowledges that they don't share that special romantic spark (although she enjoys helping him), while also admitting that his combined attraction and need for her and her abundantly compassionate nature means she constantly needs to put boundaries on the relationship. She wondered if she would keep attracting people who *need* her instead of people who *love* her. My friend may need to keep this distinction clear in her search for love: compassion is a great part of love relationship; but compassion without passion and sexual chemistry is drudgery. It's hard on the heart. If this sounds familiar, it may be important to stubbornly insist that the Universe bring you a lover for a partner—not a child, not a dependent, not a patient.

Compassion is, actually, a higher facet of love. Its function exceeds personal love, which it simultaneously happens to enrich. Compassion is, at its highest, spiritually unifying and fulfilling. It offers the satisfying experience that "we are all one." It brings us a sense of Cosmic Love. That's infinitely valuable, especially when you're going through a period of social isolation or loneliness. I remember a low point when I knew I wasn't yet ready for love, but I was feeling a little too cut off from connection. So I volunteered at a local AIDS hospice. My heart opened to these people in a new way. I didn't really know these folks I felt deeply and lovingly toward, but I experienced love, and it was on a whole other level—a compassionate level. This opened me up to a higher facet of love by deepening my connection to all of humanity. It "cured" an aching in my heart. Incidentally, it also cured me of my loneliness. I found that it's very hard to feel separate and unloved when you are linked to others in understanding. It's hard to feel alone when you're faced with very human predicaments we all face, ones that call all your compassionate resources into play.

Why is this? The opposite of compassion is separation. Anytime we separate ourself from others, regard them in judgment, hold an unkind attitude toward them, or even just think their problems aren't our problems, we're also saying, "You are not me." We are not being compassionate. The tricky thing is, sometimes our heart can hide from itself—from its own vulnerability. Even if our heart is stirred in sympathy for another, we can still say, sneakily under our breath . . . "That's not me." This is because our heart tries to avoid pain by avoiding people or experiences that bring us to the edge of our deepest fears. The ironic thing is that if we faced those fears honestly, they could bring us much-needed heart-healing. Compassion does not separate. Separation will always move us away from love.

At its highest, love and compassion merge, connecting us to a broader and vastly more soulful experience of love. I mentioned that by volunteering for a hospice, I tapped compassion to heal some of my loneliness. This also helped me face some of my deep fears, such as fears of chronic disease, social isolation, and death. By getting closer to what I feared, I finally understood there was nothing to be afraid of, because everyone has my same fears. In this way, compassion can magically dissolve almost every emotional pain. Recognizing your pain—be it existential, psychological, or physical—connects you with all of humanity. You understand people better, you find it easier to connect with folks from all walks of life, not just the "safe" ones who don't trigger your fears. It's also really good for your heart!

Compassion needn't involve altruistic motives or people with sad stories. Being compassionate only requires a willingness to investigate our fears with heart: those ideas, people, and things that shut us down, that leave us feeling separated and alone. If you noticed a theme in this chapter (and this book!), it's this: becoming receptive to love all comes down to you. The way to invite compassion into your heart as a facet of love relationships is by bringing it back to you. We all have times when we come up short on self-acceptance, and that's the right time to be compassionate. Gentle self-talk, investigating your fears, choosing to follow the things, interests, and activities that gladden your heart and put you at comfortable ease—such as doing gentle self-care, making a good soup, or baking a pie—all offer emotional respite for your predicament of the moment. These activities also ground you in basic self-compassion.

Sadly, we're often better at accepting our friends for who they are in their entirety than accepting ourself. It's so easy to focus on our flaws and miss our strengths. But the good news is we can use this information to our advantage. Friends bring us closer to our capacity to love unconditionally and therefore teach us how to be compassionate with ourself. When a friend tells you she's feeling underappreciated, unlovable, or sad, your heart is stirred with love for her. You may offer advice: "Yes, I've been there." You might begin with all the conviction and gusto of a salesperson selling compassion for a living, convincing her of her beauty, her power, her strengths. You do this until she is smiling again. Compassion love mission accomplished! You've reminded her of her connection, restored her wholeness. That's a technique for generating compassion that you can use for your self. There are more techniques you can try on the following pages.

So, yes there's a reason compassion is making a divine comeback. We need it! The world needs it! In those moments we feel separate, alone, and unloved, we can return to compassion. It will lift our spirit while adding another facet and dimension to love: the unifying power of compassionate love. It's hard to feel separate while simultaneously understanding that plenty of others are in your same shoes (or worse shoes) at this exact moment. And if we're blessed with oodles of understanding, this doesn't mean we must choose our desire for a special love over the people who need us; it means we're going to have to insist on negotiating healthy boundaries in our copious compassion. Compassion is beautiful, but we don't want to give away our kindness and lose our happiness in the exchange.

Finally, when we raise the vibration of our self-love and self-acceptance, we absolutely raise our love vibration. Just imagine a bubble of pink love surrounding you at all times. By enlarging that sphere of love to include compassion, we extend our love aura into infinity. Compassion always has this kind of effect on love because it's a universal truth. Compassion makes love bigger.

Try this at home: When you find yourself on the verge of nurturing despair, take a walk, talk to a friend, or talk to yourself as though you were your own best friend.

❧

Exercise: Let The Love Flow

Compassion is not pity for another person or for one's self. I've found that when we pity another person, it's usually because we're scared. For example, we may see a homeless person and pity them because we fear how we would feel in a similar situation. In my experience, there are two possible actions when confronted with an anxiety-causing person or situation: we can either (a) relate to our fear and by so doing regard that person with love and understanding, or (b) shut down. We always have the choice to bring compassion into a fear-causing moment and turn the situation around.

Compassion is generous with emotional feelings of connection and support; it is not an emotional swamp. Julia Cameron, a writer whose *The Artist's Way* books help artists and artistic types heal creative blocks, coined a great term, "emotional sobriety." When we're emotionally sober, things may be bad, but we see them as they are. When we're not emotionally sober, we're in a haze of self-defeat and isolation, thinking, "Things really are terrible. I must be a horrible person for letting things get this out of hand." Ungrounded in our heart, we lose our compass. The problem is, when our emotional state resembles a swamp or when we feel self-pity, love won't find us even though we may be the most compassionate person in the world. Love just can't see through that thick swamp of self-flagellation and self-rejection. Love flows. In meditation or journaling, work with this concept: connection, understanding, kindness, and melting is the feeling of compassion and it moves us closer to love; separation, defensiveness, and fear is the feeling of loneliness and disconnection and it moves us away from love. Now write down ten thoughts that make you feel separate, defensive, or fearful. Can you bring love to those thoughts? With self-acceptance and understanding in mind, flip the thoughts into their positive form. For example, "I'm overweight and I'm too lazy to do anything about it," can be changed into, "I can see that I want to have a better body image. Maybe I'll take a walk today instead of watching TV."

Fall In Love with Yourself

I don't like myself, I'm crazy about myself.
—Mae West

Hmmm, funny how we adore the people we love, but when it comes to yours truly, we can hide our light under a bush. It amazes me how many of us would rather become fascinated with someone else than with our very self.

Think about it: When we fall for someone, we become fascinated by them. We want to get to know them in the deepest ways. We want to know their family, their favorite books and pastimes, their favorite movies, how they take their cof-

K.I.S.S.

LOVE YOUR LUSTER

In astrology, your true love and your personal joy in life fall into the same house or sector of the sky, the fifth house. Yes, finding your true love is intrinsically linked to the things that make you giddy with joy! This is also the house of the self, so it follows that our talent, the creativity and joy we put into the world that brings us happiness, also leaves us feeling lustrous, blessed, and aglow with life. That special "in love" glow, the one we get when we've just fallen for our beloved, can be gotten from using your natural talents. Performing in a play, painting, knitting, and socializing (it's a talent!) all relax and open your heart. Anything you do that increases your personal happiness or brings soul-stirring beauty into your life links you to love. Love, beauty, and happiness are the same bandwidth of energy. Take advantage of this knowledge. Fall in love with yourself and attract love!

fee, and how they like their steak. We not only want to know about them, we want see the world through their eyes. Then we want to do those things with them. We want to go see their favorite painting, read their favorite book, attend the concert of their favorite performer. We want to know what makes their heart sprout wings and what makes them tick. And by gosh, isn't it as if everything and anything they are is nothing short of amazing?!

Do you do this for yourself?

Do you find yourself fascinating? Do you marvel at all the crazy things you come up with? Do you laugh at your own jokes, find your interests entertaining, and know that if left to your own devices, you will amuse yourself for hours on end? Can you see the timeless beauty in your beautiful face and body, sans makeup or your morning shower?

How can we find love if we ignore our own fabulousness?

Modern life offers plenty of opportunities for distraction and being blind to our beauty instead of truly see it, and even more ways to accomplish nothing at all. We're overworked, too tired, and too busy—we simply don't have the time. This is real. Yet when we finally stop to smell the roses, we're so cooked and stressed that we reach for the first anesthetic we can to relax: television, gossip magazines, the Internet; maybe we eat, drink, or smoke too much; or we obsessively think, think, think—hey, there's a popular one!

The list goes on. Venus, who wants to bring relaxation, love, and pleasurable happiness into our lives, is still trying, but she can only do this in one of two ways: by having magnificent experiences of aesthetic proportions, or by numbing out. When we have an aesthetic experience, we're grounded in our senses, appreciating the beauty of the moment. We leave the world of distraction in favor of the world of the senses and we become sensual. Ooh-la-la! This is love attract-ive.

Companion Spell: FALL IN LOVE WITH YOURSELF SPELL

Venus delights in creating pleasant experiences. She does this through stimulating the senses. According to dictionary.com, the definition of *aesthetic* is: "having a sense of the beautiful; characterized by a love and appreciation for beauty . . . or being concerned with pure emotion and sensation as opposed to pure intellectuality." Curiously, *aesthetic* and *anesthetic* are in direct opposition, as *anesthetic* means insensitive. You know anesthetic by the way it feels, or rather, the way it doesn't feel. It's non-sensual, there's nothing to feel. It's dull and senseless. Maybe your anesthetic is food, or watching reruns all day. About anesthetic activities, you may wonder, "Why am I doing this again?" An anesthetic is similar to the anesthesia we get in the dentist's chair—it numbs our senses. We may think an anesthetic is pleasurable, but it's not stimulating, so it can't really offer pleasure—only relief. When we're missing out on our senses, we're also missing out on sensuality, which is a key component of attract-iveness.

When it comes to conjuring up our soul mate, there's nothing soul-stirring about an anesthetic. And the only cure for anesthesia? It's a good one: surrendering the *substitute* of pleasure for *real* pleasure! As Marvin Gaye sang, "There ain't nothing like the real thing, baby."

Accept no substitutes for soul-stirring pleasure. To discover and nourish and taste your unique pleasures in life, we can look at our world the way our lover might. Become fascinated. Take a real interest in what gets you going. Ask, Is there anything soul-stirring or rapturous about my life that I'd like to do more of?

The romantic Libra artist Sting once sang that "every little thing you do is magic." Love is not sleepy, tired, or dull; it is alive, awake, and magical. Venus wants us to wake up to our sensibilities, our sensitivities, and our beauties. She asks, with a devilish grin, What gets you in the mood? Granted, this may require taking a risk, such as calling up a friend to check out a new art show in town, starting an art project, or getting up off the couch to do some gardening. Whereas loveless logic says, *Reaching toward new beauties would be too hard—and hey, I probably wouldn't even enjoy it*; I-am-loved logic says, *I'm going to make my world beautiful and inviting. Then I'm gonna share it with you!*

Spiritual Cake Batter, or Keeping the Faith

Soul Mate Secret No. 8

To attract love, let go of your need for instant results. Remain expectantly positive, even in the face of mixed results. Turn ALL results into positive synchronicities and signs that a perfect love is coming.

Undoubtedly, each of us is demonstrating his life concept now but trained thought is far more powerful than untrained, and the one who gives conscious power to his thought should be more careful what he thinks than the one who does not. The more power one gives to his thought—the more completely he believes that his thought has power—the more power it will have.

Ernest Holmes, *Science of Mind*

I may have conjured up a man, but I certainly don't take the full credit for the smashing results. It was only by mixing up and using the time-honored ingredients other seekers have used for centuries that I got my love-wish cooking and allowed that golden cake batter to rise and transform. If there is a recipe to follow (which is what I'm suggesting), nothing rises without an attitude of conscious intention and positive expectancy. These ingredients prepare your being to receive, like a Bundt cake–shaped vessel!

All form begins with thought. I see thought energy as though it were spiritual cake batter. Look around you: everything you see, the chair you're sitting on, the house you live in, even your cup of coffee, started out as a thought. The thought energy I pay attention to creates a cake pan, like a mold or a vessel for the Creator to fill with batter. By aligning your thoughts with a spiritual intention for love, you will be filled with something that will rise and transform over time. When I ask for something I need, I don't confuse myself with the cake batter substance itself, or put conditions on the time it will take to cook. I just consistently put my thoughts and my actions in the right place. I take full ownership for creating the mold, which is the intention and expectancy, but I honor the Mystery of how it will all turn out. I know that my work is to only "prepare the space" for the substance of Mystery to enter.

Carolyn Casey, visionary activist extraordinaire, often says, "If we can dream it up, we can also dream it down!" This is more than just the power of positive thinking—more like, if you don't like your reality, you can create a new one. Science is proving that spiritual energy, like prayer, is just another version of creative energy. You may have heard about water-crystal scientist Masaru Emoto, who taped words such as *love* or *fear* on jars of water, then examined the frozen crystals, discovering that the positive words created harmonious snowflakes, while the negative ones create sadly disfigured snowflakes. He also took water samples from lakes in different environments—I remember one was from a beautifully peaceful-looking but deadly nuclear waste site, on which he placed the word *love*. By repeated exposure to the word *love,* he managed to change a sad snowflake into a harmonious, lovely one. Isn't that hopeful? What we think matters, the words we read matter, the environment we live in, beautiful or ugly, matters. And we can influence all of it.

In a sense, we are each snowflakes; each of us uniquely reflecting the thoughts we think, the way we feel, the environment, and even the people we surround ourself with. Just as with the snowflakes, it's worthwhile to examine all aspects of our environment—physical, emotional, mental, and spiritual. All are obviously important, though we may not realize just how our mental environment affects what and who we draw toward us. Is it hospitable (positive) or inhospitable (negative) to love? All thoughts have power. Having a clear thought field to work with (along with a clear understanding of the principle of attraction) will help you in your soul mate search.

Science is telling us other things about thoughts, too. Just as physics tells us that the observer influences the thing that's being observed, our observations and thoughts about our situation can absolutely change it. This is compelling and supportive evidence for spiritual practices that observe the mind, such as meditation. When we consistently witness our thoughts, we develop the potential to discover the repetitive mental patterns behind many of our difficult emotions. This is cause for hope, especially when it comes to identifying those stubborn ways of thinking that sabotage our search for love. It's only by becoming aware of a pattern of thinking that we can change our experience of it. Our emotions can be absolutely changed by thinking about them.

It takes discipline to train the mind to see itself clearly, and in the kitchen of the Creator, there's much psychological prep work to do. Often we need guides, sous-chefs, and some training. Having psychological and spiritual support helps. Having a spiritual practice helps. It takes effort to work on our self, to examine our thoughts and emotions, but it's effort well spent.

Creating a love-hospitable thought environment was quite a challenge for me at first. But it began with examining the thoughts that drove my emotional responses.

When I began noticing just how tied my emotions were to my thinking about them, I was horrified to discover that my mind resembled pea soup. My thoughts were disorganized, jumbled, easily influenced by others, and basically flopping all over the place. My big epiphany was this: I had thought my emotions were run by the storyline of my life, but in reality I had no control over my thoughts! My careless thoughts were running my big emotional story. So I began to mentally train myself to become aware of the thoughts I was thinking during an emotional experience. My thoughts could make my experience emotionally complex, convincing me that a situation was more difficult than it actually was. Once I identified the thoughts I didn't really believe in, they lost all power over me. And as a thought surgeon might, I removed the negative thought and replaced it with a positive one.

The mental discipline to train the mind to stop running away with itself creates a laser-like beam that cuts through negativity and helps you focus on what (and who) you want to create in your life. The only difference between a powerful thought and a weak one is that a trained and practiced thought is far more effective at creating happiness than a vague, untrained thought. But the real difference is the amount of energy you save. By using trained thoughts instead of vague ones, you bypass the winding and potentially hazardous long way around. These mental shortcuts are what I call a spiritually elegant way of arriving at your desired destination.

Once you identify the mental ruts you fall into, you can start to use the mental shortcuts that the wise ancients have always used: affirmation, prayer, and mantra, which are elegant thought forms—simple and powerful. Repeating an affirmation, mantra, or prayer over time literally changes your energetic vibration and you will begin attracting differently. Oh, and this only works 100 percent of the time!

If I could give you a simple step-by-step plan to "create the space" for Spirit to enter, it would be this: First, prepare the space. Like weeding a garden, pull out all the icky thought weeds in your mind. Do some psychological self-examination, if you need. Orient yourself toward self-realization and personal growth. Surround yourself with people and books who have actually done what you're trying to achieve. And prevent yourself from getting stuck by planting new, positive thought seeds. Get specific about what you don't want in order to be positively clear about what you do want.

Your success with these techniques depends upon your level of mental awareness, or thought-consciousness. Remember, the Universe runs with any idea you give your attention to—negative or positive. Choose to live in the affirmative, and you will receive confirmation of your desires. This is called affirmation. You can try casual affirmation by affirming for something small: a parking spot in a crowded city. If you affirm for a free parking spot in your mind but end up walking six blocks, it's probably because you forgot to affirm for a free parking space *nearby*. Yes, in our big love experiment, you learn how to get specific real quick! Likewise, instead of affirming for a soul mate with money, affirm for a soul mate who loves his lucrative career, so you won't end up with an unhappy millionaire. With practice, you get the idea that the more you believe in your power to create, the more power you actually have.

Once you see how your negative thinking affects your emotions and joins with those emotions to create a distorted reality, you'll also discover that the opposite is just as true: positive thoughts, unclouded by murky emotions, create a clear, straightforward reality that resonates with your soul's true desires. Once you've learned to elegantly co-create with the "spiritual shortcuts" of prayer, meditation, and affirmation, you'll never want to take the long, circuitous road to your goals again! You're finally ready to receive.

Goodbye, Pollyanna

Don't believe what your eyes are telling you. All they show is limitation. Look with your understanding, find out what you already know, and you'll see the way to fly.
—Richard Bach

Okay, so in theory, positive thinking is great, but what if you can't muster the energy to think positive thoughts? What if even eking out a prayer of gratitude with your morning coffee is a Herculean effort? Mystical guru Catherine Ponder describes prayer as soul-stretching (she also says, "When your prayers haven't been answered, maybe your soul hasn't stretched enough to receive that answer"). Are you willing and able to stretch? That answer may be yes, but sometimes your soul needs to stretch a little wider. You may need to become bigger than the problems you're experiencing, but that's hard to do when your problems are happening right here and now. What to do?

There are times when life events will whack you upside the head, discombobulating you emotionally and turning your world upside down. A job changes. You lose traction with your health. A relationship's end brings up old wounds, and those wounds have teeth. Negative or positive thinking may be a moot point when you just feel terrible. Human beings are not designed to be bright and chipper Pollyannas all the time, and even depression has a purpose. When life hurts, resisting the painful situation only causes more negativity and stress; positive thinking is a superficial band-aid at these times, and only true acceptance will bring you the radical grace you need. You need to be right where you are. Insisting that you are happy when you really aren't only makes you feel more miserable. Honor your emotions, even if they are distressing.

Accepting the harsh realities of life isn't easy. My own name has provided a unique spiritual assignment: *Jessica* means "grace or gift of God." I guess I've been uniquely assigned to see alternatives and possibilities where none are apparent! If I've been given the spiritual quest of embodying grace, then my life has been the answer.

What I discovered was that, central to the most challenging times in my life, beliefs about why I shouldn't be suffering only perpetuated more suffering. I resisted suffering, and in so doing, resisted the present and all the opportunities of the present. Resistance to the present moment is the definition of suffering itself. So when I examined the belief, "I shouldn't be suffering," a voice of wisdom answered, "Why not? Everyone suffers. Are you any different? What's the problem with suffering?" What we resist persists, right? So I stopped resisting my negative thoughts about my situation and instead started accepting my experience for what it was. My negativity diminished, and over time, disappeared entirely.

The Buddha said that suffering is a fact of life. The only thing that makes it valuable is the meaning we discover in it. To finesse the suffering part and arrive at the awakened part more quickly, take responsibility for your choices, keep a positive mental outlook, and do the required spiritual work. Acceptance is the ultimate act of grace. Acceptance can miraculously change your circumstances, too. You'd be surprised by how many wishes acceptance grants. Acceptance is the ultimate magic!

K.I.S.S.

SPIRIT IS TALKING

I don't personally identify with one any religion, but I can find spiritual kernels and universal truths from many different sources not limited by religion. I can also experience God in a really great tune, a spectacular hike, my favorite paintings, and a deep conversation with a friend. To me, spirituality is everywhere—it's a point of connection to love. Spirituality is participatory and quiet, strong and feisty. It doesn't put me to sleep with a sermon but asks important questions and answers in paradoxical and sometimes playful ways. Often it's absolutely silent and asks me to search for answers in my own heart. That's my favorite thing about Spirit—good, healthy spirituality gives you the freedom to explore your answers in your own way.

Heartache, depression, disillusionment . . . all of the tough stuff will empower some of your life's greatest transformations. Mental resistance will not. Once you accept your thoughts about how you shouldn't be lonely or suffering, you are given the grace to look beyond those thoughts. When you do that, you'll discover a clear and present voice inside your head, a voice that transcends positive or negative thinking about your situation, circumstance, or condition. Listen to it. That's the voice of wisdom, and that's the voice of who you really are.

You Gotta Have Faith

There's a recipe to follow for our spiritual cake batter. First, clean up your mind (your kitchen), then build your faith muscle (practice!). Turns out, George Michael was right, you just gotta have faith! And so goes the biblical quote, "Faith is the substance of the unseen made visible." I love this saying so much that I painted it on the shelf edging of my kitchen in glow-in-the-dark paint! I couldn't see it during the day, but at night, when I stumbled into the kitchen for a drink of water, there was the message, in neon green. This creative act reminded me of how faith works. You may not see immediate evidence, but your faithful acts of co-participation in the Mystery encourage the Mystery to show itself to you. And suddenly, when you're not expecting it, you get a hint of validation that what you're doing is really working.

Having faith in your quest for soulful love is scary, because there is no proof that any of this will turn out. Especially at first, when you're seeing no results. What if your cake falls? What if it tastes like sawdust? Questions rise with the batter and you may not have answers for them. Is it frustrating? Or are you developing the grace to be receptive?

Once you start investing your precious time and energy into attracting your soul mate, it does feel like you've swum into uncharted waters. You have no idea whether your efforts will yield gold or lumpy rocks. Hey, that's called faith! To believe in miracles, let go of your need for instant results and validation. How many people never even begin to attract the person, thing, or dream of their life because it might not work out? They're afraid of wasting their time. But what if it does work out? You'll never know unless you follow through. We live in a culture of instant gratification, so it's hard to surrender the desire for instant proof, but we must. To attract your soul mate, it's essential that you stop looking for love every second of every day and just start believing that you deserve it and that it's coming. Believe in your own ability to attract and create love.

Your biggest obstacle to love is not believing in your own power to attract. Why do you disbelieve? Because you have an arsenal of experience that's told you that you can't attract—it's called your history. You believed in love before and got burned. You've been thinking positive and hopeful thoughts all along, but when the negativity creeps back into your mind during moments of self-doubt, you wonder . . . Maybe you're afraid that you really do believe the voice of self-doubt and not the voice of self-worth.

Here's the deal with self-doubt: you will doubt yourself from time to time. This is natural. The minute you recognize the doubt as self-doubt and therefore untrue, immediately turn all of your fears of loneliness, discouragement, and hopelessness over to Love/God/the Creator/the Universe. An instant way to do this is by having just one positive thought or taking a positive action to counterbalance the negative one. This gets easier over time, though it requires the diligence of a love warrior at first. You may not feel able to do it alone, so every time you get discouraged, take it as a sign to actively place your faith in something higher than yourself. Say an affirmation or mantra, get physical exercise, or perform a ritual to get back on track. In other words, engage Spirit, and snap out of it!

And when you do find faith, a little warning is appropriate: have patience. Again and again, I've noticed a rebound effect in new believers. Just when they're all excited by the positive rush of a synchronicity, coincidence, or love spell success, something goes not quite right, and they totally regress. It's like a spiritual law: soon after you find faith, that faith will be tested, and that's when you must remain ever more vigilant. A common faith-tester is patience: Remember the kitchen truism that a watched pot never boils? You're most vulnerable to jumping the gun just as your love juju gets going, believing the first likely guy you meet is The One. Instead, focus on maintaining your positive thoughts and keeping your energy high and clear. Synchronicities—or coincidental events that seem to line up mysteriously especially for you—will happen. But often, there's business to clear up first.

During this time, your faith must remain strong enough to keep you on task with your highest love wish, not just with whoever shows up. Remember, if there were an Insta-Soul Mate, you'd have found him already!

And be prepared: you will have disappointments. Your love magic won't always go in the direction you want it to go, at least at first, but you can turn that around, too. Shortly after I began doing this soul mate work, and my laundry at a new laundromat, I caught the ardor of a sweet-but-not-my-type guy. Practically every time I went to wash clothes, there he was. Smiling. Like a Cheshire cat. I accepted his idle chat graciously, but I didn't call him. I also didn't use this experience to say to myself, "I don't want *this* guy! This love magic really isn't working!" Clearly, something magical was afoot. No one had gotten sweet on me in, like, years! What I did instead was create this affirmation: "This person is living proof that my soul mate energy is building. I know someone more perfect for me is on his way. As I grow clearer, I grow closer to my perfect fit."

Faith is a muscle you build over time, much like you build your kitchen skills over time. You build faith by staying focused on your best love magic and by asking only for the highest results. Look for the lesson in those not-quite-right fits, and use all the love energy that comes your way as positive evidence that you're on love's wavelength. Do this and you'll get closer to manifesting the man (or woman) of your dreams.

Affirmation: I have faith in my power to attract the person of my dreams. And when I don't have faith, I let a higher power do the faith-making for me.

Breaking the Karma and Moving Forward

Hope is good; it is better than despair, but it is a subtle illusion and an unconscious compromise—and it has no part in effective mental treatment.
—Ernest Holmes

We can always hope for a miracle. But hope that is optimistic, not fantasy-based, is a result of something else. I suspect that that something else is faith and grace; we need faith that it will all come together and the grace to look at things differently, and that's when hope appears.

This section will deliver a "mental treatment." I learned how to do this when I was studying the science of mind, and boy, is it effective for moving out of major mental ruts! Try not to underestimate the power of this simple working; the best healings are simple, not complicated. In reading through this section with conviction and certainty, you will receive a mental makeover. Trust it. I suggest reading this step-by-step treatment when you need a jump start on your heart and soul mate work. For extra juju, copy the affirmations onto an index card and carry them with you to recite whenever you need a pick-me-up!

So without further ado, let's get started.

1. Acceptance and Forgiveness

No one in the Universe is living a life in which they haven't attracted the perfect people, situations, and circumstances for their growth, learning, and love. There's no reason to escape or to want to escape. You are exactly where you belong. No one is more uniquely qualified or has more expertise, beauty, love, or talent to live your life than you. You didn't miss the love boat somewhere along the way—you are just on your way to finding it. The universal energy is love, and it's coming to you. The Universe is conspiring for your happiness.

There are certain things you're responsible for in life, and others things you're not responsible for. If you attract difficult relationships, you can convince yourself there's something wrong with you and that you've done something to cause your disastrous love life, but there may be things you don't yet understand. Don't get stuck on the why, or you may stay stuck for a very long time. Focus on the present instead.

Now, forgive yourself for what you can't understand and move forward with the resolve of a modern-day love vigilante who is wonderfully willing to let go of the past to get closer to the future of her dreams.

Affirmation: I know that I am perfect, whole, and complete. I am uniquely qualified to rise to any obstacle in my life gracefully and beautifully. Today I release the circumstances and people who no longer bring me goodness. I only attract situations and people who want the best for me. The Universe is conspiring for my happiness.

2. Negate Your Reality

Mentally negating a reality is not is not the same as being the Queen of D' Nile. Denial is refusing to see the truth. You know someone is living in denial when their account of what's happening is at odds with the opinions and thoughts of everyone else. When negating the grip a thing, person, or situation has over you, you can clearly see the useless misery and suffering it's causing. Even if you don't understand the why or how of it, simply being tired of a relationship that keeps hijacking your happiness is reason enough to mark a big, fat mental *X* right through it.

Affirmation: There is nothing I can't change with my thoughts, choices and attitudes. No force outside of myself has power over me. Nothing is real unless my thoughts and speech make it so. I now mentally see an *X* appearing over the attitudes, thoughts, and choices that have kept me from peace, love, and happiness.

K.I.S.S.

MY SOUL MATE HAS ANGEL WINGS

Sometimes when we've done our homework with other people (or karmic mates) we get to have a soul mate relationship that feels more like a cherry on top of life's wild sundae—and this relationship is sweet indeed. But often, finding a soul mate can help us resolve our own karma, with the scales being obviously tipped toward the happiness side. I found this to be true with my husband, who fell in love with me within two months of my diagnosis with an excruciatingly painful disease—fibromyalgia. He had no idea if I'd ever be able to work again or lead a normal life, and yet he was certain he wanted to look into my eyes every day for the rest of his life. Two years later and pain-free, I do believe his love healed me. When we find a soul mate who can hold our hand through our tough karma and help us make it to the other side stronger and more healed by virtue of being together, surely that soul mate earns angels wings!

3. Affirm the Positive in Your Life

After negating your negative circumstances, affirm the positive. This is more than positive thinking—it is a powerful spiritual tool used by mystics and saints and wisely-abundant, happy, in-love people for centuries. St. Teresa of Avila, a beautiful spirit, wrote love songs to God during her darkest hours, transforming her personal darkness into light and love. The mystics call this invoking the divine mind, which basically means you attract more great things through gratitude and naming the goodness in the Universe.

Every day brings something to be grateful for. Gratitude is the most powerful prayer in the Universe. It's like a triple-whammy prayer. Being grateful fills your heart with love (which attracts more love toward you), opens your spirit to abundance, and opens your heart to receive. People with closed hearts, who have been hurt or lack spiritual tools, don't attract love because they're not receptive to love. When we're receptive, we're sending high-beam attractor lights out into the Universe. Gratitude literally opens the heart by making it spacious—creating room for more happiness where there used to be closed energy.

Affirmation: I am blessed with a beautiful personality, friends who love me, and I am successful at everything I do. My goodness is my truth and the Absolute Truth of the Universe. I expect wonderful things to happen today, and they do. When I remind myself about all the wonderful things, qualities, and people I have to be grateful for in my life, I attract even more. In gratitude, I open my heart to love.

The Power of Sound and Mantras

When I began my soul mate practice, using affirmations had the effect of wringing out my mind like a wet piece of laundry. I felt clearer after saying them, more in balance, and more peaceful. I loved the equilibrium affirmations gave me, how they removed negativity, and how a still and silent faith began to grow inside me. Yet I still considered that I might want another tool under my belt. I had a feeling there was some deeper karma at play (I had my parents' unhappy marriage to contend with, and my first and only true love happened way back in high school). As I repeated affirmations in my mind on the subway and uttered them under my breath walking to work, I began to wonder about the healing power of language and sound.

We talk to and communicate with people every day, giving voice to our spirit and letting it fly on the wind of our words. As I described in Secret No. 4, Mercury is the planet of voice and thought, the divine messenger, the celestial FedEx guy who flutters between humans and gods, delivering messages of import. Words are magical, they have wings, and from our earthbound perspective, words can accomplish impossible things. Poets have crafted words with such beauty and hope that they've brought peace to political unrest. Greek philosopher-poet-physician-astrologer Marsilio Ficino prescribed musical hymns for all kinds of ailments, and his healing methods were so popular that he was invited to join the prestigious School of Athens, the Renaissance school of genius minds. As Ficino's spoken prayers demonstrated, when set to a cadence, rhythm, or music, words can heal.

Prayerful chanting has been practiced and prescribed by many cultures for centuries. The ancient language of Sanskrit has mystical correspondences to the spiritual and magical realms. Sanskrit is one of the oldest languages on Earth, and although rarely spoken as a dialect in modern times, it has been used prescriptively over the centuries in mantras.

Mantras, as it was been explained to me, are a way of working with and transforming stubborn karma. I found mantra while in the final stages of my soul mate work. I had done so much personal growth, but I still felt mysteriously stuck. I kept returning to karma, because, after everything I'd healed, grown through and discovered, it seemed karma was the only reasonable explanation, right? Leaving no stone unturned, karma was a nice explanation for the mysterious stubbornness of my love dilemmas. That's when I stumbled upon the Eastern practice of mantra.

To understand how mantra works, you've got to understand the connection between Sanskrit language and the chakras. Sanskrit is a uniquely spiritual alphabet. It's spiritual because the letters are actually sounds that, when strung together, resonate with the body's energy centers (the chakras) in a very specific way. There are fifty letters in the Sanskrit alphabet, and each corresponds to one of the fifty petals on the seven chakra centers in the body. The energetic centers running from the base of your spine to the top of your head are said to store your life energy and, thus, your spiritual power. Eastern teachers describe the chakra centers as energetic wheels of colored light, colored lotus flowers ascending from the base of the spine to the top of the head. There is the red Muladhara chakra at the base of the spine, the orange Swadhisthana chakra at the sacrum, yellow Manipura chakra at the solar plexus, green Anahata chakra or heart chakra, blue Vishuddha or throat chakra, purple Ajna chakra at the forehead, and the violet Sahasrara or crown chakra at the top of the head.

A practitioner trained to see these energy centers can judge where our life energy is out of balance by "reading" our chakra energies. These folks can see which chakras are humming along "open," which are stalled "closed," and which are just kind of running on fumes. Apparently very few of us have seven spinning, vibrant chakra center flowers, and some centers are spinning stronger than others. The goal of mantra is to amplify and strengthen all this inner energy, so we have a full tank of gas. Then we can tap our innate ability to heal and change our condition or circumstance. One example of mantra used in the West is "Om Shanti Om," a mantra commonly used to invoke peace.

Imagine that the sounds, by virtue of being strung together and hummed/ uttered in different combinations, reach the appropriate petals on "flowers" of your body. One petal opens, then another and another. The mantra sound traveling through your energy centers moves like a ripple on a pond, outward into the space or spiritual energy surrounding you.

Over time, through working with mantra, a chakra that once looked like a drooping flower revives and stands straight and tall. The idea is that by doing mantra, you're plugging into higher energy states, which will change your physical vibration. Your energy gets clearer, more powerful, and more recognizable by the Universe. Essentially, you're increasing your spiritual wattage, and thus your energy. As with yoga, mantra generates inner strength and resilience.

Interestingly, you don't have to know the meaning of what you're chanting to activate the power of your mantra. Because the Sanskrit alphabet revolves around the energetic vibration it elicits from the chakras, the meaning of the words isn't important, the repetitive hum is. We're very used to words giving a thing mental meaning, so when you use mantra, it helps not to think of them as words, but as energetic utterances. You strengthen your energy body as your utterance speaks the language of an energetic center. Compared to mental affirmations, mantras are more like sound affirmations. This isn't logical left-brain stuff!

Besides being the most ancient spiritual system known, it was the karma thing that sold me on mantra. After all the spells and soul mate work, mantra was the final thing I added to my spiritual toolkit, and it was probably the most potent. I'd been there, done that, and now I was ready to bust through those invisible barriers. It was like the ultimate test of faith, because it really didn't make logical sense. But ancient systems stick around for a reason: they work.

I've come to view mantra as a particularly powerful spiritual tool, a sort of "pull out all the stops" prayer for help from the Divine. But there's a catch: mantra requires your total discipline and dedication. If you're not a disciplined person by nature, you may be challenged with this final assignment. I consider myself a disciplined person capable of very difficult things, and mantra practice was challenging for even me. And it was so worth it!

If you decide to do mantra, you'll have to commit to repeating the mantra 108 times, twice a day, for forty days. I know, I know—I saved the best part for last! Forty days is the standard practice time frame for this spiritual discipline, and 108 is the magic number; it is the number of beads on any Christian rosary or Vedic mala. Why? Vedic (Hindu) teachings say there are 108 astral channels within the body, so by repeating the mantra 108 times, you will thoroughly charge every channel in your body.

Here's my suggestion, modified for us busy, modern Westerners. If you find it impossible to do 108 mantras, start getting the hang of it by chanting (silently or aloud) for a set amount of time, maybe ten minutes, twice a day. Don't let the number of recitations (or how long it takes) intimidate you right away. Just get in the habit of chanting. When I really got rolling, I could do the 108 repetitions in fifteen minutes, but it took awhile to gather steam.

Here's the mantra I used for the perfect man, taken from the book *Healing Mantras* by Thomas Ashley-Farrand. The pronunciation is below.

Sat Patim Dehi Parameshwara

(SAHT PAH-TEEM DAY-HEE PAH-RAHM-ESH-WAH-RAH)

Please give to me a man of truth who
embodies the perfect masculine attributes.

Or, if you're looking for the perfect woman:

Narayani Patim Dehi Shrim Klim Parameshwari

(NAH-RAH-YAH-NEE PAH-TEEM DAY-HEE SHREEM KLEEM PAH-RAHM-ESH-WAH-REE)

Oh power of truth, please let me attract a spouse carrying the
supreme feminine energy manifesting abundance and creativity.

These are catch-all mantras, covering all bases of attracting your perfect man or woman. (Please do the Dear Cupid Spell on p. 279 before you begin mantra practice.) If you're not familiar with how mantra sounds, or need help and/or confidence before chanting it, many examples exist online. Try YouTube.com and type in "mantra chanting" to find one you like.

Remember, every mantra already contains the seed intention, even if it's in a language your mind doesn't understand, though thanks to your Dear Cupid Spell work, you will already have your own intentional blueprint laid out. Since I found it difficult to say words foreign to my brain without attributing actual meaning to them, I visualized the intention of the words as a green glow surrounding my heart chakra as I chanted. My heart center grew bigger and bigger with each mantra, so by the time I reached 108, it extended across the Universe as a beacon, guiding my soul mate to me.

Using Mantra to Attract your Soul Mate

1. Make a list of the qualities of your perfect mate (you can use the letter in your Dear Cupid Spell, p. 279).

2. Commit to a period of practice time.

    How long have you been looking for a soul mate? A year? Your entire life? If you're like most people, you've been looking a long time. It's important work finding this soul mate, and it requires an investment of time, energy, and sometimes even money (for therapy, self-help materials, or CDs). Compared to the attention, intention, and time you've already given your soul mate search, a half-hour a day for forty days is a drop in the bucket.

3. Do it. Every. Day.

    I know, I know. Accept that you will have resistance, and you will falter. And then you will think about how you don't want to get half a soul mate because you were half-assed in your practice, and so you will begin again. If you miss one session, make up for it by adding on another day. Since life is busy, you can do the urban mystic method, like I did. My first mantra session was a noontime walk by the Bay. It turned into one of my favorite, relaxing times of the day, this time spent walking and chanting. I did my second mantra session in the evening, on the train ride home from work. But if you want to make this extra special, you can do your mantra in front of a personal love altar (see "Building an Altar to Love" on p. 221).

4. Be complete.

Don't let anyone interrupt you, so turn off your cell phone and close your door. If you're on the subway surrounded by people, envision a bright white protective bubble around you so no one will ask you for money or interrupt you by starting a conversation. Make it clear: this is your sacred time.

5. Use a rosary or prayer beads.

There's a special way to use prayer beads (malas) if you're using them to count your mantra. Count off one bead for each repetition, moving in one direction. When you reach the bead at the end (called the melu) don't cross over it but instead turn the beads and count in the opposite direction. The melu bead stores spiritual power, which culminates when you finish one complete loop. Using a mala is a handy way to count off your mantra repetitions. Another fun thing is that you can wear your mala as a bracelet or love charm to charge up your intention! Rose quartz (love) or sandalwood (purity) malas or malas with stones that are special to you are available on the Internet.

6. Create a special mantra area.

Even if you don't sit in front of it while you're doing your mantra practice, give your mantra a home at your love altar (see p. 221).

I Am of Magic, I Am of Patience

Over tea, I was asked by an interested friend how long it took to manifest my soul mate with magic. "A very focused nine-month period of work," I replied, anticipating the usual deflated sigh that I hear from so many people who are waiting for their love dream, "So far away . . ."

I know, from the position of wanting, nine months sounds like a long time. And from my perspective of a dream fulfilled, it wasn't very long at all. What's even a few years in the grand scheme of life? Tell me, do you have something better to spend your time on than attracting the love of your life? It's what most of us do, anyhow, although in a far less focused way than I'm suggesting.

Instead of giving a sigh of defeat, my friend surprised me. Her eyes sparkled and she said something that rang loud and clear with truth: "I was recently told that magical time works on a different time line than our concept of time." And she was told this by a man she'd used magic to attract, no less, whom she was also now seeing a lot more of. She spoke of a soul mate spell she had done months back and casually wondered if that could have possibly attracted the relationship that was happening right now. I smiled. Yes! Yes! and Yes! I knew she knew a secret about magic.

I know magic works, but it works on a different time line than your standard Timex. It's not clock time, this magical time. The good news is that it's a lot quicker than you think; in fact, it's nearly instant. The less-good news is that it takes awhile to manifest into physical form. Imagine being in Paris, France. That was easy, *oui, oui*? Now, imagine all the steps of really going there, how many hours you'd have to work to afford the ticket; booking the ticket; the hours of preparation, planning, and packing; the coordinated effort to get to the airport; not to mention the trip itself. Okay, so when you send your magic out there and your wish is elegantly and instantly received by the Universal Creator, the Creator must also coordinate multiple efforts here, on slow-as-molasses planet Earth (you've heard of gravity, right?). All this behind-the-scenes stuff is happening to bring you your soul mate! Obviously there are many factors involved. It takes time.

But it can also feel futile. Especially when you're waiting, and it feels like it's taking *for-e-ver*. What is forever? A very long time in which your wish remains a wish, your dream is something you see only at night, and you don't expect your dream to come true. The truth is, dreams move from inspiration into reality in small incremental steps, not in one giant leap. Again, there are no Insta-Soul Mates! Yet there is something we can do, besides just wait for "something to happen" (which often just doesn't work). We can work the dream inward with magic; we can examine our thoughts and beliefs, try mantra, play with rituals, experiment with personal growth, look for synchronicities and signs, and spend time in quiet contemplation. This is proactive spiritual work, not just to get a soul mate, but to become the right person for our soul mate. That's infinitely rewarding.

Take your dream of love seriously. Believe in it. There's nothing more spiritual than a deep desire in your heart to make a dream become true, to make your dream for love a reality. And it's a sacred task assigned to only you. The Divine speaks to us through our dreams, through planting a desire in our heart. Dreams of love are never futile—dreaming of love motivates the materialization of love.

But manifestation doesn't happen in a day. It takes patience. It's a process of opening and of commitment. A prayer in the heart, an openness to play with the different ways to make it real, a willingness to examine where we've been confused or stuck in misunderstanding—that's the commitment part. We can talk, talk, talk about manifesting our desires, but to put perspective on that we're talking about—matter that's been spiritualized into being (*Webster's* dictionary defines *manifestation* as "an occult phenomenon of something materializing")—that takes awhile!

The thing about impatience is that it can lead to discouragement, inaction, or bad choices. Try not to let impatience derail you. When life isn't moving out there, when the phone's not ringing, when nothing's happening on Friday night, there's always something we can do right here, in our spirit. We might light a candle, write a letter, heal a wound, create a spell, release a past relationship, create a painting, or educate ourselves about the magical world of symbols. It gives you something to do on those Friday nights instead of sitting around just waiting!

Moving inward spiritually relieves our need to "make something happen." By doing so, we're investing in our dreams. As we take a gigantic healing leap, for example, we may find ourself propelled forward in a way we didn't anticipate. Or after weeding out some negative thoughts, we discover a powerfully positive one, and we're off and running in an unpredictably exciting direction. We experiment and we wonder and who knows where that could lead.

To marry your heavenly wish to your Earth life takes persistence, patience, fortitude, and self-examination—those wonderful virtues that vex and eventually reward us. Faith comes through patience. Faith is knowing that the Sun is shining somewhere, even when it's dark. The dark winter in your love life is not just the absence of light, it's the pregnant pause of beginning, empty and hopeful. The dark is where you'll always begin your most important life's work—like finding your soul mate.

You're Charmed and Dangerous

Soul Mate Secret No. 9

Love is, and has always been, magical and mysterious.
Restore magic and Mystery to love through
enchantment.

I put a spell on you . . . because you're mine!

SCREAMIN' JAY HAWKINS

Spellcasting 101

Keep It Simple

One thing you'll notice about all affirmations, spells, prayers, and love rituals I suggest: they're all simple. In fact, when it comes to intentional work, simple is where it's at. That said, if you tend toward overthinking, your thoughts can muddy Venus' tranquil waters. To get in a ritual or spellwork frame of mind, you'll want to be relaxed, open, and basically free of thoughts. In spellwork as in life, struggle and effort only attract more struggle and effort, and you don't want to invite that into your soul mate relationship! All love work should be done in a spirit of optimism, playfulness, and fun. This isn't brain surgery.

A Twenty-First-Century DIY Witch Gets Creative

I believe spells can be made up on the spot and still be 100 percent magically powerful. That's because the Universal Creator digs originality. Think about it: the Creator must be thoroughly modern, because he/she/it always keeps inventing new, cool things to taste and try. It's always like, "Wow, look what I just did!" Therefore, I strongly endorse following spontaneous insights, intuitive promptings, and pursuing those wild hairs that will call you during your soul mate magic-making sessions. The best soul mate conjurers have that special combination of inventiveness, confidence, and intuition that takes their magic from mere paint-by-number spellcasting to a true art. So if you're moved to do something different in the spur of the moment, by all means, do it. These spells are certainly ready-to-wear, yet I fully endorse your personally meaningful spell modifications.

You'll also notice I use the term "spell" fairly loosely. Not all these spells involve candles, herbs, incantations, and incense, though some do. Some "spells" suggest you make a piece of art, take a special bath, or even wear your hair differently. In my book, "casting a spell" is just another way to say "creative-ly intending." The premise is that when your desire and intention converge in a creative act, you can alter reality.

As far as be-witchery goes, I've never trained to be a witch or Wiccan—though my soul mate calls me his witchy woman! I wasn't attracted to the aesthetic of the centuries of witches gone before me, so I developed my own spellcasting style. As a bewitching babe with feet planted firmly in the twenty-first century, I've put a modern spin on old love magic because the here and now is always the most power-ful place to be. Today, spells needn't involve brews, brooms, and toads' feet if you don't want them—nor need they be "by the book." A basic knowledge of magical substances and ritual invocation, passed down by our ancestors, is enough to begin, and within that framework, there's plenty of room to play. Although I am not a Wiccan, I honor the women of the Craft, those who were persecuted for the same magical knowledge we get to so freely practice without harm today.

As for the magical ways and means we have access to today, it's easy to be magically charmed. But never confuse the appearances—the chants, incense, and candles— with the real magic. What's the real magic? Your spiritual intention, your whole-hearted belief that you can really pull love toward you is the real magic. Intention always charges your successes (and even your so-called failures), for when your heart is clear, you are spiritually growing in the right direction and even those "spiritually educational" mixed results will turn out to be positive.

Don't Believe in Magic. Believe in You.

It doesn't matter whether you believe in magic or not; it only matters that you be-lieve in yourself. Just as you must accept the truth that you were created in love to really feel beloved, your ability to align yourself with love so you can pull it toward you is God/Goddess given. The spells will ask you only to believe in the power of your own ability to co-create on a new level—a magical level. Believing in yourself as a powerful co-creator of magic is the basis of all magic. By trusting that you are a wonderful spellcaster already, the gift of magic making will be given to you.

But you don't have to take my word for it. No one really believes in anything until they experience it. If I told you a diamond is the strongest stone and you had no knowledge of this, you wouldn't fully believe me (hopefully) until you tested it out. As with magic, or any radically different world outlook, belief is irrelevant in the face of experience. So just experiment and have an experience. However, when you're just beginning to do magic for the first time, you may find that suspending your disbelief is helpful. Remain curious, open-minded, and open to having good things come your way—then see what good comes!

Release It with Love

If you've ever been in a really foul mood, turned on the radio to hear your favorite song, and had that song turn your day around, you've experienced the beautiful power of surrender. Release is an important part of leading a balanced life—we surrender to sleep at the end of the day and leave the remainder of our daily work unfinished. And just as the exhale follows the inhale, we each have to surrender to the fact that we have no control over what happens next. Total surrender is the final step of life and it's also the final step of magic making.

After your spell, ritual, or prayer work is done, there's one final step for you to take: release it. It's a cinch—effortless, really! Besides intention, this simple step is the most important one. Surrender the outcome. As spirituals say, give it up to God. You've done your best. You've put your heartfelt intention into the Universe and that's really the only control we ever have.

Trust that even though you can't see it yet, your wish, intention, or desire has now become a living thing. You must treat this wish with the expectant care you'd give a growing flower. Just like a flower, if you hold your wish too tightly, it can be crushed by the weight of your need or expectation for it; neglect to nurture and care for your heart's desire, and it may not grow.

Surrender is effortless. But the ego is a big believer in striving and doing. Add to that the fact that we humans usually think what we want is what our soul actually

K.I.S.S.

DO IT WITH FLAIR

One thing that struck me about the books *The Secret* and *The Law of Attraction* is that while they relay substantial spiritual principles anyone can use, illustratively and stylistically, they were real snooze-fests. It was like someone cooked a really good soup and left out the best spice. I think spirituality is far more motivating when it's fun, when it asks us to add our own individuality, creativity, and genius to the mix. What does that mean? Make everything you do personal and original. If it's an infinitely creative world, then the Universe doesn't just appreciate our individual style and creativity—it actually flourishes with it.

You don't have to choose substance over style—you can do both! You've got flair. Venus thrives on seeing just how creative you can be with the assets you've been given. The unimaginably prolific Creator didn't create merely one white flower, but hundreds of different white flowers, daisies, roses, lilies . . . You don't have to reinvent the wheel, just be willing to use your individuality and unique abilities because those make you—yes—attract-ive. So I encourage you *not* to perform your love spells as though following an instruction manual, to a T. (Few of us bother to read boring old instruction manuals, anyhow.) Instead, use these spells at the back of this book as a skeleton outline. Tap your creativity and individuality to find the right phrase or symbolic action to make things intuitively click for you!

desires. Our higher self knows this is not always the case! Inviting a third presence into your magic *will* help you release your willfulness for Thy Will, and it is this Will that *will* strengthen your spellwork (pun intended!).

Never do a spell in a state of anxiety, fear, or upset. Remember, like attracts like. If you find yourself getting anxious or obsessive about your heart's desire, try silently working with this in mind: "I release this desire to the loving Divine, knowing Thy Will be done as my own." Repeat until you're calm and surrendered once again.

Payback's a Witch

Are you a good witch or a bad witch?
—Munchkin to Dorothy in *The Wizard of Oz*

Just as what you focus your attention on exerts influence over the natural order of things (you focus on your daily work, and thus, you get it done), what and who you focus your magic on will absolutely influence the spell's outcome. This is common sense be-witchery. But there will be times when you may toy with the idea of effecting a very specific outcome, like, say, making a specific person fall in love with you.

I advise against doing this.

Why? Because payback's a witch. Magic can be powerfully coercive, but that isn't soul mate magic. Venus magic is receptive and allowing, influencing others by drawing them in with a spirit of open and playful curiosity. The other kind of magic channels the universal energy for the ego's ends. And the last thing you want to do is manipulate the natural order of things for your own personal gain.

Still, few of us are so liberated from our ego that we can separate our own desire from the Divine Will, so that's why it's necessary to totally surrender our attachments to a specific outcome and trust that the Divine has our best interest at heart. That's what the previous chapters have taught you to do! To help you out with this, always affirm that "Thy Will be done" (not *my* will be done) before each spell.

I know, I know. If you've got your heart set on someone special, this is difficult. We've all been infatuated with a person we just wish we could make love us back! But myriad problems arise when you mix the Divine Will with your will to "get" a specific person. You could end up wasting countless magical hours and energy on someone not right for you if you have your heart set on the wrong person. By focusing your love magic on a specific person, you could inadvertently sidetrack the more fabulous soul mate energy coming your way. Put another way, even if *you* are convinced a certain man is your soul mate, the Divine may know that he's not the right one for you!

There are also karmic implications to trying to attract a certain person. While the thought of messing with the will of others and potentially influencing their destiny makes me shudder, others find it tempting. Don't be tempted. Soul mate magic isn't mind control, nor is it making another person do anything that's not congruent with their heart's wish. Soul mate magic is about tapping the Universal Creator's force and saying, "I'm ready, willing, and able to receive my soul mate!"

By becoming a vessel for attracting, you open up to a power greater than little ole you. You're playing with a larger sphere of influence—spiritual energy. You do this by aligning with the greater You, your higher self, and remaining open to being lovingly guided to your mate. Unlike the ego (which often has an agenda about who to love), the higher self is pure love, has your best intentions at heart, and can be trusted completely.

That higher self knows your deepest, most soulful wish to attract a lover with all the wonderful qualities you need for maximum spiritual growth and happiness. Your higher self's desires are not your ego's desires, but since most of us get the two confused all the time, we need to periodically let go of our personal will while keeping the wish for love in our heart. When we do this, a reservoir of spiritual power is at our disposal. Put this release of ego into a ritual or spell to become doubly empowered!

Spirit is not to be personally messed with, if you catch my drift. But don't take my word for it. There are many tales of spellcasters who have paid the price for self-interested magic. While these stories may be outrageous or fictional, they're also a cleverly veiled warning about how the desire for personal gain can go awry. The teen cult movie *The Craft* is a fine example of how using magical forces for ego (a.k.a. evil or desire) creates more problems than good, as is *Practical Magic*. I understand that pain can drive us to do things we'd otherwise not consider, but when good witches lose their heads to power by doing spellwork to control a specific person, that's not keeping with the free and easy style of Venus.

That said, if you're hung up on a certain someone, I'd suggest beginning your spellwork with the release spells—the Give Me Back My Mind, Body, and Soul Spells—to keep your heart in the free and clear. Good witch!

In a modification of the warning "Be careful what you wish for," be careful *who* you wish for. While doing spellwork, you can always change your wish for a specific person into a wish for a specific type of person with similar qualities (and then throw in a few more they're lacking, for good measure). In my experience, the Universe hears our customized soul mate intentions by delivering our intended.

Now, get ready to charm their socks off!

K.I.S.S.

THERE ARE NO JUST DESSERTS

Some people believe in just desserts, the sweet satisfaction of revenge. I don't think it makes sense to torture someone for being dishonest or hurting you, unless you want to attract a tortured soul mate. One of the most useful mantras I've learned to say to myself when someone's hurt my feelings is "They didn't intend to hurt me, they're just confused." Almost all the time, I'm right. However, emotional or physical abuse is never justified, just as emotionally torturing someone else by calling and hanging up, letting the air out of their tires, or doing a spell that messes with their free will isn't justifiable. Even if it seems perfectly harmless, you're moving out of your business and into someone else's, and you're not equipped to re-organize their karma: first, because you have a limited understanding of it since it's not yours; and second, because you don't want the karmic contract to continue that relationship down the road. One of my favorite people, Byron Katie, reminds me to keep my mind on myself: There are two minds you need to think about—yours and God's. Mind your own business. Don't jump into anyone else's head. To stay in integrity with your heart, and only your heart, mind your own business and let God/Goddess take care of theirs!

Finding Your Shakti Power

What does it mean to be attractive? Is it beauty or intelligence, good Botox, or good hygiene? On the physical plane, these things may help, and they are powerful magic in their own right. But what about the spiritual plane? Don't ignore one plane for the other; we need both. As we've explored, the spiritual plane is the magical place truly capable of drawing a soulful relationship toward you, not just another warm, pretty body. In the sphere of spiritual energy, attraction is receptive magnetism. And it's something we women are especially good at (though men can do it, too!). If you can't immediately feel your attract-ive power, it helps to imagine your energy as a magnet, drawing the world toward you. I remember once seeing a postcard photograph of a woman standing on a cliff, with the wind and her dress swirling around about her in a spiral, as though she was the force at the center of a powerful vortex. I bought the photograph and kept it as a reminder of my awesome power to attract.

In the Hindu Vedas, Shakti is the embodiment of feminine power. Her power is her receptivity and generosity, her ability to give energy, not take it away from others. Shakti doesn't need to manipulate or seduce; she draws others to her with her creative-spiritual energy. She contains feminine wisdom, the quiet confidence of spacious knowingness. And perhaps the greatest power of the feminine is her ability to attract whatever she wants—beauty, love, success, power—with psychic intention.

You can gather your Shakti energy just as we've learned to harness the seemingly elusive power of the wind. It may help to collect or design symbols or visual examples to remind you of your power to attract. These symbols are feminine containers in their own right, attracting "more power to you" by becoming a portal or vessel for a very specific energy. Talismans, icons, paintings, and other magical objects have been used throughout history, and I see them as a sort of direct heart line to the Creator—totally nonverbal and mystical. You may have art hanging on your walls at home, and you can sense another dimension of energy, space, and time through looking at. If you're hung up on the words *talisman*, *icon*, or *magic*, there's nothing voodoo about hanging a picture you love on your bedroom wall for the feelings it brings you—happiness, contentedness, or relaxation. You don't call that magic, but it is the same basic idea.

Through objects, you create heart-mind associations that perpetuate a certain state of mind and being. The thing to remember about magical objects is that their power lies in the intention and purpose you give to them. And whether you worship at the altar of Isis or a hot photo of yourself or another Goddess-y woman (or you *and* another hot woman, meow!), it's the person looking at the symbol who supports the intention for love (hint: that person is you). However, I must say those fertility symbols and love icons that have been used successfully by your female ancestors for thousands of years are ultra-powerful. They have the intentionality of many, many women behind them. If you're so inclined, you can use these ancient symbols and icons, too.

Exercise: Lovely Icons

Find a love goddess or female icon that makes your heart happy. Build an altar around her as the ultimate psychic prayer. Treat your icon like the love goddess you are.

Building an Altar to Love

One of the best ways to play with your Venus power is by building a ritual altar in honor of the queen of love and romance. Altars have ancient magnetism because they've been used for centuries to answer prayers and attract desires. Altars are the ultimate symbol of feminine receptivity. Think of church altars, both a form of worship and an elaborate invitation for intervention from the Divine. By building an altar to a love goddess, you're building an altar to the part of you that resonates with love. So use your unique tastes, your sense of romance, and your creative aesthetic to craft an altar in your image. You're also wooing Lady Love into your corner, so pull out all the stops. Knowing what the mythical Venus likes will really impress her (see the lists in this chapter for some ideas). And that right there could land you a date.

Altars are also mysteriously effective at matching your beloved to your very specific wishes, so be specific and intentional in your choice of objects. Remember, everything has meaning. I created my altar with spiritual tokens, tsa-tsas (Tibetan symbols of spiritual merit), a Buddha, sandalwood prayer beads my father gave to my mother, rose quartz beads (for unconditional heart love), jade stone (abundance), saffron (richness and prosperity), and several vases and small dishes. I also made regular offerings to Venus, such as pieces of candy and flowers from my garden (she loves sweets and flowers). I love seashells, and the ocean and water are also dear to Venus, so I added a few of those, too. From my collection, I chose a set of shells that perfectly "matched"—one dark shell curled naturally into the other, lighter shell. To top off my altar creation, I made sure to include a few whimsical pieces, colored beads and little toys, because Venus loves to play.

You'll want to make your love altar lush and plush, abundant with the riches Venus herself adores. What else does Venus love? Anything you love! Tarot cards, crystals, incense, statues of deities . . . it's all good to her so long as it makes your heart sing. Make specific offerings to Venus: pile your altar high with jewels, shells, copper pennies, flowers, etc. You can use pretty bottles, shells, bowls, all types of vessels. Venus is attracted to shimmering and shiny things, so use glass beads, sea glass, and sparkly jewels. She also likes to stare at herself in the mirror for hours and primp (sound familiar?), so put some handheld mirrors on your altar, perhaps some perfume or lipstick to encourage her (your) beauty and someone else's affection. You can also choose your favorite love goddess or fertility goddess icon (if you want children with your soul mate) and place her in a prime spot, surrounded by her bounty. Lakshmi, Isis, Venus, Oya . . . there are so many wonderful women to choose from. Make regular love offerings by freshening up your altar with flowers, candy, candles, and incense to keep the spirit of love and your intention alive.

Where to build your altar? On a flat surface, raised above the floor. The best location really depends on how you plan on using your altar. If you want to kneel or meditate in front of it, choose a table at eye level. Maybe you'd like to look at it before you fall asleep at night to dream about your true love. Or maybe you're pressed for space, in which case any convenient, flat surface will do. (I built my love altar on a windowsill, which I wouldn't necessarily recommend as the first choice because according to the principles of feng shui, windows and doors are energetic exit pathways. However, immediately behind the window was a fence, so maybe that helped contain the energy. Hey, it worked!)

So I suppose you want to know how my altar synchronously matched my mate? Okay. As I said, tsa-tsas are symbols of spiritual merit, they're "good karma" tokens people like you and me offer to alleviate other people's suffering and by so doing, increase our own goodness. My soul mate has some of the best karma ever—he's what other people might call incredibly "lucky," but I know that's his spiritual generosity and overwhelming sense of optimism shining through. Of course he resonates with Buddhism, like me, and shared spirituality continues to be a theme for us (the Buddha). He has a big heart (the rose quartz), born under the sign of Leo the Lion. And he's compassionate: we fell in love and within months, I was diagnosed with the painful muscle syndrome fibromyalgia. I had to quit my job and lost a large part of my income, and John's abundance (jade, saffron) graciously allowed me to recover my health. To this day he always marvels at how "perfectly matched" we are (the nesting seashells). And finally, he is unequivocally the most fun man I've ever met (the colored beads and toys)! As my mentor and teacher said to me shortly after John and I got together, "In the past, if asked, I'd probably have described you as a sensitive and thoughtful, but serious woman. Maybe it's John's influence, but now you're lighter. I think you're finally having fun in life!"

Companion Spell: ATTRACT YOUR SOUL MATE CHARM BRACELET

Creating a Sacred Space for Love

When I became ready for love by doing this soul mate work, I prepared my house as though I were expecting the arrival of a very special guest. I was fortunate enough to live alone in a very cozy studio cabin and this gave my creativity and imagination free reign. As with so many things in magic, making your spiritual wish into a living, breathing reality not only satisfies your need to see proof that "something's happening" but also sends an instant message to Cupid: "Look, over here! I'm ready!" I figured if I was building a home for love in my heart, why not build a place for love inside my physical home? A fresh coat of paint and a few personal touches communicated my intention to Cupid—along with my hospitality for the arrival of a very special person.

The Boudoir is the most intimate part of your home. It is the place of repose and relaxation, where you dream of true love, and it's where—one day very soon—you will take your soul mate by the hand and lead him to ecstatic bliss. The goal is to make your boudoir a love den, a temple of passion, one that he'll never want to leave. Love goddess Venus absolutely adores it when you put your own special taste and style into your self-expression, so give your boudoir your signature; make it a flourished and artful expression of your intimate romantic side.

What's your fancy? If you like period French, be inspired by Marie Antoinette. This needn't be an expensive endeavor, and most rooms can be made over for under $150. Just head over to Ikea and get some cornflower linens, simple vases with sweet flowers, and antique white frames, and add plenty of girly flourishes. For a more exotic look that's more Scheherazade than Laura Ashley, go Moroccan with spicy warm colors like burnt orange, deep crimson, and plum. Artfully arrange mirrors in naughty positions, add candles, and sew dangling prisms and jewels into your curtains. This is your love den. Make it worth visiting.

If you're stumped, look at your bedroom through the eyes of someone who has never seen it before. What's great about it? What needs to go? Think about it as though you were checking into a luxury hotel for a romantic weekend—and you wouldn't be leaving the bed. Okay, does that thought excite you or make you feel claustrophobic? Be honest.

The only rule is to make sure your space is neat and uncluttered. It's a rule of thumb for any home environment magic, so you might consider applying this to your entire home and personal style. Bewitching babe Fiona Horne said, "Cleanliness is Goddessliness," and I can't agree more. If you're swamped with disorganized energy, how ever will your soul mate to find you? He might confuse the bed with the pile of dirty laundry. Your job is to keep your energy clean and clear. And as people say, your home is a reflection of how you live your life.

The Bed is the center of your love temple. I put mosquito netting around mine because I find the half-hidden, half-revealed quality very sexy. Like a woman wearing a piece of semi-revealing lingerie, there's something incredibly alluring about slipping behind the curtains. Playing with netting, flowing curtains, and big fluffy pillows has the effect of making your bedroom feel sumptuous and inviting. And who doesn't want sumptuous? Strategically placed candles are a must; candlelight flatters every body type. Fresh flowers bring fresh beauty and joy into the bedroom, so if you're lucky enough to have a garden, voilà!

Your mattress should be comfortable, and if it's not, make getting one a top priority. Who wants to sleep on a lumpy, uncomfortable bed? Also, if you're using the same bed linens you used in a previous relationship, get rid of them or do the Burn Those Sheets! Ritual (see p. 285). You don't want to carry that old energy into your new relationship.

The Toilette is no mere pit stop on the way to somewhere else, *mon cheri*, it is where you transform yourself into a love goddess every morning! You put on makeup and get ready to show your best face to the world here. It is also a place sacred to Venus—not just because you endeavor to become more beautiful here, but the bathroom has mirrors and lots of running water, which Venus adores. Remember Botticelli's *Birth of Venus* painting? The woman rising out of a bathtub on an over-sized seashell is you. Place seashells around your sink, along with copper pennies. Dressing tables have an old Hollywood glamour and have become passé, but they shouldn't be—they're an altar to Venus. Whether or not you're lucky enough to have a dressing table, treat your jewels, cosmetics, and perfumes with reverence. These aren't just beauty potions for mere mortals, they're sacred ritual objects.

Don't forget those affirmations on your mirror!

Companion Spell: AFFIRMING FOR LOVE

The Color of Love

The Universe speaks to us in many ways and languages. One of her languages is color. We may have favorite colors and color associations and, if we're perceptive, we might notice that certain colors induce memories, psychological states, and moods. I believe color is saturated with supernatural meaning. Color absolutely affects our consciousness. And whether choosing a candle for a love spell, the color to paint a room, or the best dress to wear on a date, the intentional use of color will enhance all your love magic.

When I was really young, I recall my father leaving for a meditation retreat and telling me a memorable story upon his return. His teacher had instructed him to meditate in a different-colored room for a whole day—either solid red, blue, green, or yellow. In the red room, my father experienced intense passion, anger, and energy. In the yellow room, he had a lot of cerebral thoughts. He experienced feelings of loneliness (without anyone to express them to) in the blue room. His experiences absolutely jibes with the color theory I describe below.

Red is earthy heart energy, attributed to the planet of sexuality and passion, Mars. Use red for stimulating heart passion and pure sexual energy. It is the color of the first (root) chakra, which ties you to all physical life. Use red to stimulate heart-ful sexual chemistry. When decorating, bright red can be too high in energy for some parts of the house, such as the bedroom, so deeper, jewel-toned hues can help ground this forceful color.

Orange is an exciting color for its attract-ive properties. It is Shakti-promoting, stimulates sexually creative energy and belongs to the bright battery of our solar universe—the Sun, along with Venus, the artist. Use orange to encourage procreative-sexual chemistry. This is the color of the second (sacral) chakra of sensuality and creativity.

Yellow is intelligent, happy, and upbeat. Owning attributes of self-esteem and mental optimism, yellow reigns supreme for engendering wonderful third (solar plexus) chakra feelings of mental and emotional well being, which you feel in your solar plexus or belly area. (I once heard yellow stimulates digestion, making it a great choice for the kitchen or dining room!) Use yellow to bring the sunny qualities of the Sun and mental chemistry of Mercury into your relationships.

Green is composed of both yellow (self-esteem) and blue (soul truth) and is the color of the natural abundance inherent in life. Belonging to the fourth (heart) chakra, the heart's wisdom knows love is all there is and knows, without a doubt, that love is everyone's birthright. Use green to reinforce Venus self-esteem, financial abundance, and self-love. Green contains shades of three planets: Mercury, Venus, and the soulful Moon.

Blue contains metaphysical healing protection, because the fifth (throat) chakra attribute is about remembering and speaking from our soul's deepest truths. Self-remembering, either expressed or vocalized, is healing for relationship. Use blue when you want to remember to speak your truth in relationship. Blue belongs to the dreamy, nurturing Moon, and allows us to flow with life's changes.

Indigo has spiritual properties because of it's sixth (third-eye) chakra connection to the truth and freedom in possibility. It is the color of the mind inspired by life's spiritual teachings, collective wisdom, and opportunities offered by "opening" our mind. Use indigo when you want to attract an open-minded partner, or to receive spiritual insight about someone or something. Indigo and the sixth chakra are ruled by the expansive and faith-giving planet, Jupiter.

Violet is the colorful result of divinity (white) mixed with open-mindedness (indigo). Mystical and imaginative violet brings the fruition of faith to those who be-

K.I.S.S.

IT'S ELEMENTAL

The cool thing about making magic is that it's as natural to us as the water we drink and the air we breathe. Hippocrates, the ancient astrologer and physician, determined that every organ in our body consists of four elements in varied proportions: fire, earth, air, and water. Though only God/Goddess knows the scientific formula to creating a human life (if we tried, *Weird Science* style, to make a soul mate, we'd probably end up with someone pretty strange!), we can use the four elements to clothe our wish with substance, which, with prayerful intention, is about as close as we can get to the Creator's secret. Here's how elemental magic works: A candle (fire) imbues the intention with a spark of passion, the spark of life itself. Gemstones (earth) vibrate your prayer with the physical provisions and abundance of life. A chalice of wine (water) resonates your wish with the healing, life-giving power of water while incense (air) invites the spiritual presence of the unseen into your invocation. The elements are, well, elemental to every ritual, for it's as though by symbolically invoking the "substance of life" that we can materialize our real-life soul mate. Yes, with elemental help, you too can *man*-i-fest your wish for you special man!

lieve they can co-create their reality. We tap indigo's color power by contemplating a world where all things are possible and then imagining it into being—like conjuring up your soul mate! Use violet, the color of the seventh (crown) chakra, to stimulate spirituality, imagination, and possibility. Violet is also a Jupiter color.

White is the absence of color. It's purity makes white the perfect choice for spiritual cleansing, spiritual protection, and enhancing the mystical effects of all other colors. In dress, design, and spellcasting, just like the silvery Moon, white magnifies and intensifies the desired effect of all other colors.

Black, the sum of every color, transforms obstacles by removing negative energy. This explains why black never goes out of style—it contains the mystical power of the full color spectrum! Black works wonders in a release or ending spell. The planets of endings and transformation, Saturn and Pluto, hold sway over modern, magical black.

Finally—although an amalgam of white and red, **Pink** is too important to neglect. Pink engenders romance, innocence, and playfulness, as it is the planet Venus' color, naturally!

A Ritual Primer

There's an album by Jane's Addiction called *Ritual de lo Habitual* that succinctly sums up the way we regard ritual during modern times: as habit. To creatures of habit, rituals like making dinner and going to work can go on automatic. Habit is soul-numbing. There's no better way to lose touch with magic than taking a "same stuff, different day" attitude toward the everyday.

Since almost every human being could use fewer rituals of habit and more rituals that bring heaven to Earth, in order for divine intervention to occur in our love life, we need to invite a third presence in on a regular basis.

There is sacred ritual and there's mundane ritual. There are three points that make a ritual special and sacred: (1) a spiritual presence of mind: how we hold this activity in our awareness; (2) frequency: how often we do this activity; and (3) intention: being clear about what we'd like to gain by doing the activity.

In reality, any time we invite a special third consciousness into a ritual, we elevate the ritual. My morning espresso with a piece of rye cracker and cashew butter could be considered a mundane ritual, yet quite often, it's simply divine! It's my favorite time of the day to be silent and connect and commune with taste, sensation, and simple presence. Another example of turning the mundane into divine might be the way we like to conduct our dinnertime meal—in silence, with candles, or with a prayer for those who have worked so hard to bring us our food. Ritual is not just about the trappings, it's about being present to and honoring what we're doing with gratitude and celebration. By being present to the miracle of this ordinary moment and how delicious it is to be alive, we turn ordinary moments into divine ones.

And yet, the more powerful rituals are made more powerful for being rare. This especially applies to soul mate rituals. When you do the Conjure Up Your Soul Mate Ritual Spell (see p. 249), you'll want to pull out all the stops and make it grand. Celebrate it! Plan for it in advance. It's that special, and worth treating as a holiday. Just as Christmas only comes once a year and is all the more precious for that, don't water down your wish for love by holding a soul mate ritual every week. I only perform rituals on special occasions and at those sparse times when I really need divine intervention. By doing the biggie rituals infrequently, I'm also practicing patience and faith by trusting that my prayers will be answered in divine time. I don't expect an instant result, though sometimes that magically happens!

Finally, rituals rely on your intentionality. An intention is like having a plan for your highest hopes, and articulating those plans in your mind and heart. You can frame any activity with a soulful intention. This can be as simple as washing your face while repeating the affirmation "I'm beautiful and loved." Or pulling out weeds in the garden while mindfully thinking, "I'm plucking negative thoughts out of my head, one by one."

If you really want to make your life a living prayer to love, you'll discover scads of ways to connect to love daily. Doing so is inspiring, and reinforces your soul mate wish throughout your entire being.

No Ordinary Magical Toolkit

Real magic is kitchen-sink ordinary, though, as we're exploring, it's pretty magically amazing what we can do with "ordinary." After all, nothing in this world is ordinary. We encounter alchemists every day but rarely acknowledge the transformations and contributions they're making as magical beings. Miracle workers (otherwise known as mothers and cooks) transform ordinary ingredients like flour, sugar, and water into extraordinary creations, like cake or bread! Healers transform everyday herbs like chamomile into healing remedies; songwriters distill painful love experiences into inspiring love songs; faith leaders transform difficult experience into prophetic wisdom.

Your best magical tool is your ability to take a thing and turn it into something more valuable to you and others through your own form of invention (by the way, that's one definition of alchemy).

We're each limited by the special gifts and challenges of our soul and the times we live in, and priests and priestesses of ancient times only had the resources provided by their time and place. In magic, we can only use what's available to us, but the possibilities about what to do with those resources are endless.

If you're looking for herbs, plants, and stones listed here, you may not find them at your local apothecary, but not to worry. You can come up with some of your own tools by using available ingredients that magically correspond to your desired hope.

Always, whether discovering our most valuable gift in life or cooking up a spell with the right tools, necessity is the mother of all invention. Put another way, we do our magical best with what we have!

Gemstones

These stones can be worn as a ring, made into a bracelet (you can find supplies at beading or New Age stores), placed on your love altar, or used during a spell. I've provided some helpful associations to the astrological signs and planets, but it doesn't matter if a stone does not correspond to your astrological Sun or Venus sign. Choose the stone that best resonates with your heart and soul.

Amethyst: stone of divine love, promotes healthy boundaries and safety in relationship, brings spiritual insight and supports common sense. (Neptune; Pisces)

Blue Sapphire: for steadfast and enduring love, willing dutifulness, and commitment in love. (Venus and Saturn; Libra)

Goldstone/Copper: draws admiration from others and luck in love. Helps remove personal barriers and directs one toward playfulness and personal growth. (Sun; Leo)

Green Emeralds: a stone of deep fulfillment in love, promotes loyalty, sensual abundance, material security, and overall well being. (Venus; Taurus)

Malachite: assists in uncovering unconscious blocks on your spiritual path. Transforms negativity by bringing solutions, sometimes through a crisis in awareness. (Pluto; Scorpio)

Moonstone: offers new beginnings in love, amplifies your intuition and psychic power, and draws love into your life—especially when used during Moon rituals. (Moon; Cancer)

Pearl: a stone of purity, charity, and wisdom, supports the nurturing, healing power of love. (Moon; Cancer)

Peridot: clarifies by showing untrue self-perceptions and negative or stuck thinking, promotes loving-kindness, facilitates the letting go of old baggage, and inspires psychological growth. (Mercury; Virgo)

Pink Carnelian: helps with decisiveness, fosters commitment and emotional intimacy in love, and promotes healing from abusive relationship. (Venus; Gemini and Libra)

Pink Diamonds: for timeless, enduring, and romantic love. (Venus; Pisces and Libra)

Red Carnelian: for sexual healing, a libido-promoting stone that supports confidence and the ability to express and stand up for yourself. (Mars; Aries)

Rhodochrosite: a heart-healing stone that helps resolve karmic issues inhibiting you from finding love, supports emotional maturity, and breaks down emotional barriers to intimacy. (Venus; Capricorn and Gemini)

Rose Quartz: an incredibly heart-healing stone for healing past hurts, injury, or feelings of alienation; for finding unconditional love and worth in oneself and others. (Moon and Venus; Aquarius)

Ruby: for passionate, vital, and adventurous love. (Sun and Mars; Aries and Leo)

White Diamonds: for a balance of give and take in relationships, these are the stones of pure and enduring love. (Venus; Libra)

Yellow Topaz: for faith in your own abilities, grace, wisdom, and developing an ability to see possibilities and placing trust in the Universe. (Jupiter; Sagittarius)

Incense and Scents

All the way back to the Egyptians, scents and incense were used to purify temples, as healing preventatives to ward off diseases, and in religious ceremonies. The ancient Egyptians, a very magical culture, even thought scent had a special affinity with the soul. Essential oils, known as the "scents of the gods" are found totally preserved in many burial tombs—they were that important. Modern researchers are even trying to re-create the mysterious perfumes of Pharoah (Queen) Hatshepsut, a ruler from 1479 BC!

The scents of incense and oils are interchangeable. I often use incense in ritual, as the ancients did. I like to think that the smoke carries my wishes on air (the element of Spirit) to the Divine. There's the pleasure factor, too—they elevate my mood, engage my sense of smell, and create the sacred atmosphere that enhances any experience of magic making. And it's so delicious to wear a charmed scent while out on a date—I have a special Turkish Rose attar I pull out for very special occasions!

Love: african violet, cinnamon, damiana, geranium, jasmine, lavender, lilac, magnolia, melissa (lemon balm), myrrh, neroli, rose, pansy, patchouli, plumeria, rose geranium, vanilla, violet.

Removing Negativity: bay, chamomile, clove, myrrh, sage, vervain, vetiver.

Sensuality: bergamot, damiana, neroli, vetiver, ylang-ylang.

Spirituality and Purification: african violet, frankincense, lily of the valley, lotus, myrrh, rosemary, sage, sandalwood.

Success and Spiritual Protection: bergamot, clary sage, lemon, neroli, orange, saffron.

And lastly, the one incense I constantly have in my toolkit—frankincense. It's beloved as one of the most spiritually protective and supportive of all incenses and is associated with spiritual insight and spellcasting success.

Foods

Back to kitchen-sink love magic. I love food, and to some of us (in the healthiest sense) food even equals love! It's common practice at a ritual's completion to ground yourself with a bit of yummy food and drink (cakes and ale, in the old vernacular).

Food is a wonderful addition to your love magic. I once held a tantric ritual dinner in which I only served aphrodisiacs to my guests (and all aphrodisiacs are sacred to Venus). Needless to say, that dinner was a hit!

By the way, in a ritual spell or on an altar, I suggest always plying sweet Venus with fruit or chocolate. Put a little sugar in her bowl and she'll thank you for it by putting a little sugar in yours.

Apple: The fruit of original sin. Need I say more?

Banana: A versatile fruit valued for its obvious physical, ahem, resemblance. Also useful in spells to attract the male member—pair the banana with a hot-crossed bun for a sexed-up love spell.

Chocolate: A substitute for love? Maybe. Chocolate contains the same chemicals that simulate love, and may increase the desire for physical contact. A nibble of chocolate at a ritual's close brings sweetness to love magic.

Figs: According to the Greeks, figs caused spontaneous love making.

Oysters: If there were ever a twin flame or soul mate food, it's oysters. Oysters change their sex from male to female and back again, spawning claims that by eating the oyster, you will experience both the masculine and feminine sides of love.

Other aphrodisiacal foods include almonds, artichokes, asparagus, avocados, caviar, champagne and wine (of course!), fennel, garlic, mint, mussels (any shell fish belongs to the shell-loving Venus), radishes, raspberries and strawberries, truffles, and vanilla. Anything with sweetness—like honey or sugar—is also a favorite.

Herbs and Spices

Herbs are like little magical assistants for every spell. I place a few pinches of an herb at an altar or in the middle of a ritual formation of candles. I heartily recommend baking/cooking with basil and anise, taking baths with rose buds and patchouli, or drinking light, refreshing Sun tea made from the herb damiana.

Love: anise, basil, cinnamon, damiana, dandelion, fennel, hibiscus, lemon, lemon verbena, melissa (lemon balm), nutmeg, patchouli, rose, strawberry, tansy, vanilla.

Removing Negativity: fennel, flax, mistletoe, mustard, nettle, passion flower, peppermint, rosemary, sage.

Sensuality: cinnamon, coriander, dragon's blood, lemongrass, parsley, patchouli, rye, saffron, sesame, vanilla, vetiver, yerba mate.

Success and Spiritual Protection: bay leaves, clove, poppy, saffron, St. John's wort, thyme.

Flowers

Buying flowers for your home, or planting them, is a way of sweetening up your environment and is love-magical at the same time. Flowers brighten your mood, can make you feel sexy (orchids and lilies) or innocent and playful (daisies), or simply incline you to notice beauty. You may have a favorite flower that is meaningful to you, or you can choose a flower by its language, as flower giving was a popular way of communicating love and friendship during the Victorian Era. Flowers have a special affinity with love making.

Anemone: the expectation of love
Azalea: the fragility of love
Bamboo: steadfastness and luck in love
Bird of Paradise: magnificent love
Buttercup: a sharing love
Camellia: gracious love
Cosmos: peaceful love
Daisy: innocence in love
Forget-Me-Not: remembrance in love
Gardenia: joyful love
Hibiscus: delicate beauty, a gentle love
Ivy: fidelity in love
Jasmine: grace and elegance in love
Marigold: wealth in love
Pink Rose: romantic love
Red Rose: passionate love
Stargazer Lily: ambition and love
Violet: faithfulness in love

White Rose: pure love
Wisteria: steadfast love

Sacred Days

Since I'm an astrologer, I rely on divine timing to bring my wishes. You don't have to know the intricacies of astrology to empower your wish for love; there's a simple way to use the days of the week and the Moon.

Monday: Moon day, emotional cleansing and healing spells
Tuesday: Mars day, confidence spells and taking action
Wednesday: Mercury day, spells that change your mental outlook
Thursday: Jupiter day, spiritual spells inspiring generosity and faith
Friday: Venus day, spells for love, romance, sexuality, and relationships
Saturday: Saturn day, spells for emotional sobriety, clarity, endings
Sunday: Sun day, spells for decisive energy, success, and well-being

Friday is the day of Freya, who was the Norse version of Venus. Ever notice how this is the day of the week when everyone wants to take it easy or cut out early, and can barely stay focused on work in anticipation of the weekend? That's the influence of lazy, pleasure-loving Venus! So whether you're building a love altar or performing a love ritual, choose romantic Friday to amplify Venus energies.

Moon Watching

Also consider the Moon's cycle. The Moon has long been the planet of romance, bringing lovers together (moonlit walks come to mind) and sometimes driving hearts to mad acts of passion. Shakespeare knew this when Juliet said, "O, swear not by the moon, the fickle moon, the inconstant moon, that monthly changes in her circle orb, lest that thy love prove likewise variable." Shakespeare rightly named the Moon as a powerful, variable energy in our lives.

The Moon is constantly changing. The intense pull of gravity between Moon and Earth and its observed effect allows us to use the Moon's cycle to amplify or "grow" our love wish. When the feminine (Moon) and the masculine (Sun) join—

at a New Moon—it's a particularly fertile and creative time for planting soul mate love seeds.

Those days when the Moon is in your Sun sign, a transitory "New Moon" is formed in your astrological birth chart. These days are also especially powerful magic-making days for you. Since the Moon visits every sign over the course of twenty-eight days, your "New Moon" happens approximately once a month. Consult your favorite astrological calendar or date book for the current Moon sign and phase.

The Moon's waxing cycle, from New to Full, is especially effective for bringing any form of increase and fortune, including love, to fruition. The Full Moon is famed as being one of the most romantic times. The waning cycle can serve our purposes, too. The waning cycle, or when the Moon decreases in light, from Full to New Moon, is wicked good for eliminating old energy in preparation for new developments.

The Sun and Moon are cosmic lovers, each possessing what the other needs, as one never moves without affecting the other. The feminine Moon presides over our heart and soul, while the masculine Sun presides over the ego, the self, and its glorious prizes of achievement and recognition.

Both dance through the cosmos together, yet our world clearly favors the Sun over the Moon. We basically "go, go, go" all the time trying to accomplish . . . what, exactly? We scrape for replenishing downtime, struggle with honoring the expression of our feelings, and all but neglect taking the time to listen to our heart. It's a solar world we live in, and one revolving around accomplishment, because that's the way the Sun rolls.

The tragic result is that our lunar, or heart, nature has become severely depleted, undernourished and often all but ignored. That really is a tragedy because our soul relies on attentive self-care to thrive. To know what we really want, we need to make the time to listen to our heart. If we're caught up in the Sun's world, we forget to ask, "What do I really need in this moment?" (And then we don't listen for the answer, either.) We are all but addicted to accomplishment and achievement. We may have all but stopped listening to what our heart wants, yet we wonder why we're not achieving our heart's desires. And we wonder why we're out of balance!

K.I.S.S.

A DIVINE TIME

When is the best time to cast a love spell? Look in an astrology date book or calendar for waxing Moon days (New to Full) when the Moon is in your Venus sign. For extra powerful love mojo, look for a lunation occurring in your Venus sign. For example, if your Venus is in Libra, you can count on a New Moon in Libra every year between September 21 and October 22; likewise when the Sun is in Aries, March 20–April 19, there will be a Full Moon in Libra. You can look forward to delicious Venus activity described by the style of your particular sign during these lunations. For those with advanced astrology knowledge, look for a lunation cycle that spans your 5th/11th or 1st/7th houses. The houses represent areas of life: the 5th/11th is the axis of true love and dreams come true, the 1st/7th is the axis of selfhood and partnership (to figure out what signs fall in your special love houses, consult an online chart service like astro.com, or your favorite astrologer). These special love lunations can literally light up your life!

Here are some symptoms of being out of sync with La Luna, your soul:

- feeling overworked, overly tired, and easily stressed or weepy
- placing too much attention on external, material reality, at the cost of happiness
- feeling too anxious or fearful over losing ground with goals and responsibilities to make time for your spiritual or soul needs
- not responding to a persistent intuition or nagging feeling
- struggling to keep going, but refusing take a day off to do a nourishing activity

Any or all of these can spell trouble for soulfulness, and thus for our search for the soul mate. We can remedy this by remembering the Moon. We can refill our soul, similar to the way La Luna refills herself with the energy from the Sun, by dedicating times for both action and reflection. Downtime, self-care, connecting to female figures in our life, and healing or reflective activities all feed the soul. Moon watching is an easy way to re-establish your connection to the organic and natural rhythm of change in your own being, for, just like the Moon, we are constantly shifting and changing, with new awarenesses coming to light and old patterns fading away. The more we cooperate with nature's cycles as dictated by the stars and planets, the likelier we are to be in alignment with our soul's wish and the more peaceful we'll be.

Here's a little primer on Moon watching for both emotional health and your ritual spellwork.

The **New Moon** is a changing time of both endings and new beginnings. We may bring something to an end that has been long in coming; we may sense a new beginning but have no strategy for carrying it out. Often we're flying blind here, with the Moon being basically invisible in the sky. The key to using the New Moon is knowing that it's a seeding time, a time when we can conceive a dream and nourish it to realization. We will have to be patient from conception to fruition though, sometimes waiting until the next Moon, or until many Moons have passed, since every new seed will have a different gestation period and life span. Plant an intention at the New Moon and it will grow.

The Quarter Moons, equidistant between the New and Full Moons, are times of great activity and inner prompting. During the **First Quarter Moon**, the week after the New Moon, you might find yourself getting antsy and wanting to take action. This active Moon phase feels most productive when we take a new step or two toward a goal. We generally feel gratified when we do so and dissatisfied when we don't. The Moon is still growing, so it's a good time for intentional spellcasting.

The **Full Moon** often brings emotions to a head. Some Full Moon waters are emotionally choppy and unpredictable; at other times, the energies of excitement or romance predominate. The exact emotional weather depends on the sign the Moon occupies and the other planets influencing the Moon, but something is definitely in the air! This is a good time for listening to others, responding to crisis, and cultivating more awareness. Rituals and spells performed at the Full Moon will illuminate your awareness on a heart matter.

During the **Last Quarter Moon**, the week after the Full Moon, we're prone to attitude shifts and changes in our perceptions. If we're faced with a dilemma or mental hurdle during the last quarter cycle, the most productive response is to adjust our internal attitude. In this phase, a problem may not be an actual problem—it's a way of being that we need to give up, and when we shift our outlook, the so-called problem also shifts. Rituals done now help us turn over a new leaf.

The **Balsamic Moon**, the few days before a New Moon, is a special time for finishing up business of a spiritual, emotional, or psychological nature. We may be at loose ends, sleepy, feel anxious, or be in a daze. A common physical symptom during this phase is fatigue, which comes from the French *fatiguer*, "to tire." Not conducive to starting new projects, the Balsamic Moon is appropriate for dreaming, meditating, and taking it easy. This Moon nourishes us when we surrender to healing activities and gentle release. Release and ending spells and rituals work great now.

The Moon's forte is restoring equilibrium. She illuminates whether the next step will be action, awareness, mental adjustment, or rest and release. By knowing that emotions and awareness are high at Full Moons, for instance, we can be mindful and not overreact, for this too shall pass. From the New to Full Moon, she supports the steps we take toward our heart's desire—like growing soul mate wishes—while Full to New Moon periods are fabulous for self-improvement and work of a spiritual nature.

A Divine Conclusion

"But how will I know who my soul mate is?"
    "By taking risks," she said to Brida. "By risking failure,
disappointment, disillusion, but never ceasing in your search for
Love. As long as you keep looking, you will triumph in the end."
                                                —Paulo Coelho, *Brida*

I'm in a train station in Geneva, Switzerland, with my husband. I'm preparing to settle in on a journey to a small Swiss town to visit a long lost but, through a series of synchronicities, recently reconnected friend I haven't seen in twenty years. On the ride there, I will write the conclusion to this book, as my publisher has requested. Yesterday I ignored the small voice of intuition to check out the magazine stand while waiting for the train. Today I won't do the same. I walk over to the "English Books" section, see the book *Brida*, turn it over, and read the above quote. I instantly know I'm meant to share it with you.

Soul mate love finds us exactly like this—through a series of synchronicities, which are the outward result of following our own inner promptings. When we get curious about what we feel, see, desire, and connect with, we recognize that these are calls of the soul and that our response answers it. The choice to seek out and follow Mystery aligns us with what the rest of the world calls magic, and a smaller number of us might recognize as the *Anima Mundi*, the World Soul.

For me, this grand love experiment was about stepping into the unknown, leaving behind the "rules" of the dating world. Abandoning everything I'd been told about finding love, this love experiment rocked my world. I once thought love was designed for those I call the BPs—beautiful people with no problems; now I know love is a spiritual journey. Love isn't just for people whose parents had a perfect relationship. Love makes us normal people, replete with problems and personal disasters, beautiful and perfect. All we have to do is learn how to tap into the soul of love. And since no one taught me how to do this, I figured you may need help, too, which is why I wrote this book—to share what I've learned with you.

Now that we've reached the end of our journey together, I've told you how I came to find magic, but I haven't yet told you exactly how I met my soul mate. It's high time I did just that! Every time I've told this story to others, I've felt that silent exchange of awe in the air (the sign of a soul mate meeting). Yet the reason I want to tell you the story is because it so beautifully illustrates the mysterious ways of love. We rarely realize that our life's work—of waking up to who we are, healing our wounds, dropping our illusions, and loving ourself—is preparation for meeting our soul mate. Until it undeniably is.

The events leading up to my soul mate meeting probably began in my late twenties, when I made the decision to leave a high-paying job I didn't like to become a nurse. It quickly became apparent that nursing wasn't the profession for me. However, it did lead me to accept an administrative position at a medical school, where I eventually met John.

John was first introduced as my boss. This placed a professional barrier between us, along with another barrier: I had been "warned" about him by a co-worker whose friend he once dated. Apparently, things didn't go so smoothly. So when I began working for him, I insisted on rigid boundaries and professionalism of the highest order, as any young woman warned about a single man might. I vowed to myself that I wouldn't be harassed by unruly behavior. On several occasions, I even recall telling him the expectations for the tasks he had assigned to me were unrealistic (in his version he says, "She told me to talk to the hand"). But always he listened respectfully, taking my requests seriously.

We worked together for a year before we started dating. This usually prompts the question "But, weren't you attracted to each other before then?" I'd basically all but turned off my second chakra, the energy center that "wakes up" when sexual chemistry is near. In fact, sexual chemistry had turned out to be an overrated, dismal failure for me, never yielding a soulful connection. Over and over again, when second chakra chemistry bathed everything in the liquid light of sex, it became impossible for me to get to know anyone, or for them to get to know me. I naturally concluded that strong sexual chemistry equalled a total loss of ground with soulful love, for how would they ever know the "real" me if my energy circuits were being hijacked by my second chakra? Turning off my second chakra turned out to be a very wise move, as John and I got to know one another as individuals, outside the cloud of sexual attraction.

John and I worked together for some time before we crossed that professional line. And when we did, he was so honorable and dignified, it was as if my knight in shining armor had arrived. John is a respectful Capricorn rising, and he went through all the proper channels of authority to win my hand. He also was prepared for all eventualities, like the possibility that I would view his interest as sexual harrassment. Considering I had expressed no interest myself, this was entirely plausible.

Two months before getting up his nerve to ask me out, John first asked my supervisor (who, although there were no rules against office dating, strongly advised against it), his best friend (who stayed neutral on the matter), his therapist (who provided him with a supportive script), and our workplace's agency of sexual harassment and equity.

Apparently I proved irresistible!

After all this, he invited himself on my noon-time walk, where he asked the question I'll never forget: "Do you think the line between the professional and personal is blurring between us?" He reports that I visibly gulped, saying nothing. He had stopped me in my tracks.

I examined this declaration dubiously. It was risky. I'd dated in the workplace before and the end result was always painful. Worse, John was in the power position and I was a lowly administrative assistant. If things went badly, he would be in the power seat and I could ostensibly lose my job.

Well, he'd thought of that. He had a conversation with the sexual harassment department, who would provide advocacy for both of us. If we decided to date, one of us could transfer to another department. (He then honorably volunteered himself. Good move.) He said he wanted to make sure I felt safe to explore our connection. Then, he asked me if I wanted to go out just once—as an experiment.

Experiment, indeed! No one had ever put such effort into asking me out on a date, and this man had done months of legwork! The way he approached me showed great character and integrity, qualities I'd never been shown by a romantic interest before. Was that enough, though? I had blocked all my second chakra, kundalini sexual energy from intruding on this connection, and therefore had no sense of our sexual chemistry. Alas, influenced by the wise counsel of girlfriends and the nobility of his request, I gave in. I agreed to go out on a date.

Do I really need to tell you that our chemistry was off the hook?!

He first asked to hold my hand from across the dinner table. I told him I wasn't ready for that level of intimacy, but later that night, after dancing and dinner and our first kiss, my soul spoke when, to my surprise, a voice in my head began repeating three words over and over: "I love you, I love you, I love you." That voice never stopped.

There was so much magic in our meeting. A series of inner promptings and decisions later revealed as "coincidences" leading us to one another. The nature of our meeting met all the criteria for the soul mate: compelling connection, familiarity, comfort, synchronicity, excitement, joy, and love. The timing was even divine. He had been on his own soul mate journey to me, having spent the last two years working on his own personal and spiritual growth. As I prepared to receive him, my soul mate had been getting ready to receive me.

Once we came together, our story became thoroughly steeped in soulfulness— with healing and restoration. I had developed a painful muscle syndrome, fibromyalgia, and by supporting me in a way no person had ever done before, John healed what I could not heal for myself. My soul mate gave me a piece of my essence back.

The final thought I want to leave you with is something I've said before, but it's worth repeating: you already have everything you need inside you.

You don't need magic to find a soul mate, though it helps. You don't need guidance, though that helps, too. You don't need to change anything about yourself, only keep growing, healing, and learning. Soul mate love relies only on your self-knowing. To paraphrase writer Paulo Coelho, in the search for the soul mate, you will risk failure, you will have your illusions stripped, and you will be disappointed. But in the end, because you never gave up believing in yourself and in love, your soul mate . . . will find you.

Companion Cookbook of Soul Mate Spells

The Commonsense Sutra

OMG, what was she thinking? Maybe we've said that about a friend who has a habit of bringing home couch-surfing jobless boyfriends who hang out and hang on like stray puppies. Or maybe it's you who can't decipher the writing on the wall—your new guy is giving you mixed signals, one day hot and heavy, the next he's gone. You like him, but he doesn't instill confidence in you . . . you're just not sure about him.

And years later you'll wonder, "'Why did I waste so much time on that guy?"

We sometimes temporarily lose our head to love and need an objective friend to administer that missing dose of common sense. Sanity is at arm's reach thanks to the god of reason, Saturn, from whom this sutra was inspired. Saturn is the planet of reality checks, among other things. Incidentally, he's also the planet of fathers and grown-ups (so if you suddenly find yourself sizing up dates by the very respectable standards expressed by dear old dad, you'll know why).

Because it's a sutra[1] of dedication, this spell asks for your dedication in return. To receive the honorable qualities of respect, commitment, honor, honesty, responsibility, and integrity from others, you must pledge to do that for yourself. Saturn knows it's better to be alone than to be mistreated and miserable, so be prepared to stand firm as circumstances shift in your love life—even at the cost of a relationship that no longer serves you.

That loneliness will be temporary. When we make the choice to stay in integrity, we eventually attract people who treat us by our own best standards. (But if you've been habitually dating people who don't respect you, be patient. You may have to prove to the Universe that you have it in you!) The point is, when we pledge to do right by our own self and then do it, others are obligated to do the same. It's a law of attraction; unlike a boyfriend who is all promises and no action, you can count on it!

USE IT WHEN: They're not showing you (a) Respect: they're consistently inconsistent about showing up on time or meeting obligations that matter to you; (b) Integrity: they're really good at BSing around about the important stuff, which makes it hard for you to identify what it is they stand for; (c) Responsibility: when push comes to shove, you're just not sure you could count on them. They may simply not have the ability (*Responsibility* literally means "the ability to respond"); (d) Commitment: you're offering them commitment and devotion, and they're not offering you the same.

SAY IT WHEN: You're done with child's play and ready for a grown-up relationship.

YOU CAN CARRY IT WITH YOU: In your wallet or in your car, written on a index card.

THE SUTRA (TO BE SAID 3 X): I value my time, know my self-worth, and demonstrate responsibility and dedication to the things and people that matter in my life. I attract the same loving devotion from others. I AM ready to accept a love that honors, cherishes, and respects me.

WARNING: after practicing this spell, you may start developing a penchant for mature relationships and unusual levels of personal accountability!

---

1 Sutras are Indian teaching aphorisms that simplify the teachings of more complicated ancient texts. *Sutra* means "to sew or tie things together."

Go Date Yourself Spell

This one's simple, but how often we forget! Stuck in a nine-to-five job and eternally in our routine, we may pine to escape from the doldrums. Sometimes the only way to kick up our fun quota a few notches is to bravely and courageously take ourself on a date. I've noticed that guys do this much better than gals—they hang out with friends, watch the game, and schedule social activities that provide a consistent stream of fun. And here's another thing I noticed: people who are having fun are more attract-ive. Since waiting around for someone else to have fun makes you about as attractive as a wet blanket, go date yourself! Do something you really love. Regularly!

You will need:

- A date-worthy outfit: 'cause face it, when you look good, you increase your odds of having fun.

- A destination: anywhere you love to go. The farmers' market, a movie, a nice dinner at a restaurant you love. Don't be self-conscious about dining alone, consider it to be indulgent and self-confident (this is a good way for getting over your single-girl shame).

- A play date: are you busy Friday night?

Before you leave home: Repeat this affirmation three times:

I take care of myself by making a commitment to having fun on a regular basis. This makes me an attract-ive being!

Glamour Spell

People who have glamour are easy to spot. And although their powers of enchantment are hard to define exactly, their glamour is recognizable by the way they attract worshippers as though they're under a hypnotic spell. Maybe it *is* a spell! Glamour goes far deeper than superficial beauty; in the ancient art of bewitchery, the ability to "glamour"—to possess powers of enchantment—is a supernatural and magical ability.

Marilyn Monroe had the signature planet of glamour, Neptune, prominent in her birth chart. But have you ever seen how ordinary Norma Jean Baker once looked? Actors and actresses, with a few handy props, can morph so completely that when we see them off-screen they can pass unnoticed. If you've ever seen a celebrity in real life and noticed how small and normal they appear in sweats, walking down Santa Monica Boulevard with groceries and kids in tow, you certainly catch my drift. However much money, makeup, and great stylists can facilitate glamour, consider that the power to enchant, bewitch, or seduce just might be a magical mindset.

Some people have an innate ability to be glamourous. Others work at developing it. If you're magically intent on playing with your own ability to enchant, this spell is for you!

You will need: An alter ego. Draw on your most elaborate fantasies and imagination for this, because that image you've held since childhood, your secret dream, your fantasy image, is the actual source of your enchantment.

What to wear: Wear exactly what your fantasy image would wear! Jackie O sunglasses, Grace Kelly scarves, Kim Novak pencil skirts, seamed black stockings . . . the sky's the limit. In other words, let the spirit of fashion and glamorous women move you to create your own glamour look.

Mood music: Music takes us beyond our ego by connecting us to the universal power of emotions, so as you get ready to glamour, choose music that makes you feel transcendently beautiful. The success of glamour depends on how good you are at conjuring up an altered, fantasy state.

INCENSE: Frankincense, for spiritual protection and to promote an altered, ecstatic state.

DESTINATION: A simple trip to the grocery store will do, or a drive down the strip with the top down. Seriously, the destination need not be elaborate; the task is simply to pay attention to see who's picking up on what you're putting down. In other words, if you're properly glamouring, you will get seriously noticed.

While you're getting ready, repeat this incantation three times:

> *I am an enchantress of the highest order,*
> *Calling on the goddesses who dwell at the border.*
> *I offer this body as a vessel for the glamour of the ages.*
> *I receive the powers of enchantment and superficial illusion,*
> *Knowing I will be seen for my deeper beauty within.*

Glamouring, although fun, is a power not to be messed with. This spell is designed to help you flex your confidence muscles by getting noticed and to ramp up your attract-ive powers. Yes, glamour can be only superficial, but with intention, glamouring can show you that you are way more attractive-ly powerful than you think. Oh, and that last bit in the spell, about being seen for who you really are, is a necessary precaution. If you attract a man while doing the glamour spell, this will ensure that while he's intrigued by what you're giving off, he'll see the real you, too.

And on that note—glamour away!

Conjure Up Your Soul Mate Ritual

You don't have to follow my ritual to a T—the Universe loves individuality, and your creativity truly makes the Universe giggle! Use these basic ritual elements as a skeleton outline on which to base your own version of this ritual spell.

Give yourself a couple days to begin assembling your magical materials. If you're a last-minute person, you don't want to feel frenzied or rushed, or forget something necessary for your spell.

Choose your day carefully (refer to Sacred Days on p. 235). Look for a Friday between the New and Full Moons, the Moon in your Sun sign, or, most excellent, all three!

DURING THE RITUAL:

- Make sure you won't be interrupted. Turn off all phones. Put the dog or cat outside. Buy your roommate a ticket to the movies.

- You might enjoy soft, spiritual music (no words) playing in the background, but only if it enhances the process for you.

- If you can, do your ritual at night under moonlight, or within eye gaze of the Moon. Actual moonlight makes this spell more potent.

YOU WILL NEED:

- a pink candle, a red candle, and a white candle

- a sweet-smelling stick of incense of your choice (jasmine, rose, apple blossom, and patchouli are all love scents)

- a thorny red rose

- a gemstone of your choice, if you wish: emeralds, diamonds, rose quartz, rhodochrosite, etc.; these can be loose stones, or to ramp up this spell, use a piece of jewelry that you will wear for seven days following the spell

- a pen and a piece of quality stationery paper

- a mirror, full-length if possible

- a chalice with water, wine, or juice

THE SPELL: Make your space sacred by drawing a circle (also known as a formation) with chalk, tarot cards, rose petals, or shiny decorative garden stones at your ritual spot. Arrange all your magical tools in the center of the circle in a way that makes you happy. Now step outside the space. You will step into this space once the spell officially begins.

Take a deep breath and put the thoughts of the day aside. Now call on your higher self to enter the circle with you, and step into it.

First, call in the elements for balanced love. Walk clockwise beginning at the east, pausing at each direction:

(Facing west) I call in water, for soulful love.
(Facing east) I call in air, for wisdom in love.
(Facing south) I call in fire, for passionate love.
(Facing north) I call in earth, for grounded love.

Light the incense and the candles. Sit down in the center and calmly sit with your breath, visualizing the love you want. When you're ready and clear, look into the mirror and recite this spell (or you can make up your own):

Venus, Isis, Astarte, Ishtar, Mary all. Loving goddesses who embody love,
compassion, and grace, now hear my heartfelt request:

I am a vibrant, enchanting, and attract-ive being
Whole, complete, and perfect just as I am!
With this spell, I deeply commit to loving myself as I am
And make my readiness for the appearance of my true love known

I have love to give, and love to receive
Art to create, a life together to build and to share
My beloved is arriving, my equal in life, my soul mate
Placing my faith in this love, I completely open to receive my beloved

I feel it inside, my heart's fulfillment already begun
This heart prayer, a kiss, carried on the winds of love blown
Closer to me, and closer, now arriving
My soul mate is here.

Now take your pen and paper and write down the attributes of your soul mate. This can be a new list, an extension of what you wrote in another love spell. You might try:

My soul mate makes me feel attractive and beautiful by telling me so.

My soul mate honors my thoughts and opinions.

My soul mate expresses his love for me in spontaneous ways.

My soul mate is physically demonstrative and passionate.

My soul mate cherishes my essence.

Once you feel your list is complete, prick your finger with the thorny rose, drawing a little blood. There will be times when your soul mate's love feels prickly; they will get under your skin. Your blood is the blood of your heart, and this symbolizes your willingness to accept all facets of love. Fold your letter and seal it with a drop of wax mixed with your blood. Now release your letter.

RECITE:

> *True love comes to me in divine timing, not my own. I recognize that the people who are about to come into my life are leading me to my soul mate. I patiently take the time to explore their mystery. If they are not meant for me, I honor their mystery by releasing them to their highest good and moving forward with renewed hope and renewed resolve. These people are a necessary step for me to find the person I truly love. I know my soul mate comes to me in perfect timing. And so it is.*

Take a sip from your chalice to drink your intention into your body, blow out the candles, and step outside of the formation. Place your soul mate letter on your love altar or in a special box, and re-enter your love life with a sense of positive expectancy—your soul mate is coming!

SUPERCHARGE YOUR WISH: If you used a special piece of jewelry in your spell, wear it for the next seven days. Also, you can light your candles every evening for seven nights while meditating on your wish for love. However, you don't need to do any of these if they prevent you from releasing your wish.

Fall in Love with Yourself Spell

While you're waiting to fall in love with someone else, try falling in love with yourself. One of the easiest ways to do this is to take an interest in your interests.

How to do it: Take an active interest in what turns you on, just as your dream lover would do!

Preparing a new food can turn you on, but so can listening to music or making your own music. The art of creating a rarified and fantastic aesthetic is the "art of romance," and just like you, your aesthetic (or romantic) side craves simple pleasures and intelligent stimulation. What romances you? That simple question evokes the constant process of self-discovery, and it's the little things that make the most difference.

More suggestions:

Explore new scents, sights, and smells. A friend of mine discovered that burning jasmine incense after she gets home from work transforms a workday frame of mind into an enchanted evening full of creative possibilities.

Research your pleasure principle. A triple Scorpio client of mine (Sun, Moon, and Venus all in Scorpio) was intrigued by the idea of exploring how she could use her super-charged sexual libido in non-sexual ways. I talked to her about the myths of the sexual priestesses who, through focusing their sexual energy, used it as a form of service to the Divine. This opened up a wealth of creative possibilities for her. There's nothing better than deepening your appreciation for a pleasure you already enjoy.

Sex it up a notch. Speaking of sexy, maybe you've always wanted to dress sexy, but your personality is more modest than your everyday self-expression allows. Sexuality taps the power of desire in a way that nothing else can; just look at the way advertising uses women's bodies to generate desire! If you're feeling out of touch with your sexuality or blasé about your passions, try experimenting with what makes you feel sexy.

Just follow your instincts. When I felt my soul being sucked away from working as a cog in the corporate wheel, I'd come home after a particularly grueling day, put on some hot pants and sexy music, like "Ava Adore" by the Smashing Pumpkins, and dance in front of the mirror. That act dropped my dark mood of the day, reclaimed my sexy side, and made me remember how much I loved dancing (dancing is an ancient form of Goddess worship, and dance has been used magically to raise feminine and procreative energies—and love).

Falling in love with yourself is about attending to those wants and wishes floating around in your head. Rock climb, pole dance, take language lessons, or travel to Rome . . . just get to it! No matter your situation—a demanding job or family, too much work, too little money—there's no excuse good enough for not reaching out and grabbing happiness. You can take a class after work or make a collage/altar for the trip you'd like to take. You can write down the date on your calendar when you will meet your dream. You can take one micro-step toward a fun goal—a micro-step is one that takes less than five minutes, e.g., signing up for a language class or posting an advertisement that you're looking for a salsa partner at a dance studio.

What creative act would wake you up and help you fall in love with yourself all over again? If you're using magical thinking, nothing is too big or too impossible. These are the "little things" that keep love energies circulating around you like invisible cupids, angels, and faeries. When you find yourself bogged down with the excuses, remember, the only one who pays the price for not reaching for the stars is you. Not your employer, not your family, not anyone else.

Meditate on Your Magnetism Spell

When we're in touch with our innate magnetism, we're also in touch with the temptress archetype within, Venus. Venus' joyful, playful receptivity equates to an openness to what others have to offer.

We've also explored that attract-iveness isn't how you look or what jeans you're wearing it's a state of mind. By being receptive and positively expectant, focusing on what holds joy for you and holding a mental picture for love in your mind and heart, we achieve a level of mental magnetism.

There's a physical-spiritual-sexual aspect, too. Attraction is a sexual and sensual experience, and our sensuality is connected to how present we are in our body and senses. The sexual vibes that we do or do not send out and how we share our sexual energy with others (easily and open or closed and controlled) also influences our attract-ability. We can tune in to our magnetism and amplify our signals by meditating.

BEFORE YOU BEGIN: Explore your Venus sign (Secret No. 4). Identify which archetype you most resonate with. For example, as a Venus in Aries, you may identify with the magnetism of a desert rose.

HOW TO DO IT: Allow yourself the space and time to meditate on that mental image. Getting comfortable will help you get in the sensual mood Venus requires to reveal her secrets: you might play soft music, wear a favorite essential oil, or surround yourself with warmth and light.

Invite your archetype image into your body and into your second chakra, located behind your kidneys. Allow the image to get into your body; really open yourself to resonating with the entire experience of that image. You may feel your sexual center tingle in excitement—feel the power here!

Once you have contacted the image and feel the power center, ask yourself:

- Does she/Do I feel safe to come out and play? If not, why?

- Does she/Do I feel validated and empowered?

- Does my archetype feel misunderstood? If so, why is that?

- What qualities have I underappreciated in her/myself?

- Does she/Do I feel beautiful, magnetic, and attract-ive?

- Can I see why people really like her/me?

- Is there any joy or excitement that I can offer my archetype?

Through the dialogue of awareness in your body, notice how your Venus archetype has consciously or unconsciously played a starring role in all of your relationships. This may have had implications on your self-esteem, but don't judge your archetype (or yourself!). Just allow the energy to unfold within. Let your Venus sign inform you of your magnificent magnetism, and of her ways. Thank your Venus archetype for sharing when you feel complete.

Write down your insights in your journal so you can better integrate them into your being. Carry your Venus insights with you into your life, in a new sensually-conscious and empowered way.

Command Your Spirit Back Spell

Power is your birthright. And your magical work is far more effective with your power strong and intact. However, many of us women feel our power being chipped away in minor or major ways every day. I used to work for a woman who drove me crazy with her complaining about how she hated her job—and she was my boss! I knew she was a reflection of my feelings of being creatively stifled and underutilized in my own work, but here I was still stuck in this job, at least until I could figure out what to do next, listening to her litany of complaints.

I knew this relationship was draining my power because every time she stopped by my desk, and I had to listen to her go on and on, it wasn't only uncomfortable and negative, it was just taking too much juice out of me. I would come home exhausted and negative myself. So after trying to look busy or pull a disappearing act when she came on the scene (didn't work), I decided to put it into spirit. What she was showing me was that I needed to perform some psychic surgery on myself.

UNDERSTAND THE SECRET LANGUAGE OF POWER: The secret language of power is this: it's invisible and always for you, not against you. That's both the good news and the great news. It's good news because someone only has power over you when you're unconsciously under their spell. They may truly want something from you and you may never fully understand what that is, but you don't have to understand their trip. The great news is that with conscious awareness of your body and a little inner magical work, you can render negative, spirit-sucking people powerless over you.

WHO TO DO IT ON: Energy vampires.

WHEN TO DO IT: When you feel your power being drained. It will only take about 30 seconds.

OBSERVE YOUR BODY: Practice observing yourself when a person is actively pushing your buttons—notice where your energy (power) is going. Do you feel tightening around your chest or your throat? Is your face tight, your head aching? Are you feeling angry, irritated, annoyed, or trapped? Notice the questions that arise as you start fully feeling your body. One of them might be, "Why is this person causing me to lose power?" Or, "I wonder what they are trying to accomplish by doing this?" Don't try to do anything about it—just watch.

HOW TO DO IT: Get in touch with those prickly feelings. Now you're ready to call your power back to you.

In the body, power can be seen as invisible cords of light energy that, once recognized, you can command. Imagine these energy cords of light emanating from your solar plexus and root chakra (those areas around your belly and kidneys). Sense their electrical voltage. As you sense them, imagine these cords going into this other person. Or, if you want to really get clear on where you're power is going, imagine the cords running to all the people in your life, from your best friend to your neighbor to your boss.

Feel the charge you both receive and give in relationship. How much are you giving? How many amps is each person taking/receiving from you? As you sense which relationships feel energetically balanced and which are imbalanced, gather the cords of energy in your body and silently command:

> *In the midst of my experience with this person, I command my spirit*
> *back to me. My spirit is eternal. It is unbound by any physical,*
> *emotional, or mental circumstances. Spirit, return to me now!*

Imagine those power cords dimming, returning energy to your core. Since you've shifted your energy, your feelings of disempowerment around this person will shift, too. This is transcendence, real power. Power on!

Venus Healing Spell

Guess what? The best way to get out of a relationship while keeping what's rightfully yours is to bless the other person. Antagonistic energy truly accomplishes nothing in life.

I used this spell to settle a score with someone I was receiving negative energy from but still needed to maintain right relations with, because they owed me money. I needed this money, as it was a sizable sum, but I also didn't want to nurse a grudge. Attachment and self-righteousness would only push the money away and prolong the relationship, so I created a nursery rhyme spell. You can use this with any person you need to receive healing from. I like the light, singsongy feel of this spell. (And yes, the money eventually came!)

> *Venus, star of morning bright*
> *Star of deepest winter's night*
> *Leave the bondage of heart behind*
> *Heal this body, soul, and mind*
> *Return to me what is rightfully mine*
>
> *Compassionate and generous, I manifest the highest in you*
> *Embodying grace in everything I say and do*
> *In all my relations virtuous, loving, and true*
>
> *I secure these blessings with gratitude.*

Magical Bath

I sometimes give this Bath of Aphrodite Erotic Love Potion to girlfriends at bachelorette parties. Fun! I usually package it up in a small red or pink cloth pouch, the kind you get at craft or jewelry supply stores, with the below recitation typed on a piece of paper. I was flattered when, during my girlfriend Marie's wedding ceremony, I spied this satchel o' love on her wedding altar!

This spell is courtesy of Wiccan Priestess Phyllis Curott, *The Love Spell* (Gotham Books/Penguin, 2006). Used with permission.

> Water is the element of the emotions, of love and dreams. It's also the element associated with many goddesses of love such as Aphrodite, Venus, Yemaya, and Lakshmi. Bathing in a love potion is a wonderful way to make magic. And what a wonderful place to make love, with the water connecting not only your bodies but your souls.

INSTRUCTIONS: In 2 cups of water, combine 2 tbsp rose petals, 2 tbsp patchouli, 3 tbsp damiana, and 1 cinnamon stick. Boil for 20 minutes. While the mixture boils, stir it clockwise, visualizing your true love coming to you or making love with you.

Strain the herbs from the water and pour the potion into a tub of warm water. You may also add 3 drops each of musk and almond oils to the bathwater and light a single red candle carved with your name and "True Love." Get in the tub and recite the spell invoking Aphrodite, goddess of love.

> *Aphrodite from the sea*
> *Hear my call and come to me!*
> *Bless me with your radiant power*
> *And open me as passion's flower!*

Remain in the bath, dreaming of your lover's touch until you feel his/her presence approaching. Then rise from the bath and feel Aphrodite rising with you. See her in your eyes and feel her in your body.

Lose This Man: A Spell of Personal Protection

I recited these prayers casually, several times a day over a period of several weeks, to lose a man I began to recognize as off-center, a little not-quite-right. He would call me all the time, and even though I had caller ID and never picked up, I wanted those phone calls to stop. When I was just short of changing my phone number (this man was hard to shake!), this spell hastened his departure.

Choose either one of these casual affirmations, write it on a slip of paper, and carry it with you, reciting the prayer until you have it memorized. Repeat casually, for instance while you're riding the bus to work, or on your noontime walk, three to ten times a day, or as needed.

1. *You have no power in you to hurt or destroy any good thing. In the name of (God, Mary, Goddess, All That Is, Buddha, the Divine, the Creator) you are now finished. You are permanently let go from my life.*

2. *We are complete. I now place you lovingly in the hands of the (Father, Creator, Divine Mother, Universal Good). I release you to your own good, and I will follow mine. That which is for your highest good now comes to you in your own time and your own way.*

Attract Your Soul Mate Charm Bracelet

I designed these bracelets as wedding gifts for my single gal-pals in the wedding party. One of my girlfriends, Justine, took this to heart, wearing her bracelet every day until she found the man she wanted to be with. They married less than a year later. This is the note I included with the bracelets:

This charm bracelet was made in deep, delicious, juicy, romantic, passionate, healthy, committed love . . . to bring you love. Use this bracelet as prayer beads (mala) to recite wishes or prayers with as you're fingering the beads; as a bracelet to attract and perpetuate love blessings; or as a magical tool for your love altar.

The magic is always in the meaning and energy you give your special objects to draw love toward you. I can tell you that this bracelet has the positive vibration of two people very much in love, but only you can feel it and make it real. The process of magnetizing love is feminine, the principle of Venus, Aphrodite, Yemaya, and Lakshmi, and it is available to every woman.

If you've found your soul mate, wonderful! You can design love spells for the things you'd like to enhance or attract: passion, romance, deeper commitment, or keeping that in-love feeling alive forever.

The magical beads in these bracelets are rose quartz and goldstone.

Often called the "love stone," rose quartz is said to open the heart chakra to all forms of love: self-love, family love, platonic love, and romantic love. Emotionally, this gemstone is believed to bring gentleness, forgiveness, compassion, kindness, and tolerance; raise self-esteem; and remove fears, resentments, and anger. Some also say rose quartz can heal and release childhood traumas, neglect, and lack of love, in part by enhancing inner awareness. It is attributed with power to ease reconciliation with family and ease overwhelming or unreasonable guilt.

Goldstone is said to be an uplifting stone, associated with vitality and energy, which helps reduce tension. It is believed to be helpful in securing love, protection, riches, and diplomacy. It's further believed to attract positive energies. It is also flecked with copper, a metal sacred to Venus.

How to do it: Customize your soul mate wish by using a very personal combination of gemstones, as listed in No Ordinary Magical Toolkit (p. 229). For example, do you need a more playful (goldstone), light-hearted approach to love (rhodochrosite)? Perhaps you want to bring more self-confidence (red carnelian) and self-acceptance (rose quartz) into your relationships? Visit a bead or craft store for stones and bracelet-making supplies. Because I made quite a few bracelets, I used a simple elastic string with jewelry glue, but fishing wire, copper, or leather is a stronger and smarter alternative, especially if you're going to be wearing your charm bracelet every day.

Self-Esteem Charm

Once while on vacation in Hawaii, my sister told me about a friend who, although cute, single, and available, seemed to push love away. After describing this woman's personality tendency to be in control, it became clear that while she was looking for someone to love, she needed to start loving herself first.

So we visited a crystal and gemstone store and found the perfect stone for her—a rose quartz bracelet. Rose quartz melts hearts hardened by pain or grief, offering healing and unconditional love to the wearer. My sister's friend carried the stone close to her heart, in a hidden pouch, which reminded her that she was loved. Within months of wearing her everyday self-esteem charm, she attracted a fabulous guy, and they're together to this day!

Emily's Aphrodite Candle Spell

My friend Emily is a true love enchantress who attracted the love of her life using a simple ritual with a pink candle, emeralds, and sea shells. She burned this candle every night for seven nights and her true love appeared shortly afterward!

You might try finding a special pink candle and surrounding it with emeralds and sea shells. Burn the candle every night for a week and meditate on goddesses of love, including Aphrodite and Venus.

Heaven Help Me Release My Negative Emotions Spell

Negative emotions cloud the clear silver stream that connects us to our magical power, our higher self, our real truth. Sometimes we're doing the work but we just need that extra little push, some positive, pick-me-up angel help. We don't have to do it all—when we're feeling overwhelmed with life, we can solicit the heavens for help. I recited this when I started getting emotionally cloudy or discouraged to re-align myself with good and to move to the creative, positive side of the love equation. Recite it as many times as you need until you feel heaven has helped you!

> I, (your name here), am a perfect manifestation of that One Power
>   which is infinite. I reaffirm my life with positive experiences only.
> I dissolve and release every negative influence, visible and invisible,
> And replace it with positive good.
> I take full responsibility for my actions, without judging myself.
> I now redirect my life, taking full responsibility for my positive direction.
> For the Good of All, so make it be.

Mourn the Little Losses Spell

On the day I lost my favorite pink camisole at the laundromat, I was devastated. As trivial as that might sound, it was symbolically the straw that (almost) broke this camel's back. That cami was symbolic of the femininity I felt I was missing. I hadn't felt sexually attractive to a man (at least one I wanted to attract) in so, so long—and I wore my soft, nubby, lacey pink cami around the house or while gardening so I might grow in the power of pink—feminine beauty, lovability, and sexy allure. Without that cami, I felt like *Sex and the City* diva Carrie Bradshaw, when she lost her signature "Carrie" necklace while in Paris with Petrovsky—and with it her life-line to her New York identity. Like lost Carrie in Paris, I became bereft.

"Frivolous, silly, unimportant"—those were my mental judgments to my mournful and emotional reaction. But hey, who was I to judge my heart? It was *my* heart, after all. I had loved this cami because when I wandered around the house in it, it was like I was trying on my own desirability. I had asked, Am I attractive? And she answered, Infinitely! Am I sexy? Again, Oh-so! "Maybe this loss means I don't really deserve love after all," one part of me thought, while another, more sane voice told me maybe I should just let it out and cry. After all, I reasoned, I'd really been cultivating this non-attachment business lately and I thought my heart was supposed to be made of Teflon—nothing and no one will ever stick again, right? I was afraid the people and things I loved would roll right off of me. I was afraid that I was supposed to emulate some mystic saint or sexual abstinent, and I'd forever and always have to give up everything I desire. I was afraid that everything and everyone I loved and wanted in my life permanently would eventually leave me.

There it was. My heart had spoken.

Sometimes a little loss just nails us and taps our deepest fears.

So I wrote this poem, "For My Pink Cami."

> *Pieces of clothes take their leave of me.*
> *In absence of something I've grown to love, I've come undone.*
> *It's only material, cloth and thread, but the color made me feel like a Queen;*
> *the furry nub on my skin comforted my wearied spirit—the holes and*
> *tears in my soul, softly laying on the threadbare coat I wear on the inside.*

Each day, new becomes wear and tear again, the world's a giant washing
machine on spin cycle!
Taking my quarters and giving back clean, but not-quite-white whites. Eat-
ing my favorite pink camisole and the single socks of the good people of the
world.
I've spun out.
I loved it. I miss it. Take me with you.

I had uncovered the taproot of my loss. My heart was vulnerable, and it was afraid.

I don't think it's at all silly to mourn the little losses. Mourning them is an empowering, self-nurturing act. I do know that everyone's heart is vulnerable. Those day-to-day griefs that add up over time chip away at your emotional confidence if you don't honor their deeper message. An overreaction is often just your inner self screaming, "Hey, crazy lady—over here!" Making the space to honor those feelings—emotionally, ritually, and artistically—restores clarity and peace to the heart.

By the way, remember how Carrie thought her necklace was lost and then found it again in the lining of her bag (where it had been all along) at the perfect moment for her perfect epiphany: that she was meant to return to New York and Big? Well, I found my pink cami again—actually I'd never lost it in the first place. I found out that I had really had it all along.

THE SPELL: Everything your heart cares about—its wants, desires, and feelings—are sacred and important. Honor them by creating a living homage to your losses. It needn't be a somber affair, though many funerals are. Others are joyous; it all depends on what you need.

Write a poem if you're a poet. Sing if you're a songwriter. Build an altar to all the things and people you've loved and lost. Make a photo collage if you're a scrapbooker. Draw, chant, or do a death dance. You could even create fabulous floral funeral arrangements to honor those little losses.

Flowers of My Heart Spell

Once I did this very simple ritual of planting flowers to keep a particular lover in my life and the result was a mixed bag. It wasn't the spell's fault; the magic worked flawlessly. Unfortunately, he wasn't the lover I ended up wanting to spend the rest of my life with, which is a common magical user-error that can happen with any spell. You think you want to be with this person, oh, you know it's so true, but then one day, you realize it's not meant to be. It's all part of the process. I've mentioned this before—you will probably kiss a few frogs who won't turn into princes, despite your readiness and your best mugwort! However, you'll find that with every spell you do, you'll get closer to The One. I definitely can't say this spell wasn't successful, because it was. But it was also a lesson in being careful whom you wish for . . .

WHAT YOU'LL NEED:

- annual flowers because they bloom anew every year (perennials are seasonal—in other words, brief—which is fine if that's how you like your affairs!)

- all flowers have meanings, so look to a reliable source for one that works for you (or see below)

- a garden plot, pot, or hanging basket

Here are some great flowers to get your love garden growing (see p. 234 for more on magical flowers):

Red roses, of course, for true and passionate lasting love

Pink roses, for romantic love

White roses, for spiritual love

Violets, for faithfulness and constancy

Jasmine, for good luck, prosperity

Orchids, for ecstasy

Simply hold the man in your heart while planting the appropriate flowers and watch your intention bloom!

Yes, I did this spell for a very specific man (a precarious intention at best; see Payback's a Witch, p. 217). It had been years since we'd been together, and I wanted to rekindle our flame. The morning before I picked up this man from the airport, I planted pansies, a member of the violet family, while holding a desire for this man in my heart. During our visit, he said that over the years he'd never forgotten about me, having dreamed about what might've been had we stayed together. Despite a mutual attraction and affection, this was not a soul mate match. Much later I stumbled upon an alternative meaning for pansies which was "remembrance and telepathic magic." How appropriate for a past relationship that had been rekindled through long love letters and imaginative, dreamy soul confessions to each other!

As with the search for true love, there's no failure in spell-making, just feedback. This semi-success gave me the experience I needed to design this next flower spell, Growing In Love, which really worked!

Growing in Love Spell

Since I had the good fortune of having a garden while doing my love spells, I took full advantage of the opportunity to put the ultimate Miracle-Gro on my roses—love magic. Rose bushes are absolutely the favorite flower of Venus, so you'll get on her good side by planting or even enjoying cut roses. Roses symbolize constant and undying love but they also bring joy and beauty to the beholder. And planting and tending a flower is such a great way to care for, nourish, and see your wish grow.

I planted my rose bushes with a little wishful spell: that I would grow in love as they grew. As you plant, recite these words:

> *As these roses grow in strength, beauty, and health, my love will bloom in radiant wealth.*

I vividly remember the first night my soul mate and I spoke on the phone for four hours, because it was there, while talking on the phone under the full moon-light, that I noticed my intentional love magic had indeed come full bloom, too: my very first rose, an exquisite white-pink-coral beauty, was in full bloom.

Sexual Power: The Pomegranate Spell

Sex and Power. Yin and Yang. Pomegranates and Persephone. The presence of one always requires the other, right? In astrology, sex and power are esoterically joined in the sign of Scorpio for, just as pomegranates are linked with Persephone and her journey to the Underworld, we always have the choice to remain empowered throughout a difficult relationship.

If we don't feel confident and healthy in our sexuality, or if we're unwillingly bound to an unhealthy relationship through irresistible magnetism, the story of Persephone is a reminder that while we all lose our innocence, we can reclaim our power at any time. Persephone's fruit is the pomegranate—the only fruit with sexual seeds. When she ate of the sexual fruit, she sealed her fate to live with her man, Hades, six months of the year, and with her mother for the other half. Our sexuality is undeniably bound to our choice and to our personal power. By becoming conscious of our sexual power, we realize that it's sacred, and it's our choice alone as to what we wish to do with it.

This spell is about imbuing your sexuality with consciousness and personal choice, and, if need be, reclaiming your sexual power from the sexual hall of shame. We all need to renew our sexual energy periodically to tap it for a source of power. Persephone's story reminds us that relationships from hell and/or the misuses of sexual energy can offer us a very real opportunity for a more conscious and empowered relationship to our own sexuality.

When to use this spell:

- you're tired of meaningless, casual sex

- a sexual attraction is all-consuming and feels disempowering

- your sexual connection to someone has an addictive quality; it's as though there are invisible bonds keeping you from moving on when you know you should

- you want your sexual power back

You will Need: A pomegranate.

WHEN TO DO IT: The best time of the year to do this is either while the Sun is in the sign of Scorpio, approximately October 21–November 20, or during a Scorpio Moon, which happens for about two and a half days every month (consult your favorite astrological calendar or date book to find out).

THE DESCENT: Ask Persephone to be your guide, close your eyes, and allow her to guide your awareness from your head downward, down, down . . . into the wisdom and personal power of your womb, your sexual center. If you have a consuming sexual issue, a personal power concern, or a trauma, you'll feel it here. Wait silently for an insight or just sit with your concern. Noticing what you feel is enough.

THE RITUAL: Take the pomegranate and crack it open. Spoon out some seeds with your hands, letting the juice stain your fingers. Red symbolizes the blood that connects your heart to your emotions to your life force. Imagine each seed as a kernel of sexual wisdom you already have concealed inside you. As you eat each seed, one by one, imagine taking your sexual authority into your womb. If you like, you can imagine that a lover is feeding you these seeds, and you are the source of his/her desire.

THE SPELL: Affirm your desire for a healthy and empowered sexual relationship by proclaiming (or writing your own variation):

> *I have served time in relationships from hell, and I now reclaim my sexuality and personal power. With each seed I eat, I celebrate my sexual emancipation from powerless passions, loveless liaisons, and dead-end affairs!*

Now retrace the path of the pomegranate all the way back up to the crown of your head. Send a sexual shimmer of power up your first, second, and third chakras— these are at the base of your spine (your root safety and power chakra), your abdominal area (your creativity and sexuality chakra), and your solar plexus (your self-esteem chakra). Continue sending energy upward through your heart center and your throat (and self-expression) center, guiding that connection of liquid light through your third eye and to the crown of your head. Feel this shimmer from your base to your crown. Your sexual power is now connected to your higher self, and your sexuality is entering into a sacred contract with the Divine. Your spiritual aspirations for a soul mate are exciting, vibrant, sexy, and alive.

Open your eyes. Your fingers and lips are probably stained with the pomegranate juice. You are officially juicy!

The next time you're about to get sexually intimate with a partner, the body memory of doing this spell will remind you that your sexuality is a precious choice, one that inextricably binds you to the sacred in life.

Give Me Back My Mind, Body, and Soul Spells

I once made the mistake of returning to a past relationship that didn't work out the first time. I'm sure you've been there, done that, too.

I had true affection for this person, but there was a reason it didn't work the first time. He would often court me with gifts (like a true Libra). I, however, was never convinced that our relationship was meant to be and didn't respond to the gifts as he'd hoped. Unfortunately, when I treated one of his gifts a little too casually he called me mean, and that's when the relationship really fell apart.

A one-line email from him arrived out of the blue, years later, during the time I was doing my soul mate spellwork and I deeply reconsidered our breakup. Had I been wrong? Was there something here for me? Guilt pulled at my heart strings. I still liked this man, so I decided to give our relationship another go.

Over the next few months, the same old problems reappeared. When he invited me to L.A. for a weekend, he sank into a depressive funk on New Year's Eve, fell asleep early, and didn't get out of bed until a few hours before my flight left the next day. This time I really was pissed! Oh, he didn't like my anger—the same issue that separated us the first time around.

I was angry, hurt, and confused. He'd somehow wormed his way back into my heart, body, and soul. I decided extricating him from my life was essential.

Give Me Back My Mind Spell

This is a double-dipper spell because it works on two levels. I wanted to release this man, but I also wanted him to release me. The energy cords that tie us to others may be invisible, but they're super powerful.

I knew this man had created a mental picture, a fantasy, about me. Although a part of me was flattered, now I was a little disturbed by the amount of magnetism he had been sending my way. Through using his desire and imagination, just as I've suggested you do (he had Venus in Scorpio joined with the planet of divine imagination, Neptune), he had conjured me back into his life. Perhaps he was doing spellwork of his own!

I used this affirmation to successfully release myself from the mind and imagination of any person with whom my business was finished:

> *I now release and am released from those who are no longer part of the divine plan of my life, as they now release me and find their good elsewhere. I expand quickly into the divine plan of my life where all conditions are permanently perfect.*

I also chose to honor the divine meaning of this relationship in my spiritual and creative growth (after all, good did come out of it—many of my spells are a result of this relationship!). As difficult as it felt at times, I was dedicated to harboring no ill feelings or resentment. As the song goes, there's a thin line between love and hate. Resentment and anger are as powerful a form of attachment as love. Anger and ill feelings are another way of staying in connection with a person. I recited this affirmation over time and it eventually worked its magic on me:

> *You are in my life by divine appointment. You have crossed my path so that I may learn something from you, and so that I may give you my blessing. I now do this and you are released to your highest good.*

Give Me Back My Body Spell

These men, they get into our hair, our clothes, our bodies! I loved the way I felt about myself with this particular man, but only most of the time. I loved feeling desirable and lovable again, but I didn't love him. That's an important distinction to make, and sometimes we just need to spell it out for ourselves. I liked the version of me he had created, which by the way was a pretty elaborately gorgeous fantasy! Who wouldn't like that? The reality was that he never really knew the real me. We'd get to the part where I'd get real, and I felt totally obscured by the fantasy, never seen for who I was. That's when I realized how easy it is to get drawn into someone else's fantasy of you. I also realized that I could draw myself right back out of it, literally, and still keep that gorgeous creature he saw in me.

So that's what I did—I got out my canvas, pencils, charcoal, and paints. By drawing myself, I also drew him right out of the picture.

WHEN TO DO IT: When you're alone! I drew in the buff for this one, so if you have roommates, send them out for a movie night. You need to feel uninhibited, without the fear that someone else will walk in on you. Relax, let your guard down, and get into art appreciation of the self-ish sort—appreciating your own beautiful body.

YOU WILL NEED:

- newsprint drawing paper and a charcoal pencil

- a canvas and acrylic paints

- magazine photographs of aspects of artistic renderings of the female form; artsy-fashion magazines with great photographers who have an appreciation for the unusual or unconventional beauties—like *Interview Magazine* or *Rolling Stone*—are best; look for a lovely curvature of the back, perfectly pedicured feet, great chunky bed-head hair, or any other titillating element you might superimpose on your self-styled image

- a full-length mirror

- sexy tunes to get you in the mood (Paula Cole's *Greatest Hits* album comes to mind for me)

THE SPELL: Notice your womanly curves. View yourself from all angles, through your lover's eyes, noting your best and sexiest angles. Come on, every woman on Earth has 'em! Focus on one angle or body part that is erotic for you and build your drawing around that. Try sitting with your back to the mirror, kneeling to see how gorgeous your hourglass figure looks from behind. It's one of our most flattering angles!

Don't worry if you don't consider yourself an artist—you don't have to do a full portrait, just a piece. You can always use the great hair or other visual perfection from the pictures as your muse. You can even use tracing paper. You can collage a whole image of yourself if you'd like, but do include your own favorite feature in order to make it personal.

The whole point of this exercise is to own your beautiful assets. And because we often only see those by looking through the eyes of love, as you do this, allow the essence of how this man made you feel to be the guiding force at work. Caress the canvas or paper with the touch of a lover.

When you're done, step back and appreciate your work. See that beautiful creature? That's you, girl! That beautiful body belongs to you and no one else!

Give Me Back My Soul Spell

This is a holistic balancing spell for those times when we feel emptied of soul, emotionless, or just plain stuck. When we feel out of balance, stuck in an emotional rut, this spell draws down the healing, intuitive side of the Moon by making Moon water. Fun, yes, but also scientific. Water represents our emotions, the blood of life, and composes around 70 percent of our bodily fluids. We are water-babies.

While balancing and purifying our soul, Moon water heightens intuition and enhances spiritual seeing. Moon bathing (bathing under moonlight) can clear the body. Moon water is also good for clearing the negative or stuck energy of ritual objects, jewelry, or stones. I like to give my jewelry a cleansing moonlit bath by washing and laying them on a windowsill, which restores their luminescence and glow.

You will need:

- a Full Moon

- a chalice filled with your favorite clean water

Place the glass of water in a moonlit window overnight so the Moon infuses the water with her magical healing rays. Drink the cup of water the next night under the moonlight, chanting three times:

As I drink this water bright, my soul is restored by moonlight.
Purifying my past pain and sorrows, making for brighter tomorrows.
My heart no longer wanders alone, as my soul is called back home.

Prepare to receive a Moon missive from your soul!

Venus Alchemy Spell

This spell was inspired by Alanis Morissette's song *So Unsexy*. She's a Gemini Sun sign, born under the sign of the Twins, so she's good at synthesizing opposites. Alchemy, the art of unifying the opposites within the self, plays a role in all healing and is integral to becoming a whole person.

You will need:

- a white candle and a black candle (white for cleansing and spirituality; black for absorbing negativity)

- incense

- a mirror

- mood music; put on some tunes that reflect a part of you that is in conflict with another part; since she's got a Twin in her, I recommend any Alanis Morissette song, like *So Unsexy, Hand In My Pocket, Ironic,* or *You Oughta Know*

The ritual: Light your candles and incense and go deep into your feelings. Face yourself in the mirror and remember a time you felt ashamed, humiliated, angry, or just plain ugly. Maybe you felt wrongly judged, or you judged yourself harshly. If another person brought up that nastiness inside you, invite them into your imagination so you can really get into the spirit of things! Remember all those icky feelings and remember the potential they have to poison you and even cause you to want to undermine others. If you feel hostility, feel it so completely that you taste it.

Then dance with your feelings. Literally. Dance like you mean it. Scrunch up your face, jump up and down, do what you need to do to contact the evil twin in yourself.

If you're a writer, write it down, uncensored. If you're a talker, give voice to your feelings, no matter how ugly they sound. If you're moved to do something physical, contort and twist your body into unattractive positions, the kind you'd be ashamed to let anyone else see (just remember to drop the blinds). Let the dance move you.

When your other, less-evolved self feels satisfied and starts to get a little bored, ask your higher self this question: If I'm such a good, sweet, beautiful, loving, compassionate, and spiritual person, how can I be so Goddess-forsaken ugly?!

Then listen for the answer.

> *I am this ugly and this beautiful.*
> *I am this nasty and this kind.*
> *I am this hostile and this compassionate.*
> *I am this judgmental and this tolerant.*
> *I am this resentful and this forgiving.*

Repeat the above three times and make up a couple of your own. Now say, once:

> *By my will and candle bright*
> *I free my shadow into light*
> *Her power and beauty I have absorbed*
> *This truth I speak releases me from discord.*

Release the misunderstandings you've had within your self and with others into the candlelight as you blow it out. (If you wrote, drew, or crafted anything physical, you can burn your nasty art in the flame, too, if it's safe—it's a good idea to destroy the evidence to avoid having it fall into the hands of someone who might misinterpret it.)

Thank the Goddess for helping you restore your balance of light and dark!

Bluebeard's Booty Spell

I have a confession to make: I wear my heart on my sleeve, and I do it often. My confidantes are great at giving me a new perspective. Once I was retelling the story about a man I fell for and how, to my horror, he seemed to carry around a collection of women from his past, gilding each one of them with his memory. But for some reason, none of those past relationships seemed to work out. I became spooked, mainly because I was thinking about pursuing a relationship with him. When people tell you who they are, listen up! In this scrapbook of doomed-to-fail relationships, I imagined an empty slot waiting for my picture. It was as though the spirits of these girls were trapped, without their knowledge. I felt a chill move through my heart. Imagining him carrying around all these women in his mind for life was horrific, but imagining myself as one of them was even worse.

Then my friend made the connection between this dude and the legend of Bluebeard. Bluebeard was a wealthy aristocrat who was looking for a new wife; however, no one knew exactly what had happened to his three previous wives, so the wise local gals avoided him like the plague. So Bluebeard traveled to a neighboring village, where he found a sweet young flower who took residence at his castle after marrying him. He gave this girl everything she wanted except one thing—a key to a locked room at the end of the hall, which he told her she must never enter. Soon she became persistently awakened at night by noises; it sounded like crying coming from that locked part of the castle.

So one day when Bluebeard was away, she found the key and broke into the forbidden room. What she saw was horrific—skeleton corpses of his previous brides hanging from the rafters. Bluebeard returned, and since blood from her discovery got on her clothes and on the key, he knew where she had been. He was clearly a violent man. The girl ran into the tower and locked herself in it. Just as Bluebeard broke down the door and wife number four was about to become a statistic, her brothers appeared on the scene and bludgeoned old Bluebeard to death.

This story chilled me. It wasn't a stretch of the imagination to think that this man had a secret mental room of horrors that rivaled Bluebeard's. I didn't think he was a violent man, but then there was clearly a dark, locked dungeon full of rotting exes in his mind. The story spoke to me, and I felt the necessity of putting a healthy amount of self-protection between my heart and his. As my Bluebeard sparked my imaginative processes, I decided to put the clanging chains of this relationship to rest once and for all—to bury him (symbolically, of course) with this spell.

You will need:
- a paper, wooden, or clay doll (or any biodegradable substance) of your lover or past lovers
- candles
- wine or juice, feast food
- a shovel
- burial ground

The spell: Make a doll resembling the person you want to bury and set free, then have a little doll party. Light some candles, drink some wine, and have a little celebration with your former lover, remembering the good times, before it all went south. Then take it south. It's time for him, and his entourage, to go downtown. Take your doll(s) to a place where you know it is unlikely to be dug up, like an offbeat mountain path or a place in your backyard. If you prefer fire, you can perform a purifying cremation and just throw the doll in the flames. Watching him (the doll) go up in flames feels exceptionally liberating (by the way, you can perform "purification by fire" rituals for just about anything you're ready to symbolically eliminate).

After doing this spell, I was no longer Bluebeard's booty. I do believe I set myself, and my sisters, free.

The best day to do this is on a Saturday—the day of Saturn (endings)—or any day during the waxing cycle of the Moon. A Saturday during the waxing Moon is super effective. Yet if you're looking for your own magical ending, check out this next spell.

Change the End of the Story Spell

When we're getting over a love affair, we can hear a song or see a movie and become a puddle of emotions. There's something about the way the world speaks to us when our heart's been broken open; everything has that tenderhearted poignancy—the world's become a mirror for our misery, right? Memories drift in and out of our minds, a couple in love walks by and it's like a dagger through our heart, or someone we see at the gym reminds us of who we used to love. The temptation is to believe we're moving backward, to think that our pain is closing us down, when it's actually opening us up to living more soulfully and open-heartedly.

Carl Jung once said, "The only way out of the darkness is through it," and I believe the only way to live soulfully is to live from the heart, even when it's in darkness—no matter how blown open and raw this feels. This means not shutting down to our pain, but experiencing it as though it were an invitation to really feel, to finally be really, totally alive.

Sometimes it's all about our story. It just gets too intense in our head and heart. That's when it helps to get some distance by seeing your story as a reflection of a more universal tale. Sometimes this happens spontaneously—we serendipitously have our heart mirrored back to us in a movie or book—as happened for me when I told my friend about my heartache. But we often create our own tragic story, and then we believe it.

The difference between the story we tell ourselves and the one that speaks through the ultimate storyteller, the Universe (in the form of a movie, myth, or fairy tale), may be slight, but the healing power is strong. I propose that all tragic love stories that really speak to us open our heart to heal it, but that not all love stories need to end tragically and without healing resolution. That's the tragedy of many modern movies, and many of us have that message programmed in our mind: instead of believing that we can have it all, we have internal contradictions, pulling us this way and that, and staying in conflict always leads to the same tragic ending.

We can change the ending! Believe you me, "I'm doomed to dead-end love affairs" is no one's true destiny.

You will need:

- your love alchemist's notebook

- a white candle

- myrrh incense for purification

The spell: Curl up in a safe, comfy spot and guide yourself into the imagination of your heart. Imagine a past love story that didn't end the way you wanted. Then rearrange the ending to your own satisfaction. Pull out all the stops to make your story conclusively and utterly heart healing. What prevented you from experiencing this version of events? You may find that you're now being honest with your feelings about the person for the first time, and that you had neglected to communicate those feelings. Or you may discover a conflict between your head and your heart that prevented a happy ending. As you record your stream of consciousness thoughts about how you wanted things to be, you may discover how they really went down. You can continue to write, draw, paint, or sing your new ending.

Imagine what would happen if Scarlett of *Gone With the Wind* had said what she really wanted to. Imagine she gave that tough-gal act of hers a rest and revealed her feelings (uh-oh, she'd be vulnerable!). When Rhett said, "Frankly my dear, I don't give a damn," she'd jump into his arms crying, "But I do, Rhett! I just now realized how scared I am to love you! I've been defending myself against my own feelings. And I do love you, I do, I do!" And they'd kiss.

It's never too late for a happy ending when we can change the end of the story at any time!

Dear Cupid Spell

This letter-writing thing is growing in popularity—I just read an article in *O, The Oprah Magazine* about a woman who, having already lost two soul mates through death, was advised by a clairvoyant to make a list of all the qualities she wanted in a mate . . . and to wait for him. She knew she'd found her soul mate, when, several years later she took out that list and checked off 98 of the 100 qualities. When she showed her list to her soul mate, he actually broke down and wept. Why? Because she had given voice to qualities that no one ever acknowledged so clearly but which he clearly possessed. Gorgeous! The larger part of falling in love is being seen for who we are.

I'm convinced that so many women I hear from who are "looking for love" have yet to define who it is they're looking for. Is it really a sense of humor, putting the cap back on the toothpaste, a good-looking millionaire—or does it go deeper than that? In my experience, we've spent too long overlooking our own spiritual needs and denying ourselves the gifts that someone else is aching to be acknowledged for, to give to us. Isn't it true that the receiver must learn to recognize the giver? And until we look beyond the obvious, even we ourselves can remain unopened presents with our finer qualities overlooked.

How do we envision our soul mate right into reality? I like to start with a feeling. How would your soul mate make you feel? Or here's another: what is your version of soul mate heaven? Maybe it's a big teddy bear who wraps his arms around you and makes you feel safe. Or how about someone who is emotionally self-aware, who respects your opinion and truly cares about your needs? If you don't know where to even begin, examine your near-miss and not-quite-right relationships—there was something in him (and him, and him) that you truly appreciated and/or loved. You can use that hard-earned wisdom to fuel today's heart request.

When I decided to write down what I wanted from my soul mate, I knew I'd have to plumb the depths of my heart to figure it out. I'd try to be as specific as possible and to frame it with positive, hopeful expectancy. If you're like me (and you take the time to reflect on everything your heart desires in a soul mate), you'll come up with a very specific and lengthy list. That's good, because you're going to be spending the rest of your life with this person (if you want to!). My claim is that everyone has a prince or princess charming in hiding, and that's where they'll remain if you don't call them to you.

1. Put it into words. This all comes back to intention. If you cannot define who it is you're looking for, you're sending an empty love letter to the Universe. And yet it's also true that many of us don't know what or who it is we're looking for until we really put some energy into the matter. Writing down something, putting pen to paper, literally puts "the word" into matter and is powerful magic in itself.

2. Speak positively. Clearly outline who it is you're looking for by naming their positive qualities. Be as specific as possible. When I was looking for my soul mate, I wrote a five-page letter about my perfect mate. Write it in present tense terms, because this person already exists, he's just waiting for you to find him. "My soul mate is . . ." passionate about life, committed to spiritually growing and evolving with me, emotionally mature (that's mine and you can use it, it's a good one), intellectually brilliant, interdependent, gives me the independence and space to explore my creative needs, happy with his career, financially prosperous, sexually attractive to me . . . and so on.

3. Name your no. Sometimes we're ambiguous or uncertain about who we're looking for. This is the time to discover that truth. One of my favorite sayings is "You've got to find your no to find your yes," and this certainly bears out in the dating world! When it comes to finding anything worthwhile in life and love, there's a necessary process of trial and error to arrive at your heart's de-sire. But the beauty of this list is that you can divine your yesses from all those nos by examining all your relationships that didn't work out.

   And when you do find your no, flip it from the negative (lack) to the posi-tive (abundance). For example, "no deadbeat losers" isn't a love-attracting in-tention. Flip it to "my soul mate is responsible," or better, "my soul mate holds himself accountable to others." The more specific you can be, the more heart and soul you put into it, the better. Instead of "my soul mate is not un-employed," try "my soul mate earns a reliable, comfortable income in a career he loves."

4. Dig for gold in your relationship mines. When I made my list, I also used all the wonderful qualities that attracted me to men I dated or loved in the past. One person was a musician, and I loved having artistry around, so I included that. Another was a seeker, like me, and I wrote that down. Definitely pull on your nonromantic relationships, qualities you love in your favorite friend, for instance. Remember, difficult or amazing, you can plumb the people who had the most pull on your heart to your fulfillment. Watch those relationships you thought were heavy leaden weights turn into gold!

5. Unfurl your imagination. List the fantasy and everyday qualities you know you couldn't live without. Imagining the reality of living with a person day in, day out can help you get real specific, real quick—especially if you're vulnerable to romantic love or can't even fathom what a day-to-day relationship would actually look like. Examine your own energies for more clues. What are your concerns? What have you learned about yourself from past relationships? For me, staying in energetic balance was an issue in the past. Certain relationships drained me, so I stated, "My soul mate matches me energetically." Maybe you love to hang out at home, or conversely, you're a sociable person who likes going out a lot. You might write something like "We share the same interests and pastimes." Many of us are born romantics, and if that's you, you've got this next piece of advice covered: don't be afraid to dream.

6. Handle with care. So what do you do with your love letter once you've written it? It's up to you, but above all else, treat it like a first-class message—as though it were meant for the Queen of England or another very special person. You can tuck your letter away in a safe and special place, write it on special stationary, seal it with wax in an envelope, or wrap it in a pink or red silk scarf and put it in a magical keepsake box. I wrote mine in a pink sparkly pen and put it on my love altar, underneath a seated Buddha. I also made love offerings to my intention on a regular basis by placing fresh flowers, rose petals, and copper pennies on my love altar.

By the way, when I found my soul mate, I scored better than 98 percent—he had every single quality on that list!

Affirming for Love

When I met Kim in an astrology class, she was on the hunt for a husband. She'd been dating around for quite a while. She'd tell me stories about near misses and not-quite-right guys, but she faithfully held out for The One. At the time, I was more interested in getting my life together than getting a man, but I always remembered this affirmation because it was the first one I employed to attract a job, a sustainable income, and then finally, love. I've put my intention into these words over and over again since, with fabulous results. Here it is:

> ***My perfect mate comes to me in divine timing.***

That's it. Just one sentence—it's too simple, right? That's by design.

This affirmation taught me the power of simplicity in prayer. When you make your prayer simple and clear, you're likelier to get the message through, just as writing clearly gets the message across. An easy way to write simply is to write in rhyming poetry form, or to make up a little song. So many witch-y spells are done in a singsongy rhyme, not just because it's catchy, but because they're more easily memorized.

The second thing I like about this affirmation is the release of the timing. As I've said before, magical timing works differently than clock or calendar time. Divine timing has a clock; we just don't know how to read it. Always treat your request for love as though it's already happening by stating it in the present. Try considering that the reason you haven't yet met The One yet is because they have some valuable lessons to complete before they're ready to meet you. Trust that a higher presence is guiding you both to each other, in divine timing.

Post this affirmation, or any other one you like, in the bathroom, where you can see it when you brush your teeth at morning and at night. When I got really into affirmation writing, they started coming out quick and easy, like a prayerful stream of consciousness. I put them on 3 x 5 notecards and placed them on the dashboard of my car, my computer workstation, or wherever I could see them. The trick is when you put an affirmation in a place you visit often, you don't really have to read it; you just begin to passively absorb the message. Watch out, affirmations really work. Before you know it, you'll start believing your own words!

Hair Spells

Men have a thing about hair. That's because back in the hunter-gatherer days, a woman who had shiny hair was far likelier to bear healthy offspring than a woman with dull hair. Hair has biblical roots: in the myth of Samson and Delilah, the women who cut off Samson's long locks also cut away his strength. Think about how you feel after you get a haircut—how you want to either show it off or run and hide, depending on the cut—and it's easy to see the power, beauty, and vanity bound up hair. Great hair has great power. A good hair day can give a girl a kind of confidence you just can't buy in a bottle (or maybe you can, if it's some fabulous styling product!).

Hair also has magical "roots." In the practice of witchery, long, unruly hair was far more magical than short, tidy locks. In folklore of many traditions, a witch with untamable hair went against the prevailing grain of the day. Yes, messy and un-kempt hair has defiance in it, wildness even. Mystical traditions say that hair is an extension of our thoughts, so that when one sees a person with curly hair in dreams or in visions, it's indicative of a character with uniquely prolific, rebellious thoughts. Even modern-day wizard Harry Potter's mop top of hair was no accident—it de-noted his rebellious spirit. Hair magic is powerful, and fun!

The Haitian Hair Cure

This one was passed down via oral tradition, for I have searched and searched and never found the origin of this spell. So the source I'll attribute this to is a second Kim, who advised my friend, the first Kim (who was looking for a husband), to try it.

Wear seven "do's" in seven days. Every day of the spell, you simply wear your hair differently than the day before.

Pony tail, braid, a flower tucked over your ear, straight, curly, half up/half down, scrunched, blown out, headband or glitter barrettes. You get the picture. By day seven, expect your new do's to attract a new date.

Within a week of doing this spell, a cute guy asked Kim out. Here's my line of reasoning: aside from the cavemen theory, men are visual creatures. Even if they can't quite put their finger on the fact that yesterday you had hair, and today you're sporting a *G.I. Jane* buzz cut, they really do notice when there's something different about you, even if they have no clue what it is. Yep, it's your hair.

I'm Gonna Wash That Man Right Outa My Hair Spell

My dear hairdresser once confided in me about the mistake her clients make most often. By and large, it was having one's locks lopped, chopped, or changed immediately following a stressful life event, such as a break-up, or losing a job. I think hairdressers are for women what bartenders are for men—amateur psychologists who can see into a woman's soul. It is during those times, my hairdresser said, that our judgment is most askew and we're in a hurry to hasten a transformation, which normally takes time, so we force an instant change—on a perfectly fine head of hair.

As a counselor, I notice this phenomenon as well. Right in the middle of a mild earthquake in their life, people often want to up the ante and change everything. Change is liberating, but we've also got to give ourself the space to process that change and to allow our emotions to find equilibrium again.

The desire to have our outer appearance mirror our changed inner landscape is a real phenomenon, and in the right head space, I have no problem saying, "You go, girl!" Yet going from wild-haired woman to an asymmetrical pixie cut can add another crisis to the mix—hair trauma. There is a less drastic spiritual-into-physical morph we can do that leaves us looking and smelling great. It only involves a bottle of shampoo.

YOU WILL NEED:
- a great-smelling shampoo; I like Pureology (for color-treated hair) because it has sandalwood and rose oil in it, two magical oils with love properties
- the Weather Girls' version of the song "I'm Gonna Wash That Man Right Outa My Hair," available online

Put the song on and hop in the shower. Sing, lather, rinse, and repeat as necessary!

Burn Those Sheets! Ritual

This is a good spell for two kinds of situations. First: you keep attracting empty sexual relationships with people who are so far away from your perfect spiritual partner that you think Cupid's somehow crossed wires between you and Mae West.

Second: you've moved on from your last relationship, but your sheets haven't. You've washed them many times, but like Lady MacBeth ("Out, damn'd spot!") there must be trace fragments remaining on your sheets because you're still dreaming about him. Of course you are—your sheets retain the familiar memory of his secret fluid. Eeewh! Name one good reason (aside from 750-thread-count Egyptian) to *not* burn those sheets.

WHAT TO DO: Sit on your bed. Light a few white candles for purification and declare your intention to attract only positive and healthy soul mates into your bed.

HOW TO DO IT: Recite one of the following, your choice.

> *I now eliminate all unwanted influences from my personal space. As goddess of love is my witness, I make this sacred vow to myself: I will only invite positive and healthy people into my life and into my bed. So it is.*

Or:

> *I now eliminate all unwanted and past influences from my personal space. As goddess of love is my witness, I am now totally free for new love and will happily dream about my new beloved as I sleep. So it is.*

Now, burn those sheets! If you don't have a metal drum, use a fireplace or have a beach bonfire. If you do not have access to a fire, you can always symbolically burn them by putting on a song like, "Burn Baby Burn (Disco Inferno)" and dancing around the sheets as through they're on fire. But you must get rid of them afterward. Toss them in the trash and remove them from the house. However, don't give the sheets to Goodwill, 'cause even sheets can have karma, and you don't want to pass that bad love juju on to someone else.

Come To My Boudoir Spell

Here's an original spell my friend Jessica came up with when she was feng shui-ing her house for love and decided she was ready to turn her single bed into a double sleeper.

Get a second pillow.

Not a spell? *Au contraire.* I like this spell because it reminds me that the only difference between an ordinary act and a sacred act is attention and intention. We're all natural spellcasters, and that little nudge to live creatively, to go out on a whim and follow the urge to whoop up some love magic, is actually an angelic presence named Venus whispering in our ear.

And yes, Jessica got her relationship!

Affirmation: I am the living light of love. There is no other reality. I know I am attracting love to me right now. My perfect mate comes to me in divine timing.

Collage Spell

Sometimes the world just doesn't seem to want to oblige our wishes. And the message of desperation we send out only sends back more desperation. When dreams feel so distant, we need to employ divine intervention of the magical sort. My wish come true was living proof that the Universe recognizes real need, and when coupled with divine desire, miracles happen.

Once, desperate for a place to live, I took a flat in Haight-Ashbury in San Francisco. I very literally hated the Haight; the all-night noise and crazy folks just outside my window made me miserable, yet I had spent all my money getting into this situation and had no idea how to get out. Being sensitive to my living environment, the negative activities taking place, and a roommate whom I had nothing in common with began hitting my self-esteem hard. So one sleepless summer's night, to the sound of drunkards outside my window, I put my misery into creative action with paper and scissors. In my mind, my ideal housing situation would be . . . outside of the city, quiet and tranquil, surrounded by green trees, maybe in the mountains, and next to a quiet lake. Cut, cut, cut. Magazine pictures filled the pages of a notebook. I got so carried away, I even put a writer's desk in my house, because I wanted to start writing (I hadn't yet), and I also put a heart jewel at the crown chakra of the house, because I didn't want to live in one more house that had no love in it. On yet another page, I pasted a plush bed with luxurious pillows and blankets (I was sleeping on an air mattress at the time). I wanted a garden. I wanted to live without roommates. Cut, cut, cut.

Snap! That energy shifted in only a few months, which is a relatively short time on the magical time line. That autumn, my roommate told me that he was moving to L.A. and even though this meant I would be without housing, I saw this as a wonderful opportunity to manifest my dream. I received an email from a friend of a friend: "Cozy cabin in the mountains, minutes from the freeway. Perfect for one—or two people very much in love." What?! How could it be? It was exactly as I'd wished. Synchronicities abounded: the house was surrounded by northern California eucalyptus and redwood trees and even had a garden, a rarity for the pricey Bay Area. There were hiking trails a few blocks away, leading to a lake. And most miraculous of all, it was cheap; I could afford it. As a housewarming present, my girlfriend Justine found an abandoned desk on a street corner—which I refurbished by hand into my dream writer's desk.

I'd manifested the abode of my soul. I spent a blissful two years in that "cozy cabin . . . Perfect for one—or two people very much in love." I built a life I loved and learned to love myself there. I now live with my husband, in the mountains, with a garden and a lake nearby. I'm also a writer. I'd had to work from the root chakra up to build the foundation of a really exceptional life before reaching the crown jewel of my true home: someone to share my love with!

THE SPELL: Gather a stack of magazines and cut, cut, cut your way to your dream situation, man, or relationship. Don't worry about being overly realistic, just create your dream and admire seeing it in physical form.

Tattoo Love Spell

At one point in my search for love, I was moved to make a dramatic and personal statement to the Universe: I decided to get a tattoo. I didn't undertake this decision lightly; I thought about it long and hard. Why did I want a tattoo? Angelina had to get "Billy Bob" removed, and Johnny Depp's "Winona Forever" turned into "Wino Forever." After that, tattoos were soooo cliché, and so permanent. Yet I know the power of symbols and of symbolic acts; I am a magical astrologer, after all. What better way to express to the Creator just how committed and ready I was to manifest my sexual juiciness and my creative ripeness than with my willingness to go under the needle, to commit to a lifelong tattoo?

I decided this creative act would be a powerful magical statement. It would be about my feminine shakti power to create something out of nothing in all areas of my life, specifically in love and career. So I got out my colored pencils and got started on a design.

Lately, I had been studying the secret Dakini according to Buddhist texts. The concept of pregnant space (called *chogyam* in Buddhism), the exciting idea that empty space isn't negative but full of creative possibilities, really appealed to me. Symbolically, this was pictured as two triangles—the feminine and masculine—laid over each other, with empty space in the middle. I read that the outer sharp boundaries of the triangle represented the sharp wisdom within every woman who guards her inner magic—that sounded just up my alley! Inside the space I drew the symbol for Venus, the goddess of love, beauty, and balance, and universal feminine as I knew her. Around these merged triangles, which resembled a star, I drew lotus petals for compassion and love. I chose colors specifically too: orange for passion and creativity, yellow for self-esteem and strength, and turquoise for protection. I even made the length of the lines of triangle on an abbreviated scale with the golden mean, the mathematical measure developed by Pythagoreas, who said the mean defined the underlying harmony for every shape in the Universe. Indeed, the golden mean appears in art, architecture, and even the human body. (The golden mean calls for the ratio of a:b to equal the ratio of a+b:a. A little esoteric, but there it is.)

I googled around for tattoo artists, and when I saw a parlor named Sacred Roze (the rose is sacred to Venus), I knew I had found my artist.

On the day I went to the tattoo parlor, a romantic triple play involving Saturn, Venus, and Pluto was in the celestial air. The planet of permanence, Saturn, had just entered Leo—the sign of true love, creativity, and artistry—to co-join Venus, also in Leo. This is an aspect of enduring love bonds. Both planets received a sweet kiss from Pluto, bringing a layer of sexy soulfulness and honesty to this romantic, creative pairing. This was totally intentional. I knew it was a good energy to have a tattoo: Saturn in Leo was all about quality artistry and I knew I'd be pleased with the result. But I also knew this energy reflected my intention: to unfurl to the world the creative-expressive-sexual energy that had been building inside of me. I was ready to rock my artistic side and declare my readiness for passionate love. I had the tattoo done on my back, over my second chakra, which is the energy center of sexual passion and creativity.

Less than a month later, I began dating John, my soul mate, who is a fun-loving Leo. And a few months after that, I was offered my very first creative-writing job.

THE SPELL: If you're so inclined, you may choose to craft your own soul love quest tattoo. Make this a personal and meaningful piece of body art. For a less-permanent but similarly charged exercise, get a henna tattoo that makes you feel sexy and soulful. Keep in mind that henna tattoos aren't permanent and should only be used in soul mate magic for qualities that you want to enhance on a short-term basis

Once You've Found Him: A Binding Ritual

I'm not a witch. I'm your wife!
—The Princess Bride

Handfasting is a ritual that ties two people together with the use of a cord or ribbon. The custom has origins in many different cultures, the Celts and Romanian Gypsies, especially. A handfasting ritual is a formal or informal way to bind two lovers together, for as long as you both choose, as handfasting has no hard and fast rules about how long you stay together. I personally like the Wiccan idea of "a year and a day," in which you rededicate your vow to be together every year through ritual. As individuals need change, commitments aren't static. I think much suffering would be spared if we had set dates to renew our vows and rededicate our choice and commitment to each other, just as we renew our driver's license.

Handfasting has been a part of traditional Irish weddings for centuries, where tying two souls together in front of God/Goddess is as binding as the exchange of rings is in America. Of course, without an officiant, handfasting isn't legally binding, but that doesn't make this symbolic act any less powerful! Many witches handfast to their true love without a formal certificate and in the privacy of their own home. My soul mate and I did this ritual before we decided to get married, then performed it again publicly at our wedding ceremony.

WHEN TO DO IT: Whenever you want to celebrate your decision to be together! June is a good month for this ritual (June is named after the goddess of fidelity and marriage, Juno), as are Fridays when the Moon is waxing.

WHERE TO DO IT: Choose a private and romantic area of your house or garden, and light strategically placed candles. Everyone looks wonderful by candlelight! You might want to scatter rose petals, too, or light incense. You may also choose a sacred site; John and I chose a woman-made labyrinth.

YOU WILL NEED:

- two pieces of silky ribbon or cord; I used white, for pure, spiritual love, but you might like red, the color of passion and true love

- small scissors

- anointing oil of your choice: rose, lavender, or jasmine, for instance

- a chalice filled with a red beverage (wine or juice)

- a candle; white is appropriate

HOW TO DO IT: Read this affirmation together:

Today we come together as two individuals, joined as one heart and one soul. We vow to love, respect, and cherish one another through all times, good and trying. Bound together in love and understanding, by honoring each other, we create love's happiness and its fulfillment. So it is.

Light the candle. Step into your ritual area. Call in the directions/elements:

(Facing west) I call in water, for soulful love.
(Facing east) I call in air, for wisdom in love.
(Facing south) I call in fire, for passionate love.
(Facing north) I call in earth, for grounded love.

Facing each other, one person offers a sip of wine to the other, saying, "May you never thirst." The other partner then does likewise.

Both partners anoint the candle with lavender oil. They then anoint each other's third eye with oil, saying, "You are my light."

Each cuts a snippet of the other's hair (take it from the back), saying, "You are my strength." Put the hair aside in an envelope.

Each takes a sip of wine, saying, "We are now one."

Finally, tie the ribbon or string around your partner's wrist, saying, "You are bound to me."

Take the hair from the envelope and scatter it to the wind.

Blow out the candle and celebrate your union!

You can leave your ribbons on as long as you wish. I've heard of handfasting rituals in which the two partners are bound together (either with one ribbon or with many ribbons contributed by ceremony guests) and they don't untie themselves until making love on their wedding night!

APPENDIX B

Venus Ephemeris 1955–1999

To FIND YOUR VENUS SIGN, simply find the date that most closely precedes your birth date. The signs listed here are calculated for Greenwich Mean Time, so your sign may be different depending on the exact time and location of your birth—obtain a full natal chart for more information. Basic natal charts are available online at sites such as www.astrology.com. For your personal Venus report, visit Jessica Shepherd's website at www.moonkissd.com.

Aries	♈
Taurus	♉
Gemini	♊
Cancer	♋
Leo	♌
Virgo	♍
Libra	♎
Scorpio	♏
Sagittarius	♐
Capricorn	♑
Aquarius	♒
Pisces	♓

1955		
Jan.	6	♐
Feb.	5	♑
Mar.	4	♒
	30	♓
Apr.	24	♈
May	19	♉
Jun.	13	♊
Jul.	7	♋
Aug.	1	♌
	25	♍
Sep.	18	♎
Oct.	12	♏
Nov.	5	♐
	29	♑
Dec.	24	♒

1956		
Jan.	17	♓
Feb.	11	♈
Mar.	7	♉
Apr.	4	♊
May	7	♋
Jun.	23	♊
Aug.	4	♋
Sep.	8	♌
Oct.	5	♍
	31	♎
Nov.	25	♏
Dec.	19	♐

1957		
Jan.	12	♑
Feb.	5	♒
Mar.	1	♓
	25	♈
Apr.	18	♉
May	13	♊
Jun.	6	♋
Jul.	1	♌
	25	♍
Aug.	19	♎
Sep.	14	♏
Oct.	9	♐
Nov.	5	♑
Dec.	6	♒

1958		
Apr.	6	♓
May	5	♈
	31	♉
Jun.	26	♊
Jul.	22	♋
Aug.	15	♌
Sep.	9	♍
Oct.	3	♎
	27	♏
Nov.	20	♐
Dec.	14	♑

1959		
Jan.	7	♒
	31	♓
Feb.	24	♈
Mar.	20	♉
Apr.	14	♊
May	10	♋
Jun.	6	♌
Jul.	8	♍
Sep.	19	♌
	25	♍
Nov.	9	♎
Dec.	7	♏

1960		
Jan.	2	♐
	26	♑
Feb.	20	♒
Mar.	15	♓
Apr.	9	♈
May	3	♉
	28	♊
Jun.	21	♋
Jul.	15	♌
Aug.	9	♍
Sep.	2	♎
	27	♏
Oct.	21	♐
Nov.	15	♑
Dec.	10	♒

1961		
Jan.	4	♓
Feb.	1	♈
Jun.	5	♉
Jul.	6	♊
Aug.	3	♋
	29	♌
Sep.	23	♍
Oct.	17	♎
Nov.	11	♏
Dec.	4	♐
	28	♑

1962		
Jan.	21	♒
Feb.	14	♓
Mar.	10	♈
Apr.	3	♉
	28	♊
May	22	♋
Jun.	17	♌
Jul.	12	♍
Aug.	8	♎
Sep.	6	♏

1963		
Jan.	6	♐
Feb.	5	♑
Mar.	4	♒
	29	♓
Apr.	23	♈
May	18	♉
Jun.	12	♊
Jul.	7	♋
	31	♌
Aug.	25	♍
Sep.	18	♎
Oct.	12	♏
Nov.	5	♐
	29	♑
Dec.	23	♒

1964		
Jan.	16	♓
Feb.	10	♈
Mar.	7	♉
Apr.	3	♊
May	8	♋
Jun.	17	♊
Aug.	5	♋
Sep.	7	♌
Oct.	5	♍
	31	♎
Nov.	24	♏
Dec.	19	♐

1965		
Jan.	12	♑
Feb.	5	♒
Mar.	1	♓
	25	♈
Apr.	18	♉
May	12	♊
Jun.	6	♋
	30	♌
Jul.	25	♍
Aug.	19	♎
Sep.	13	♏
Oct.	9	♐
Nov.	5	♑
Dec.	6	♒

1966		
Feb.	6	♑
	25	♒
Apr.	6	♓
May	4	♈
	31	♉
Jun.	26	♊
Jul.	21	♋
Aug.	15	♌
Sep.	8	♍
Oct.	2	♎
	26	♏
Nov.	19	♐
Dec.	13	♑

1967		
Jan.	6	♒
	30	♓
Feb.	23	♈
Mar.	20	♉
Apr.	14	♊
May	10	♋
Jun.	6	♌
Jul.	8	♍
Sep.	9	♌
Oct.	1	♍
Nov.	9	♎
Dec.	7	♏

1968		
Jan.	1	♐
	26	♑
Feb.	19	♒
Mar.	15	♓
Apr.	8	♈
May	3	♉
	27	♊
Jun.	20	♋
Jul.	15	♌
Aug.	8	♍
Sep.	2	♎
	26	♏
Oct.	21	♐
Nov.	14	♑
Dec.	9	♒

1969		
Jan.	4	♓
Feb.	1	♈
Jun.	5	♉
Jul.	6	♊
Aug.	3	♋
	28	♌
Sep.	22	♍
Oct.	17	♎
Nov.	10	♏
Dec.	4	♐
	28	♑

1970

Jan.	21	♒
Feb.	14	♓
Mar.	10	♈
Apr.	3	♉
	27	♊
May	22	♋
Jun.	16	♌
Jul.	12	♍
Aug.	8	♎
Sep.	6	♏

1971

Jan.	6	♐
Feb.	5	♑
Mar.	3	♒
	29	♓
Apr.	23	♈
May	18	♉
Jun.	12	♊
Jul.	6	♋
	31	♌
Aug.	24	♍
Sep.	17	♎
Oct.	11	♏
Nov.	4	♐
	28	♑
Dec.	23	♒

1972

Jan.	16	♓
Feb.	10	♈
Mar.	6	♉
Apr.	3	♊
May	10	♋
Jun.	11	♊
Aug.	5	♋
Sep.	7	♌
Oct.	5	♍
	30	♎
Nov.	24	♏
Dec.	18	♐

1973

Jan.	11	♑
Feb.	4	♒
	28	♓
Mar.	24	♈
Apr.	17	♉
May	12	♊
Jun.	5	♋
	30	♌
Jul.	24	♍
Aug.	18	♎
Sep.	13	♏
Oct.	9	♐
Nov.	5	♑
Dec.	7	♒

1974

Jan.	29	♑
Feb.	28	♒
Apr.	6	♓
May	4	♈
	31	♉
Jun.	25	♊
Jul.	20	♋
Aug.	14	♌
Sep.	8	♍
Oct.	2	♎
	26	♏
Nov.	19	♐
Dec.	13	♑

1975

Jan.	6	♒
	30	♓
Feb.	23	♈
Mar.	19	♉
Apr.	13	♊
May	9	♋
Jun.	6	♌
Jul.	9	♍
Sep.	2	♌
Oct.	4	♍
Nov.	9	♎
Dec.	6	♏

1976

Jan.	1	♐
	26	♑
Feb.	19	♒
Mar.	14	♓
Apr.	8	♈
May	2	♉
	26	♊
Jun.	20	♋
Jul.	14	♌
Aug.	8	♍
Sep.	1	♎
	25	♏
Oct.	20	♐
Nov.	14	♑
Dec.	9	♒

1977

Jan.	4	♓
Feb.	2	♈
Jun.	6	♉
Jul.	6	♊
Aug.	2	♋
	28	♌
Sep.	22	♍
Oct.	16	♎
Nov.	9	♏
Dec.	3	♐
	27	♑

1978

Jan.	20	♒
Feb.	13	♓
Mar.	9	♈
Apr.	2	♉
	27	♊
May	21	♋
Jun.	16	♌
Jul.	11	♍
Aug.	7	♎
Sep.	7	♏

1979

Jan.	7	♐
Feb.	5	♑
Mar.	3	♒
	28	♓
Apr.	22	♈
May	17	♉
Jun.	11	♊
Jul.	6	♋
	30	♌
Aug.	23	♍
Sep.	17	♎
Oct.	11	♏
Nov.	4	♐
	28	♑
Dec.	22	♒

1980

Jan.	15	♓
Feb.	9	♈
Mar.	6	♉
Apr.	3	♊
May	12	♋
Jun.	5	♊
Aug.	6	♋
Sep.	7	♌
Oct.	4	♍
	30	♎
Nov.	23	♏
Dec.	18	♐

1981

Jan.	11	♑
Feb.	4	♒
	28	♓
Mar.	24	♈
Apr.	17	♉
May	11	♊
Jun.	5	♋
	29	♌
Jul.	24	♍
Aug.	18	♎
Sep.	12	♏
Oct.	8	♐
Nov.	5	♑
Dec.	8	♒

1982

Jan.	22	♑
Mar.	2	♒
Apr.	6	♓
May	4	♈
	30	♉
Jun.	25	♊
Jul.	20	♋
Aug.	14	♌
Sep.	7	♍
Oct.	1	♎
	25	♏
Nov.	18	♐
Dec.	12	♑

1983

Jan.	5	♒
	29	♓
Feb.	22	♈
Mar.	19	♉
Apr.	13	♊
May	9	♋
Jun.	6	♌
Jul.	10	♍
Aug.	27	♌
Oct.	5	♍
Nov.	9	♎
Dec.	6	♏
	31	♐

1984

Jan.	25	♑
Feb.	18	♒
Mar.	14	♓
Apr.	7	♈
May	1	♉
	26	♊
Jun.	19	♋
Jul.	14	♌
Aug.	7	♍
Sep.	1	♎
	25	♏
Oct.	20	♐
Nov.	13	♑
Dec.	8	♒

1985

Jan.	4	♓
Feb.	2	♈
Jun.	6	♉
Jul.	6	♊
Aug.	2	♋
	27	♌
Sep.	21	♍
Oct.	16	♎
Nov.	9	♏
Dec.	3	♐
	27	♑

1986

Jan.	20	♒
Feb.	12	♓
Mar.	8	♈
Apr.	2	♉
	26	♊
May	21	♋
Jun.	15	♌
Jul.	11	♍
Aug.	7	♎
Sep.	7	♏

1987

Jan.	7	♐
Feb.	4	♑
Mar.	3	♒
	28	♓
Apr.	22	♈
May	17	♉
Jun.	11	♊
Jul.	5	♋
	30	♌
Aug.	23	♍
Sep.	16	♎
Oct.	10	♏
Nov.	3	♐
	27	♑
Dec.	22	♒

1988

Jan.	15	♓
Feb.	9	♈
Mar.	6	♉
Apr.	3	♊
May	17	♋
	27	♊
Aug.	6	♋
Sep.	7	♌
Oct.	4	♍
	29	♎
Nov.	23	♏
Dec.	17	♐

1989

Jan.	10	♑
Feb.	3	♒
	27	♓
Mar.	23	♈
Apr.	16	♉
May	11	♊
Jun.	4	♋
	29	♌
Jul.	23	♍
Aug.	17	♎
Sep.	12	♏
Oct.	8	♐
Nov.	5	♑
Dec.	9	♒

1990

Jan.	16	♑
Mar.	3	♒
Apr.	6	♓
May	3	♈
	30	♉
Jun.	24	♊
Jul.	19	♋
Aug.	13	♌
Sep.	7	♍
Oct.	1	♎
	25	♏
Nov.	18	♐
Dec.	12	♑

1991

Jan.	5	♒
	28	♓
Feb.	22	♈
Mar.	18	♉
Apr.	12	♊
May	8	♋
Jun.	5	♌
Jul.	11	♍
Aug.	21	♌
Oct.	6	♍
Nov.	9	♎
Dec.	6	♏
	31	♐

1992

Jan.	25	♑
Feb.	18	♒
Mar.	13	♓
Apr.	7	♈
May	1	♉
	25	♊
Jun.	19	♋
Jul.	13	♌
Aug.	7	♍
	31	♎
Sep.	24	♏
Oct.	19	♐
Nov.	13	♑
Dec.	8	♒

1993

Jan.	3	♓
Feb.	2	♈
Jun.	6	♉
Jul.	5	♊
Aug.	1	♋
	27	♌
Sep.	21	♍
Oct.	15	♎
Nov.	8	♏
Dec.	2	♐
	26	♑

1994

Jan.	19	♒
Feb.	12	♓
Mar.	8	♈
Apr.	1	♉
	26	♊
May	20	♋
Jun.	15	♌
Jul.	11	♍
Aug.	7	♎
Sep.	7	♏

1995

Jan.	7	♐
Feb.	4	♑
Mar.	2	♒
	28	♓
Apr.	21	♈
May	16	♉
Jun.	10	♊
Jul.	5	♋
	29	♌
Aug.	22	♍
Sep.	16	♎
Oct.	10	♏
Nov.	3	♐
	27	♑
Dec.	21	♒

1996

Jan.	14	♓
Feb.	8	♈
Mar.	5	♉
Apr.	3	♊
Aug.	7	♋
Sep.	7	♌
Oct.	3	♍
	29	♎
Nov.	22	♏
Dec.	17	♐

1997

Jan.	10	♑
Feb.	2	♒
	26	♓
Mar.	23	♈
Apr.	16	♉
May	10	♊
Jun.	3	♋
	28	♌
Jul.	23	♍
Aug.	17	♎
Sep.	11	♏
Oct.	8	♐
Nov.	5	♑
Dec.	11	♒

1998

Jan.	9	♑
Mar.	4	♒
Apr.	6	♓
May	3	♈
	29	♉
Jun.	24	♊
Jul.	19	♋
Aug.	13	♌
Sep.	6	♍
	30	♎
Oct.	24	♏
Nov.	17	♐
Dec.	11	♑

1999

Jan.	4	♒
	28	♓
Feb.	21	♈
Mar.	18	♉
Apr.	12	♊
May	8	♋
Jun.	5	♌
Jul.	12	♍
Aug.	15	♌
Oct.	7	♍
Nov.	8	♎
Dec.	5	♏
	30	♐

Bibliography

Work from the books below have been either referenced in the text or have influenced and informed the material I've presented. All authors/teachers are directly relevant and highly recommended.

Ahlquist, Diane. *Moon Spells: How to Use the Phases of the Moon to Get What You Want.* Avon, MA: Adams Media, 2002.

Ashley-Farrand, Thomas. *Healing Mantras: Using Sound Affirmations for Personal Power, Creativity and Healing.* New York: Ballantine Wellspring, 1999.

———. *Shakti Mantras: Tapping into the Great Goddess Energy Within.* New York: Ballantine Books, 2003.

Beak, Sera. *The Red Book: A Deliciously Unorthodox Approach to Igniting Your Divine Spark.* San Francisco: Jossey-Bass, 2006.

Brockway, Laurie S. *A Goddess Is a Girl's Best Friend: A Divine Guide to Finding Love, Success, and Happiness.* New York: Perigree, 2002.

Cameron, Julia. *Walking in This World: The Practical Art of Creativity.* New York: Tarcher/Penguin, 2003.

Casey, Caroline. *Making the Gods Work For You: The Astrological Language of the Psyche.* New York: Three Rivers Press, 1998.

Chodron, Pema. *The Wisdom of No Escape: And the Path of Loving-Kindness.* Boston: Shambhala Publications, 2001.

Cunningham, Scott. *Cunningham's Encyclopedia of Magical Herbs*. St. Paul, MN: Llewellyn Publications, 1998.

Forrest, Jodie, and Steven Forrest. *Skymates: Love, Sex and Evolutionary Astrology*. Chapel Hill, NC: Seven Paws Press, 2007.

Forrest, Steven. *Yesterday's Sky: Astrology and Reincarnation*. Borrego Springs, CA: Seven Paws Press, 2008.

Holmes, Ernest. *The Science of Mind: A Philosophy, A Faith, A Way of Life*. New York: Tarcher/Putnam, 1998.

Horne, Fiona. *Bewitch A Man: Simple Ways to Add a Little Magic to Your Love Life*. New York: Simon Spotlight Entertainment, 2006.

Katie, Byron. *Loving What Is: Four Questions That Can Change Your Life*. New York: Harmony Books, 2002.

Myss, Caroline. *Sacred Contracts: Awakening Your Divine Potential*. New York: Harmony Books, 2001.

Ponder, Catherine. *The Dynamic Laws of Prayer*. Marina del Ray, CA: DeVorss & Company, 1987.

Roach, Geshe Michael. *The Tibetan Book of Yoga: Ancient Buddhist Teachings on the Philosophy and Practice of Yoga*. New York: Doubleday/Random House, 2003.

Simmer-Brown, Judith. *Dakini's Warm Breath: The Feminine Principle in Tibetan Buddhism*. Boston: Shambhala Publications, 2002.

Webster, Richard. *Soul Mates: Understanding Relationships Across Time*. Woodbury, MN: Llewellyn Publications, 2006.

Williamson, Marianne. *A Woman's Worth*. New York: Ballantine Books, 1993.